The Social Psychology of Language 2

General editor: Howard Giles

Language and Social Knowledge:

Uncertainty in Interpersonal Relations

Charles R. Berger
Northwestern University

James J. Bradac
University of California
Santa Barbara

Edward Arnold

© Charles R. Berger and James J. Bradac 1982
First published 1982 by
Edward Arnold (Publishers) Ltd
41 Bedford Square, London WC 1B 3DQ

British Library Cataloguing in Publication Data

Berger, Charles R.
   Language and social knowledge.—(The social
   psychology of language)
   1. Interpersonal communication
   I. Title   II. Bradac, James J.
   III. Series
   302.2   BF637.C45

ISBN 0-7131-6196-5

Text set in 10/11 pt Times Compugraphic
by Colset Private Limited
Printed and bound by Richard Clay (The Chaucer Press) Ltd
Bungay, Suffolk

Contents

Preface

In Europe and North America as well as in some countries in Asia and South Amercia, there is increasing interest in the field of communication by both social science researchers and communication practitioners. Many books have been published in such research areas as mass communication, organizational communication, political communication, and interpersonal communication, and there are large cadres of researchers in each of these fields who publish copious research reports in various communication journals. For most of these researchers, communication as an area of study is an interdisciplinary enterprise. Writers and researchers in each of these fields of communication study feel quite at home with the literatures of such allied disciplines as anthropology, linguistics, political science, social psychology, sociology and sociolinguistics. However, unlike many researchers in these allied disciplines, communication researchers view the process of communication as *central* to the understanding of a wide variety of social phenomena. Rather than focusing solely upon the outcome or product of social interactions, the communication researcher is interested in how persons use their communicative abilities to produce certain outcomes, whether these be attitude formation, information gain, or emotional change.

It is within this broader context that the authors as communication researchers operate. The general focus of this volume is on interpersonal communication, but this work is not a broad-spectrum, introductory treatment. In our experience there are many such introductory books available in North America and we suspect in other parts of the world as well. By contrast to the usual smorgasbord approach, the present volume advances a coherent theoretical position and attempts to show the utility of the theory by drawing on a number of different research traditions. In the spirit of the communication discipline, these research traditions involve linguistics, sociolinguistics, experimental psychology, and social psychology as well as original work by communication researchers themselves. Because of this integration, students and researchers in these areas should find this book to be both relevant and useful.

The specific focus of this volume is on the relationships among language, social cognition, and the processes involved in the development of interpersonal relationships. Our purpose is to show how language and the ways in which we think about ourselves and others influence the ways in which we develop relationships. Although there are a number of volumes which have addressed issues concerned with relationship development, this volume is unique in that it provides a new theoretical perspective for explaining relationship growth, maintenance and decay. This perspective relates communication processes to the acquisition and use of social knowledge and links social knowledge to relationship development processes. This account of relationship development differs considerably from the usual explanations of relational growth and decline which rely upon such constructs as rewards and costs. While such social exchange accounts are plausible, they usually ignore the study of communication itself. In such approaches, communication is *assumed* and the products of communication are examined. The present approach places language and communication along with social knowledge at the very *centre* of relationship development. Language and communication affect the kinds of social knowledge that persons will acquire about themselves and others, and in turn social knowledge affects how persons communicate. We think that this reciprocal relationship between communication and social knowledge is critical to a number of relational issues.

In no particular order, we want to thank (most of) the communication faculty and graduate students at Northwestern University and the Universities of California (Santa Barbara) and Iowa; both sets of parents; Emilda; Pooh, Sidney, Fluppers and Todd; Howie Giles; Larry Martin; Hans Castorp; John Waite Bowers; Joan, Douglas, Daniel and Matthew; and ANTHONY J. DUCKWINGZ (an acronym comprising the initials of the names of *all* those entities who deserve to be thanked which spatial limitations prevent us from acknowledging).

1

Uncertainty and the nature of interpersonal communication

If a man will begin with certainties, he will end with doubts; but if he will be content to begin with doubts, he shall end in certainties.

Francis Bacon

Every day we come into contact with and talk to several different persons whom we know in differing ways. Many of these encounters are with the same persons and are repetitive and routine. Whether we are communicating with close friends or strangers, a majority of our interactions are 'carried off' without a great deal of difficulty. Having to spend considerable time consciously thinking about what to say and when to say it either before or during a conversation is the exception rather than the rule. Of course, sometimes interactions with others require considerable planning or forethought. Most of us require some time to plan and rehearse a public speech, a presentation to the board of directors, or our responses in a job interview. We might also engage in similar planning before talking with a close friend about an important issue having to do with the status of our relationship with that person; for example, telling a close friend that he or she has offended us in some way.

In this book we are concerned with the roles that our thoughts about others and our communication with others play in the development of interpersonal relationships. Most of us have had the experience of meeting a total stranger and developing a relationship with that person to the point that we are willing to call the person a 'friend'. We have also had the experience of witnessing the disintegration of these close relationships. We feel that a close examination of how persons form impressions and think about each other and how they use language to relate to each other will tell us a lot about how relationships are developed, how they are maintained, and how they disintegrate. Obviously, there are numerous reasons for the development and deterioration of friendships, professional relationships, marriages, and family relationships. Although all of these cannot be addressed in this book, we feel that by concentrating upon both linguistic and social cognition processes we can gain much insight into relationship development.

Since we will be using the term 'interpersonal communication' throughout this book, it is important to clarify what we mean by this term. The term *interpersonal communication* has been defined in a number of different ways by various writers and researchers. Some of these writers (King 1979; Smith and

1

Williamson 1977) have chosen to limit interpersonal communication to situations involving two persons and no more. A second group of researchers has studied face-to-face interactions within health care, legal and business situations. These researchers take the view that interactions within these situations or contexts are unique and determined mainly by the situation itself. A third group of writers has examined communication in terms of the functions it serves (Dance and Larson 1976). Finally, some writers have looked at interpersonal communication from the perspective of how persons develop relationships with others (Knapp 1978). In the sections which follow, we will consider the potential strengths and weaknesses of each of these approaches. We shall also propose an approach which is both functional and developmental in nature. We believe that this combination approach provides us with a more powerful tool for understanding the roles that language and communication play in the development of relationships than any approach taken alone.

On the nature of interpersonal communication

As we pointed out above, there are a number of different perspectives from which to view the process of communicating interpersonally. In this section we will examine some of these alternatives and suggest a conceptualization of interpersonal communication which we find useful for the purposes of this book.

The numerical perspective

One way to define interpersonal communication is to assert that communication that occurs between two persons or among small groups of persons is interpersonal. By contrast, communication which occurs between a given individual and a large group either in a face-to-face context or a mass-media context might be labelled 'public communication'. Obviously, such an approach to the definition of 'interpersonal' hinges upon the number of persons participating in the communication situation and not upon what is being talked about.

While it is tempting to argue that persons talk about intimate matters in situations with relatively few others present and that public communication situations are not arenas for the disclosure of personal information, there are numerous examples of persons who have made highly personal disclosures about themselves in public contexts. A number of years ago Betty Ford, the wife of President Gerald Ford, disclosed that she was undergoing treatment for alcoholism and drug abuse. Billy Carter, the brother of President Jimmy Carter, explained the treatment he received for alcoholism on nationally televised news. These examples illustrate the point that disclosure of what most of us would deem personal information can occur outside of what some persons would call 'interpersonal' communication situations; that is, if we were to define the notion of interpersonal communication solely by reference to the number of persons in the communication situation.

It is also the case that in many everyday communication situations in which we interact with one or two other persons at a time, relatively little personal information is exchanged. Most sales transactions in which we engage are highly ritualistic and highly impersonal. Even routine interactions between family members may take on ritualistic and impersonal qualities. These examples suggest that defining interpersonal communication by employing the criterion of the number of persons in the communication situation is of relatively limited value.

The situational approach

Another way in which to view interpersonal communication is to focus upon particular types of communication situations. For example, one might study interactions between such individuals as doctors and patients, students and teachers, husbands and wives, parents and children, and so on. This approach to the study of interpersonal communication might be defended by arguing that there is something unique to each of these situations, so that they need to be considered separately. For example, doctors and patients do not interact in the same ways that husbands and wives do.

Although the above approach has strong intuitive appeal, there are at least three problems with it. First, the situational approach directs attention away from finding *general patterns* of communication which may operate in most or all of the different kinds of situations one might be able to discern. There may be more features in common across different kinds of situations than there are differences. Second, the situational approach would appear to lead to the almost endless listing of different communication situations. It takes little imagination and time to generate a long list of potentially different communication situations. Thus, in addition to the situations listed above, one might study communication between bus drivers and riders, car salespersons and car buyers, ticket agents and ticket purchasers, therapists and clients, etc. While studies of these and other particular situations might produce valuable information, one would hope, for the sake of drawing generalizations, that there are processes which are common to these situations. Finally, most probably, the range of possible communication which can occur within each of these situations can vary considerably. Some persons interact with the bus driver they see every day in an impersonal manner, while other persons consider the same bus driver their 'friend' and disclose highly personal information to him or her. The same range could be found in several of the situations listed above; therefore, to assert that there is *one* kind of doctor–patient communication which differs from other kinds of communication might well be misleading.

The functional approach

Basic courses in public speaking generally require students to present at least three different kinds of speeches: a speech to entertain, a speech to inform and a speech to persuade. This division of public speaking activities implies that communication can serve different functions; that is, communicative activity can be used to induce different emotional states, communication can be used to impart information, and communication can be used to change attitudes and behaviours. While all of these functions can take place within the context of face-to-face interactions of a more informal nature, there are additional functions which communication can serve in interpersonal relationships. For example, the symbolic interactionist George Herbert Mead (1934) suggested that language and communicative processes were critical in the development of self-conception. He asserted that it is only through interaction with others that persons become conscious of themselves as social beings. In addition, communication may serve to validate the self-concept once it is formed. Simply by acknowledging messages which are sent by others we inform the persons who send these messages that they are noteworthy and that they are recognized as individuals.

One limitation to the functional approach to the study of interpersonal communication is that, like the situational approach, it is possible to generate numerous functions which communication might fulfil in interpersonal relationships. For example, in their insightful treatment of the functional approach, Dance and Larson (1976) argue that human communication serves the three functions of: (1) relating self to the environment, (2) developing higher mental processes, and (3) regulating human behaviour. Although they cogently argue for the importance of these functions, it is also possible to consider additional functions which communication might serve. Moreover, the functional approach, if widely employed, would most likely lead to the development of lists of functions which would overlap and as a result produce long but relatively trivial arguments over the labelling of functions. Thus, by itself, the functional approach to the study of interpersonal communication appears to have some important limitations.

Developmental approach

The final approach to the study of interpersonal communication to be considered here is one which focuses upon the various trajectories which relationships traverse. During our lifetimes we come into contact with numerous persons outside our families; however, we develop only relatively few close friendships within this pool of potential eligibles. Some research we have done (Berger, Gardner, Clatterbuck and Schulman 1976) suggests that when persons are asked how many close friends they have, the average number of close friends designated is around five or six. We have obtained these averages for both college students and older persons.

The developmental approach to interpersonal communication seeks to answer such questions as: What factors are responsible for the escalation of relationships from the acquaintance stage to the close friendship or lover stage? Once relationships are formed, what factors are responsible for their maintenance? When such relationships deteriorate, what factors are responsible for their demise? One difficulty with these questions is that some of the answers to them may not necessarily involve communication processes directly. For example, Altman and Taylor (1973) assert that perceptions of relative rewards and costs by relational partners affect the growth and decline of relationships. When relational rewards exceed costs, relationships tend to escalate; when costs exceed rewards, relationships tend to decline. Although communication processes may be involved in generating perceptions of relative rewards and costs, it is also possible that non-communicative factors such as relative levels of education and income might also affect judgements of reward/cost ratios. By simply taking a developmental approach to the study of interpersonal communication, it is possible that one might be led away from the study of language processes to the study of non-linguistic variables.

The functional-developmental approach

Given the four options outlined above, we feel that one of the more productive approaches to the study of interpersonal communication is to focus upon a particular function that communication plays in the development of inter-personal relationships. For our purposes, the communication function we have chosen to concentrate on is that of *uncertainty reduction*; that is, how com-munication functions to help us attain knowledge and understanding of ourselves and others. We recognize that language can be used to reduce uncertainty, but it is also possible that language can be used to increase uncertainty as well. Although communication is vital to the process of relation-ship development, we feel that the role played by communication in the development of relationships is mediated by uncertainty reduction.

The approach outlined above is unique in that the usual treatments of relationship development tend to focus upon the variables which are correlates of *liking* or *attraction* between persons. Our approach does not deny the importance of attraction, but shifts the focus of the study of relationship development more toward problems associated with the attainment of *inter-personal understanding*. In our view, the relationship between understanding and attraction is best illustrated by the notion 'to know him/her is to love him/her'. Previous approaches to the study of relationship development have emphasized the latter part of this relationship. The present treatment focuses upon the former, and communication is critical to the process of interpersonal knowledge acquisition.

Before discussing the notion of uncertainty in detail, we should note that there is considerable variation in the way that researchers view the concept of communication. To some (Watzlawick, Beavin and Jackson 1967) *all* behaviour is communicative. These authors assert that when two persons are in each other's presence, persons *cannot not communicate*. Every action, whether intended or not, has potential communicative significance. By contrast, both Rommetveit (1968) and Blakar (in press) contend that it is necessary to dis-tinguish between behaviour and communication. These authors make this distinction by arguing that only messages which are *intentionally* encoded by a source and sent to a receiver are communication. Unintended messages and unconscious behaviours which a source emits are not communicative events, even though they may have an impact upon a receiver.

We will not debate the relative merits of these two positions at this juncture; however, it should be recognized that casting the debate in terms of these two polar extremes ignores the fact that when persons engage in social interaction, their levels of awareness concerning goals, intentions and actions vary along a continuum. It is a mistake to assume that persons are either aware or unaware of their goals, intentions and actions; awareness can occur at many levels. A person may be very aware that he or she is angry toward another person, but be unable to describe in great detail specific responses that he or she makes in a given situation. A person may be able to recall various *topics* which were covered in a conversation, but be unable to give a *verbatim reconstruction* of the conversation.

Perhaps a more fruitful way of approaching the issue of intentionality and awareness is to recognize that persons' levels of attention to their actions vary during the course of most social interactions. Sometimes persons are highly aware of what they wish to achieve in a given situation, e.g. a job interview, while at other times persons may be only dimly aware of goals and intentions *vis-à-vis* the other person in the interaction, e.g. cocktail-party conversation. Moreover, at times persons may monitor their verbal and nonverbal behaviours very closely in order to achieve some kind of goal. They may even rehearse their performance. At other times they may pay little attention to what they are doing or saying and how they are doing or saying it. This view suggests that important variables to consider in the study of ongoing social interactions are the levels of awareness of self and other. We believe that the issues of awareness and intentionality are most fruitfully viewed as research areas rather than definitional issues. As we shall see in Chapter 2, a considerable number of researchers have begun to explore the role that awareness plays in social interactions.

Uncertainty and interpersonal communication

Since we see uncertainty reduction as critical to the process of relationship development, it is necessary to spend some time explicating the concept of uncertainty. One way in which to view the concept of uncertainty is from the perspective of information theory (Shannon and Weaver 1949). Under this view, uncertainty is determined by the number of alternatives that could occur in a given situation and the relative likelihood of their occurrence. As the number of alternatives increases, uncertainty increases. For example, if you are asked to guess the next letter of an English word which begins with the letter 'Q', the number of potential letters which can follow is very limited. Most words in the English language which begin with the letter 'Q' have 'u' as their second letter. By contrast, given 'T' as the first letter of a word and being asked to guess the next letter is considerably more difficult since there are a number of potential letters which might follow the initial letter 'T'. Relative to the situation with the letter 'Q', the 'T' situation is much less predictable or much more uncertain. However, even if there are an equal number of alternative possibilities in two situations, uncertainty or predictability can differ. For example, let us assume that there are two letters in the English alphabet which, when they are used as initial letters in words, are followed by an equal number of other letters; however, one of the initial letters is followed by a particular other letter 95 per cent of the time, while the alternative letters which follow the other initial letter occur with about equal frequency. Because there is a dominant alternative in the first case, there is less uncertainty in that situation. In the second case, since the alternatives are close to equally likely, there is more uncertainty.

When we meet persons for the first time, we are faced with prediction problems which are similar to those discussed above. When we begin to converse with a total stranger, generally we have little direct knowledge of the person's beliefs, attitudes and preferences; although, as we will see in Chapter 2, we may infer a person's beliefs, etc. from his or her appearance, dress or accent. Also, we cannot be certain how this person has behaved in the past or how he or she will behave in the future. Yet, when we come face-to-face with such a person, we are expected to say something to him or her. Silence is awkward, unless the social context 'allows' for it, for example, sitting in the waiting room of a doctor's office. Upon meeting a person for the first time, we not only are faced with problems of retrodiction and prediction, we are also faced with problems of explaining *why* the person behaves and believes the way he or she does. Uncertainty, then, can stem from the large number of alternative things that a stranger can believe or potentially say. Further, even if we can predict what the stranger will do or believe, we still have the problem of explaining why they behave or believe in a particular way.

Everything that has been described above can also be applied to *ourselves* in interactions with strangers. There are any number of alternative ways in which we might behave in such interactions; that is, there are any number of alternative things we might say or do when we come into contact with a given stranger. Also, we might be willing to modify or change our beliefs, attitudes or preferences in a number of ways depending upon the person with whom we are interacting. The point is that not only do we have the problem of predicting what the stranger is likely to do in the situation, we also must try to select from our own behavioural and preference repertoires those responses which we think will optimize the interaction goals we have set for ourselves in the situation, if we are aware of such goals. In general, one goal in such initial interactions is to carry off the conversation in as smooth a manner as possible so that neither party suffers embarrassment (Goffman 1959). Of course, we may have other interaction goals depending upon the person with whom we are interacting. For example, we might be trying to exact some kinds of financial rewards from the person or we might be attempting to form a friendship with the person. In either case, however, most persons prefer an amiable, relaxed, and conflict-free interaction to one which is unfriendly, saturated with tension, and conflict-ridden. In order to achieve these kinds of interactions, it is imperative that uncertainty be reduced.

There are at least two kinds of uncertainty which can be discerned in inter-action situations. First, there is what we will call *cognitive uncertainty*. This term refers to uncertainty we have about our own and the other person's beliefs and attitudes. Second, *behavioural uncertainty* concerns the extent to which behaviour is predictable in a given situation. These two kinds of uncertainty may or may not be related. For example, in initial encounters persons may know very little about each other's beliefs, attitudes and preferences; however, they may be able to communicate with each other in a very fluent manner. Indeed, there are initial interaction rituals in which persons exchange such information as where they are from, their occupations, and where they went on their last vacation. There have been a number of studies of these initial interaction rituals (Berger 1973b; Berger, Gardner, Clatterbuck and Schulman 1976; Calabrese 1975; Motl 1980). In all likelihood, these rituals have been developed to cope with the problem of high levels of cognitive uncertainty in initial interaction situations. So, two persons who know very little about each other can behave as if they have high levels of cognitive certainty. Of course, once the ritual is over, congnitive uncertainty may lead to disfluencies in talk, which is one sign of behavioural uncertainty.

Levels of knowledge

Another way to think about the role of uncertainty and uncertainty reduction in interpersonal relationships is to look at the reverse side of the uncertainty coin, that is, knowledge. When we say that we 'know' another person, there are a number of different things we might mean by that statement. For example, we might say we 'know' who Malcolm is in the sense that we can identify Malcolm in a crowd of strangers. At this level of knowing we can remember that the person named Malcolm possesses a unique configuration of physical attributes which enable us to associate his name with his person. It is quite amazing that we are able to identify hundreds of persons at this level. Moreover, when we are asked to describe how such persons look, we can talk about a number of attributes like height, weight, hair colour, eye colour, etc. which we use to identify them. This level of knowing we call *descriptive*. We 'know' who a person is in the sense that we can reliably identify him or her.

When we say that we 'know' what a given person will do or say or how a person will react in a given situation, we have moved to a second level of knowing. This level we call the *predictive* level. In this case we are not only sure who the person is in the sense of identification, we are also more or less certain that we can reliably predict what the person will do or say. Furthermore, our predictions may extend beyond the person's behaviour to their beliefs and attitudes. The descriptive and predictive levels of knowing are related in that finding out things about another person may give rise to predictive activity. Numerous studies have shown, for example, that persons who are more physically attractive are predicted to be more successful in certain kinds of situations (Berscheid and Walster 1974). Knowing that a person is a mill worker may give rise to certain predictions about that person's political attitudes and beliefs. Similarly, knowledge of gender may influence certain predictions about preferences and attitudes.

The importance of prediction-making activities in interpersonal communication situations has been emphasized by Miller and Steinberg (1975). These authors argue that in order to be successful in interpersonal communication episodes, one must be able to make a reasonably accurate set of predictions about the person with whom he or she is interacting. Moreover, these authors assert that the ability to make accurate predictions enables one to exert more control in the relationship. Finally, being able to wield greater amounts of control in the situation raises the likelihood of achieving one's interaction goals. Accurate predictions enable us to make more optimal choices among the messages which may be sent to the other person in the interaction. This state of affairs lowers the chances of offending or embarrassing the other person; unless, of course, that is our goal in the interaction.

Although accurate prediction is critical to the exercise of effective control in interpersonal relationships, there is yet one higher knowledge level. This level involves our ability to *explain* why persons say and do what they do. We might be able to predict with a high level of accuracy the way in which a given individual or group of individuals might respond to a particular message or set of messages we might send to them; however, even granting this high level of predictive knowledge, our ability to explain *why* they respond the way they do might be very limited. Of course, in any given communication situation, we might only be interested in being able to predict responses. Explanation might not be of critical importance to the outcome of the situation. However, for some relationships our ability to explain the conduct of the other person is very important. In general, the more our outcomes depend upon the other person and the closer the relationship we have with that person, the more interested we become in obtaining explanatory knowledge about that person. Explanatory knowledge takes considerable time and energy to develop; so, there are relatively few persons in our lives whom we know at this level. When we say that we know why a person did or said something or when we claim that we know what makes a person 'tick', we are making claims about explanatory knowledge. Explanatory knowledge is extremely powerful since it may enable us to modify more efficiently another person's behaviour or attitudes; that is, knowing why a person believes or behaves in the way he or she does gives us more possible ways in which to influence that person than if we can only predict what they will do.

It should be pointed out that the three levels of knowledge discussed above can be applied not only to our knowledge of other persons but can also be applied to self-knowledge. At first, it might seem as if we all have large amounts of knowledge about ourselves at each of the three knowledge levels; however, it is literally true that some persons with severe psychological disturbances are unable to identify themselves let alone make predictions about their actions or provide explanations for them. While most of us have a fairly large fund of self-knowlege at the descriptive level, at times we may have difficulty predicting how we will respond in a given circumstance. These self-prediction problems are likely to arise when we enter new situations in our own culture or when we engage in interactions in a new cultural context. Finally, there are circumstances under which we might ask the question 'Why did I do that?' or 'Why did I say that?'. Answers to these questions can be difficult to come by at times. Just as we can be uncertain about other persons and ourselves, so too can we have differing levels of knowledge with respect to ourselves and others.

In our discussion of the three levels of knowledge we have talked about knowledge as something which we either have or do not have. This view should be tempered by the idea that in everyday life persons *think* they know things about themselves and others when in fact they may be in considerable error. It is probably safe to say that it is impossible to know one's self or any other person completely. Think of the number of times you have been surprised by unpredictable actions of persons whom you thought you knew well or the number of times you have been surprised by your own actions. Granting the imperfection of knowledge of self and others, we are still called upon to open our mouths and say things to other persons. Thus, most of us are forced to interact on the basis of what we think to be the case rather than what might actually be the case in some objective sense. Again, it is somewhat amazing that we are able to carry out as many successful interactions as we do given the fact that we almost always operate upon flawed knowledge. Of course, it is also the case that sometimes we do make large predictive errors which in turn produce equally large *faux pas*.

Levels of interpersonal communication

Not only do we know persons at different levels, we also exchange information with them at different levels. Miller and Steinberg (1975) have suggested three levels at which we might communicate with others. At the *cultural* level we communicate with others on the basis of shared cultural norms and conventions. In white, middle-class American culture, for example, when we see someone we have met before, it is not uncommon to greet that person with such messages as 'Hi there'. or 'Hello, how are you?' Cultural conventions also dictate that when we send such a greeting to another, we can *expect* that the person who is addressed will reciprocate the greeting. If we fail to meet these cultural expectations, the consequences can be negative. Failing to greet a person or to reciprocate a greeting may induce the other person to feel rejected or slighted and will most probably lower the attractiveness of the person committing the communicative sin. Notice, however, that we can communicate at this cultural level with relatively little knowledge of the person with whom we are communicating.

As long as the person speaks our language and appears to be from our culture, we can make certain assumptions concerning how to go about interacting with that person. However, as Hall (1959, 1966) has pointed out, we can encounter considerable difficulties in trying to interact with persons from other cultures because we fail to recognize that these persons employ a different set of communication conventions and norms. For example, when compared with characteristic distances between conversants in North America, persons from the Near East stand considerably closer to each other when they talk. Thus, when persons from North America converse with persons from the Near East, the North Americans may feel that they are being 'crowded' or that the persons from these cultures are 'pushy', while the persons from the Near East might judge the North Americans to be 'stand-offish' or 'cold'. Conceptions of time also differ among cultures. For example, it is quite acceptable in Korea to be as much as 45 minutes late for an appointment with a friend. Americans in Korea have great difficulty adjusting to what they call Korean Standard Time when they have made an appointment to meet a Korean friend.

A second level at which persons can communicate, according to Miller and Steinberg (1975), is the *sociological* level. At this level persons exchange information on the basis of group membership and social roles. These group memberships or roles might be based upon the interactants' occupations, ages, genders, races, ethnic backgrounds, or social classes. There are certain communication conventions which are tied to group memberships and roles. We tend to communicate with professors, doctors and the incumbents of other roles on the basis of characteristics that are shared in common by persons who occupy these roles. This is so because we tend to make certain predictions, sometimes inaccurate ones, regarding persons who are members of certain groups or persons who occupy certain roles. We then communicate with these persons, at least to some degree, based upon these predictions. Just as predictive errors can be made at the cultural level, so too can such errors be made at the sociological level. We may assume that as a lot, professors are not very athletic persons. Upon meeting a professor and talking with him or her, we may be surprised to find that he or she spends part of his or her spare time playing amateur soccer or semi-pro football. These 'surprises' or 'jolts' that we sometimes experience when meeting someone and talking with them are simply the product of violations of our predictions about how members of particular social groups behave and believe. Obviously, such erroneous sociological predictions can create considerable communication difficulties.

The importance of group differences in social interaction has also been recognized by Tajfel and Turner (1979) and Street and Giles (in press). These authors assert that some social interactions can be viewed as primarily based upon interpersonal relationships and individual characteristics (inter-individual encounters) while other social interactions may be based upon memberships in social groups (intergroup encounters). Tajfel and Turner (1979) argue that as the encounter moves toward the intergroup pole, the more persons are likely to treat members of the other group in a less differentiated fashion. Behaviour toward the other person is likely to be based upon stereotypes of the social group to which the person belongs rather than individual characteristics which the person possesses. In terms of uncertainty reduction and knowledge levels, we might say that in the inter-individual encounter, uncertainty is reduced by taking into account the unique characteristics of the individual. By contrast, in the intergroup encounter, uncertainty may be reduced in a subjective sense by employing a stereotype with which to guide action. Obviously, the latter process invites considerable room for error, since the person being stereotyped may differ drastically from the stereotype in terms of his or her individual characteristics.

A final level of communication discussed by Miller and Steinberg (1975) is the *psychological* level. This level of communication involves predictions that are based upon knowledge of the other person as an individual. At this level we think of the other person as an individual who has a unique configuration of beliefs and attitudes as well as a unique pattern of behaviour. At this level of communication we individuate the other person. In order to communicate at this level, we need to know what the other believes about certain issues and what kinds of things the other person prefers. We must also be able to predict how the person is likely to react in both routine and non-routine social situations. When compared with the other two levels of communication, the achievement of the psychological level requires considerably more investment of time and energy. Furthermore, in order to maintain knowledge at this level, it is necessary to monitor the other person in order to detect changes in that person's beliefs and behaviour over time. Because of the difficulties involved in both the generation and maintenance of the psychological level of knowledge, there are relatively few persons in our lives with whom we communicate at this level.

It should be emphasized, as it is by Miller and Steinberg (1975), that in any given communication transaction, all three levels of communication can be operative. Interactions between very close friends or lovers may take place primarily at the psychological level; however, there may be cultural norms which act to regulate communication even at this level. Also, persons may occasionally exchange very 'personal' information within the context of relationships that occur primarily at the cultural or sociological levels. Nonetheless, in most of our relationships, one of these three levels is more prominent than the other two.

There are two additional points that can be made. First, movement through the three levels of communication is parallel to movement through the three knowledge levels we discussed earlier. In order to move from cultural to psychological levels of communication, one must move from description to prediction and explanation. To communicate efficiently at the psychological level requires higher knowledge levels. Secondly, as we move from the cultural level through the sociological level to the psychological level, our communication becomes less impersonal. In fact, Miller and Steinberg (1975) argue that communication which occurs primarily at the cultural level is *non-interpersonal communication*, while communication, which takes place primarily at the psychological level is *interpersonal communication*.

Since the orientation of this volume conceives of communication as serving the function of reducing uncertainty, there is an obvious affinity between our view of interpersonal communication and the view advanced by Miller and Steinberg (1975). Both our orientation and the Miller and Steinberg view recognize that persons can and do communicate with each other on the bases of different knowledge levels. Furthermore, both conceptions assert that the range of communicative activities in which persons can engage is, in part, determined by the knowledge bases upon which interactions take place. Thus, although two persons might be uttering words and sentences which make sense to them, these sensible utterances may or may not constitute interpersonal communication. Interpersonal communication is a relatively unique form of communication the appearance of which depends upon relative knowledge levels of interactants.

It is important to point out that in many social arenas, persons have expectations that interpersonal communication, as we view it, should and will take place. Family members, close friends, and marital partners generally have such expectations. It is interesting to note how persons are disappointed when such personal and therapeutic communication does not take place in these contexts. Persons who get divorced frequently attribute the dissolution of their relationships to communication problems such as the inability to provide comfort, etc. Our analysis would suggest that these expectations for interpersonal communication are not met because persons do not have enough higher-order knowledge about each other to communicate at the interpersonal level. Family members and spouses may literally not know each other well because of the social forces which pull these persons away from each other. The notion of family members and spouses as relative strangers highlights the advantage of viewing interpersonal communication from a social knowledge point of view rather than a 'situational' viewpoint. Simply because persons happen to be in social situations which generally give rise to communication at more personal levels does not mean *ipso facto* that persons communicate at these personal levels in these situations.

Uncertainty reduction in ongoing and severed relationships

The preceding discussion of the role of uncertainty in social interactions has highlighted the problems of uncertainty reduction in initial encounters. We would like to stress that uncertainty reduction can become an issue in relationships that are 'established' and relationships which have 'burned out'. In fact, we would argue that in order for a relationship to continue, it is important that the persons involved in the relationship consistently update their fund of knowledge about themselves, their relational partner and their relationship. We assume that persons' beliefs, attitudes and goals are in a constant state of evolution and flux. Given this assumption, it is obvious that as persons change through time, it is necessary to either update one's knowledge base along the dimensions cited above or suffer the potential consequence of 'growing apart'. Nowhere is the necessity for uncertainty reduction in ongoing relationships more apparent than in situations where relational partners spend considerable amounts of time away from each other because of occupational demands or other reasons. We suspect that absences which are frequent or long generally do not 'make the heart grow fonder'; rather, such extended absences may make the interactions of relational partners more tentative and difficult when the partners are reunited.

Similarly, after relationships have ended, persons involved in these terminated relationships must also engage in uncertainty reducing activities involving both prediction and explanation. First, as we will see in Chapter 2, persons generally develop explanations for the demises of their relationships. Secondly, persons may become concerned with the predictive issue of whether future relationships will come to the same end. These two uncertainty reduction activities are most probably related. Persons who fail to explain in any terms why their relationships have ended may be very reticent to embark upon new relationships until they have generated adequate explanations for the terminated relationships. Furthermore, persons who explain relational demises in terms of negative attributes that they possess may be prone to feel that they can never have a long-term relationship with another person because of these undesirable characteristics. Persons who explain their relational terminations in ways that are not related to themselves may be more willing to initiate new relationships. These possibilities demonstrate the importance of uncertainty reduction activities in both ongoing and terminated relationships.

Prospect

The subsequent chapters of this volume will examine in greater detail a number of the issues raised in this chapter. In the next chapter we will focus upon the knowledge generating processes and strategies that persons use to come to know each other. Here we will discuss attribution processes, strategies that persons employ to gain knowledge about others, and the extent to which persons use social knowledge in a conscious way to guide their communicative conduct. The third chapter will consider the role that language plays in attribution generation and the creation of impressions of others. The communicative conduct of others is something which we sometimes seek to explain and we also use communication to help us generate social knowledge. The fourth chapter will deal with the relationship between language and social interaction. Chapter five will examine how the verbal and nonverbal conduct of participants in a relationship can be used to index the state of the relationship and how persons in the relationship can themselves control the state of their relationship through their message exchanges. The final chapter will deal with both theoretical and practical implications of our approach to knowledge processes and interpersonal communication.

2

Uncertainty reduction and the generation of social knowledge

The first condition of having to deal with somebody at all is to know with whom one has to deal.

Georg Simmel

In the previous chapter we discussed the notion of uncertainty and its importance in social interaction. If we are unable to explain why we and others believe and behave in the ways we do, we become less able to know what to say and how to behave in social situations. Uncertainty lowers our ability to exercise control in the situation and decreases the probabilities that we will obtain our goals in the interaction, whatever these goals may be. This chapter will focus upon the strategies and processes we employ to reduce our uncertainties about ourselves and others in social situations. We will begin by describing some specific strategies persons use to gain knowledge about others and strategies that persons might use to remain unknown to others. We will then consider three theories which have been developed by social psychologists to explain how we come to attribute dispositions and causes of actions to ourselves and others. These attribution theories are vitally concerned with the generation of what we have called predictive and explanatory levels of knowledge. Finally, we will consider some potential limitations upon the extent to which persons in social interaction situations can be aware or mindful of the strategies and processes they use to achieve their goals in interaction situations.

Knowledge acquisition strategies

In this section we will address two questions. First, under what conditions do persons become especially preoccupied with reducing their uncertainties about others. Obviously, in our everyday lives, there are many persons whom we meet but do not feel the need to get to know well. Thus, we can ask what conditions prompt a heightened concern for uncertainty reduction. Second, given that uncertainty is at a high level and a person wishes to reduce it, what strategies might the person employ to reduce his or her uncertainty?

Conditions prompting uncertainty reduction

Recent studies have suggested that it is only under certain conditions that

14

persons become preoccupied with explaining another's actions. For example, Pyszczynski and Greenberg (1981) found that persons attended to relevant explanatory information about a person only when their expectations of the person's behaviour were violated. When their expectations were met, they showed few signs of concern for acquiring relevant information about the person. Their findings suggest the broader proposition that when persons *deviate from norms or expectations*, persons become more concerned with reducing their uncertainties about the person being observed. When persons act 'normally', observers experience little uncertainty regarding the person observed, and do not concern themselves with knowledge acquisition. Thus, one condition for the creation of uncertainty-reduction concerns is that of unpredictability or deviation from some kind of standard.

There is evidence, other than the Pyszczynski and Greenberg (1981) study, to suggest that when persons encounter novel or unpredictable behaviours, they behave in ways to reduce uncertainties. For example, Newtson (1973) had subjects look at videotapes of individuals doing mundane tasks by themselves. While they observed the tapes, the individuals were instructed to press a button when they felt that a meaningful action began. The button presses defined what Newtson called 'break points'. Newtson found that when he introduced novel or unpredictable actions into an action sequence, the rate of button pressing increased; that is, observers segmented the ongoing behaviour into more perceptual units. When the actor returned to behaving in a 'normal' manner, observers pressed the button fewer times; that is, they segmented the ongoing action into larger units. Newtson (1973, 1976) interpreted these findings as indicating that when persons encountered an unpredictable act in an otherwise normal action sequence, they tried to restore predictability by more closely monitoring the stream of ongoing behaviour. Finer unitization of the deviant behaviour was an attempt by the observers to gain a better understanding of the behaviour. Newtson (1976) also reported that still pictures representing segments where most observers of a group recorded a break point (consensus break points) were more accurately sorted with reference to their actual sequence in a film than were still pictures taken from non-break-point segments of the film. According to Newtson, these findings indicate that break points contain more information than non-break points. It should be pointed out, however, that recently some investigators have questioned what Newtson's break-point measure actually indicates (Ebbesen 1980). Ebbesen suggests that break points may not be indicative of some kind of basic 'chunking' process involved in the processing of social information.

The above evidence suggests that when persons encounter unexpected events, they tend to engage in actions which are designed to help them reduce their uncertainties. However, when behavioural events occur the way they usually do, persons are not preoccupied with uncertainty-reduction concerns, at least in terms of the person with whom they are interacting or the person whom they are observing.

A second condition which motivates uncertainty reduction is *expectation of future interaction*. When persons expect to interact with each other in the future, they will monitor their present interaction more carefully and try to reduce their uncertainties about each other more. This principle is illustrated by several studies. First, Kiesler, Kiesler and Pallak (1967) studied the effects of commitment to future interaction on evaluations of persons who conformed to or deviated from social norms. When persons were led to believe that they would be interacting with a norm violator in the future, they rated the norm violator's behaviour more negatively than did persons who believed that they would not have to interact with the norm violator in the future. Furthermore, persons who thought that they would be interacting with a person who conformed to norms found that person to be more attractive than did persons who thought that they would not be interacting with the conformer in the future. In short, expectations of future interaction made deviators less attractive and conformers more attractive. Kiesler (1969) has also pointed out that commitment to future behaviour can exert considerable influence upon present behaviour. Persons who know that they will be interacting in the future are likely to surpress behaviours which might make them less attractive. Persons who know that they will never see each other again may be willing to say and do things which are somewhat less socially desirable.

More directly related to the relationship between anticipation of future interaction and uncertainty reduction is a study by Calabrese (1975). In this study, pairs of strangers were asked to get acquainted with each other. They held a conversation for 13 minutes. Unknown to the conversational participants, their interaction was tape-recorded. Before beginning their conversations, half of the pairs were told that they would be interacting in the future. The remaining pairs were given no such instructions. Calabrese's (1975) analysis of the content of these conversations over the 13-minute period revealed that persons who thought that they would interact in the future exchanged more background information with each other than did persons who believed that they would not converse again. These findings are consistent with the uncertainty model advanced by Berger and Calabrese (1975) which suggests that biographic and demographic information, which dominates initial interactions between strangers, is exchanged in order to reduce uncertainty.

If the notion that anticipated interaction heightens concern for uncertainty reduction is correct, we might expect persons anticipating future interaction with others to be able to remember more about those persons. There are at least two studies which show this to be the case. First, Berscheid, Graziano, Monson and Dermer (1976) had subjects agree to let the experimenters decide whom they would go out with or date. Some subjects agreed to let the experimenters control their dating choices for a short period of time (1 week), while other subjects agreed to let the experimenters determine their dates for a longer period of time (5 weeks). These investigators then let the subjects view videotaped discussions in which their prospective dates were allegedly participating. After viewing the tapes, persons were asked to recall as many details as possible about the prospective dates. Those persons who expected to date the person for five weeks showed better recall than those persons who expected to date the person for only one week. Harvey, Yarkin, Lightner and Town (1980) conducted a study in which some persons were led to believe that they would be interacting with one person who was involved in a videotaped discussion which they observed. Other subjects were not lead to expect interaction with any person who was part of the discussion. These investigators found that recall for details of the discussion was better for those who anticipated interaction.

Taken together, the results of the above studies suggest that when persons anticipate interaction with others, they act in ways which are likely to reduce their uncertainties about each other. Anticipated interaction increases exchanges of biographic and demographic information during interactions and heightens recall of conversational content as well as details about the persons with whom one is interacting. Also, when persons anticipate interaction, the consequences of norm violations and norm conformity become more pronounced. The available evidence provides strong support for anticipated interaction as a determinant of the magnitude of concern for uncertainty reduction.

A final condition which gives rise to needs for uncertainty reduction is the extent to which the outcomes of an interaction are likely to be rewarding or punishing. There are numerous theories of social interaction which emphasize the rewards and costs exchanged in the relationship as determinants of relationship growth and decline (Adams 1965; Altman and Taylor 1973; Blau 1964; Homans 1961; Miller and Steinberg 1975; Thibaut and Kelley 1959). In brief, these theories assert that persons involved in relationships with others attempt to maintain a balance between ratios of rewards and costs they give and receive in the relationship. When reward/cost ratios for one's self and the other are roughly equal, the relationship remains stable; however, when these ratios are unequal, inequity is felt and steps are taken to correct the inequity. It is important to note that these models do *not* assume that rewards and costs must be equal for equity to be obtained. It is only necessary that the ratios be equal. Also, rewards and costs in relationships go beyond material goods and include emotional satisfactions and dissatisfactions as well as relationships foregone by participation in the present relationship.

Within the context of uncertainty reduction, we postulate that when persons become concerned with the rewards and costs that another person can mediate for them, they will become more concerned about reducing their uncertainties about the other person. By contrast, if the other person does not have the power to reward or punish us in significant ways, then our concerns for reducing our uncertainties about the other person are reduced. In support of this relationship, Berger, Weber, Munley and Dixon (1977) found that when persons were asked to indicate what factors made specific others attractive to them, they indicated that understanding, rapport, reinforcement and loyalty were very important. These variables were all associated with a general factor which these authors labelled *supportiveness*. Thus, persons are attracted to those who give them understanding as well as material rewards. While there are no doubt a number of other specific conditions under which persons might become preoccupied with reducing their uncertainties about others, we feel that perceived deviance, anticipated interaction and anticipated rewards and punishments are among the most important general factors which are responsible for heightened uncertainty-reduction concerns.

In addition to the above findings, Giles and Powesland (1975) report that when persons want to exchange rewards with each other or become attractive to each other, they tend to *converge* or become more similar with respect to a number of speech characteristics like accent, dialect and speech rate. When persons wish to emphasize their differences, they tend to *diverge* along these speech lines. Within the context of uncertainty theory, these findings could be taken as support for the notion that when persons wish to establish a relationship, they reduce their uncertainties about each other by becoming more similar to each other in terms of speech characteristics. However, if persons are not interested in pursuing a relationship, they are likely to maintain or even diverge with respect to speech characteristics in order to discourage the other person from continuing to try to get to know them. This interpretation is further supported by data from a study by Clatterbuck (1979). Clatterbuck (1979) developed a scale called CLUES which is designed to measure persons' subjective feelings of uncertainty about others. Clatterbuck's scale asks the subject to indicate the degree to which he or she feels able to predict various things concerning a person about whom the subject is thinking. For example, one item asks the subject to indicate how good he or she feels about predicting the way in which the person being thought about would behave in a particular situation. A number of similar items are included in the scale. In a summary of several experiments, Clatterbuck (1979) found that when persons were asked to think of a person whom they liked and to fill out the CLUES scale, they displayed lower levels of uncertainty than when they were asked to fill out the CLUES scale for a person whom they knew well but disliked. When we conclude we dislike a person, we cease trying to get to know them. Thus, there may be a tendency for us to want to reduce our uncertainties about persons who will give us rewards and to not reduce uncertainty about those who might punish us. However, there are circumstances under which it is highly adaptive to 'know your enemy'. So, in all likelihood, uncertainty-reduction concerns are heightened when others can reward or punish us, but perhaps more for those who can reward us.

Strategies for knowledge acquisition

In the previous section we considered three conditions which give rise to uncertainty-reduction concerns: (1) observation of deviant behaviour, (2) anticipated interaction, and (3) high probabilities of receiving rewards and punishments from others. We now assume that one or more of these conditions is present and that we are concerned with reducing our uncertainty about the other. Another way of expressing our desire for uncertainty reduction is to speak of knowledge gaining or knowledge acquisition. The question we will examine in this section concerns the strategies we use to generate knowledge about the other person. In our discussion we will consider three general classes of strategies. *Passive strategies* are those in which we as observers gain knowledge of other persons by observing them without them knowing that we are observing them. These strategies do not involve direct interaction between the observer and the person being observed. *Active strategies* are those ways of gaining information which require the observer to do something to affect the response of the actor but do not involve direct contact between the observer and the actor. Finally, *interactive strategies* are those in which the observer gains knowledge about the actor by engaging in face-to-face interaction with the actor. Within each one of these general classes of strategies are specific strategies that can be used to acquire information. We now turn to these strategies.

Passive strategy I: reactivity search

The question being asked as we consider the passive strategies for knowledge acquisition is, what do persons look for in the behaviour of others to try to find out things about them. At the most basic level we would contend that observers tend to prefer situations in which the target person being observed is actively engaged in some activity rather than in a passive state. Further, we would argue that observers prefer to watch the target person reacting to other persons rather than to observe the target in solitary situations. This is the case even if the observer is unable to overhear the conversation taking place between the target person and the other person or persons present. We learn more about another person by observing him or her react to others rather than observing the person react to objects or things because the behaviour of other persons is considerably more variable than the behaviour of most objects. Thus, the variations in the behaviour of others is more likely to require similar variations in the behaviour of the target person.

There is evidence to support the above reasoning. Berger and Perkins (1978) took colour-slide pictures of a target person in a variety of solitary and social situations. In some pictures the target person was reading a book alone or typing alone. Other pictures showed the target person simply in the presence of others or actively talking with others. Subjects were shown pairs of these slide pictures. In one experiment, one member of the pair of slides was a solitary situation and the other member of the pair was a social situation. Subjects were asked to assume that they wanted to get to know the target person and that they had the opportunity to observe the target person without the target person knowing that he or she was being observed. Subjects were told to assume that they could not talk to the target person. The task for the subjects was to choose the slide which they thought would give them the most information about the target person. The results of this experiment were dramatically clear. For 12 comparisons of social and solitary slides, the minimum percentage of subjects choosing the social slides on any comparison was 70 per cent. In general, the percentages of subjects choosing the social slides was considerably higher than 80 per cent. Thus, subjects showed an overwhelming preference for social as opposed to solitary situations in terms of their information value.

A second experiment reported by Berger and Perkins (1978) employed only social slides in the judgement task. In this situation, subjects were asked to choose between slides which varied in the extent to which the target person was involved in interactions with others. In some slides the target person was depicted as highly involved in the interaction, in others the target person was shown to be uninvolved in the interaction. In this experiment, subjects overwhelmingly preferred slides in which the target person was actively involved with others for information gaining. However, it was felt that the overwhelming preference for active, social situations might be a product of what Berger and Perkins (1979) called the 'Matthew Effect', named after the youngest son of the senior author. When the slide pictures were shown to Matthew (when he was 8 years old), he overwhelmingly preferred the active social slides to the inactive social slides or the solitary slides. When asked why he preferred the active slides, he stated that by listening to the persons talk to each other in the interaction slides, he could find out where they live. He could then go to their house, talk to them, and find out more about them.

Berger and Perkins (1979) in another series of experiments attempted to discern whether the overwhelming preferences for active social situations in the previous studies were due to a widespread belief on the part of subjects that they could overhear the target person interacting with the others present in the picture. In one of their experiments, Berger and Perkins (1979) told half of the subjects making judgements that they were to assume they could *not* overhear what the persons in the pictures were saying. The other half of the subjects were not given these instructions. The results of this experiment revealed that regardless of the instructions, the patterns of choices were very similar between the two groups. Both groups preferred slides in which the target person was highly involved with the others present. These findings support the view that persons prefer socially involving situations as sources of information about a target person not because they assume that they can overhear what the target person is saying but because of the kind of reactivity the target person is likely to display while interacting with others.

Passive strategy II: disinhibition search

The research discussed in the previous section consistently showed that persons prefer to gain information about strangers by observing them in social contexts where they are actively involved in conversations. However, there are any number of social contexts within which such conversations might occur. For example, we might have the choice of observing a given target person interacting with a minister after a church service or observing the same person having a conversation with some friends over a few brews at the local pub. One of the more striking differences between these two situations is their formality. We would expect that the conversation with the minister would be more formal in that each person in the interaction would inhibit more behaviours than they would in the pub situation. Certain topics would most likely not be talked about in the after-church conversation; however, these same topics might be more than acceptable in the pub conversation.

Given the communicative constraints of formal interaction situations, we would argue that observers would find out less about a person as an *individual* by observing him or her within such formal contexts. Obviously, some things can be learned about persons by observing them in formal situations, but the range of things is generally more limited than that provided by informal contexts. Thus, we reasoned that when given the choice, persons would prefer to observe others in informal contexts as opposed to formal contexts for knowledge gaining purposes. Berger and Douglas (1981) reported a study in which persons again judged the information value of slide pictures of a target person shown in a variety of different situations. In this study, over 200 slide pictures of a target person were taken in different public and private situations. In some of the slides the target person was alone, while in others she was with other persons and interacting with them. In this particular study, persons judged a randomly selected subset of 15 of the slides. Before making their judgements, half of the persons were informed that they would be meeting and talking to the target person shown in the slides after making their judgements. These persons were actually taken to a room where the target person was seated alone reading a book. Persons anticipating interaction with the target were also told that their task would be to try to get the target person to like them as much as possible during their conversation. The other half of the participants were not led to believe that they would interact with the target person.

After reviewing their instructions, all participants made their judgements of the information value of the 15 slide pictures. These judgements were then analysed using a multidimensional scaling procedure which extracts the perceptual dimensions used by the judges in making their preference judgements for the various slides. The two dimensions found in the multi-dimensional scaling analyses are shown in Figure 2.1

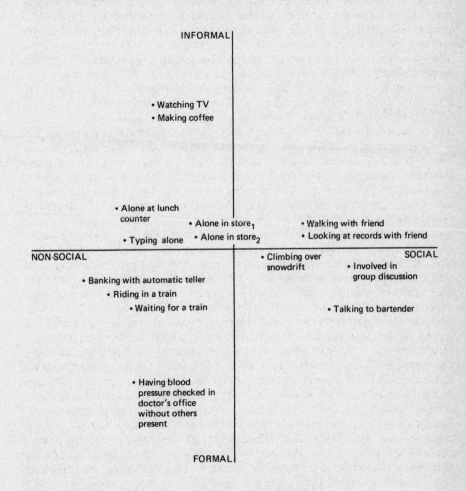

Figure 2.1 Locations of 15 stimulus pictures in two dimensional space

As Figure 2.1 indicates, the dimension represented in the horizontal axis is related to the non-social-social dimension discussed in the previous section. The slides on the right side of the axis generally represent situations in which the target person is interacting with others. Those on the left-hand side represent situations in which the target is alone. This dimension underscores the importance of reactivity for knowledge gaining. The vertical axis of Figure 2.1 is related to the issues discussed in this section. The situations in the upper part of the figure are ones in which the target person is depicted in her apartment or in other more informal situations. Those in the lower half of the figure show the target person in public and more formal situations.

The analyses of the judgement data further revealed that persons making the judgements overwhelmingly preferred the slides in which the target person was engaged in social interaction to those in which she was alone. In terms of the formal–informal dimension, there was about an even split between the judges in their preferences. However, there was a significant tendency for those who anticipated interacting with the target person to prefer the informal slides and for those who did not anticipate interacting with the target person to prefer the more formal slides. Furthermore, those who anticipated interacting with the target person rated themselves as more similar to the target than did those who did not anticipate interaction. The similarity rating was completed immediately after the slide judgements were finished. These findings show that when persons anticipate interaction with a stranger and they have the opportunity to observe that stranger in a number of different contexts, they will prefer social to solitary situations and informal situations to formal situations. In addition, it appears that anticipated interaction has the effect of inducing persons to feel more similar to the person with whom they will interact. A study reported by Larsen, Martin and Giles (1977) also demonstrates the impact that anticipated interaction has on similarity; however, in this case these authors examined perceptions of speech similarity. Their experiment revealed that persons who anticipated interacting with a person whom they heard on a tape judged their speech to be significantly more similar to the person on the tape than did persons who did not anticipate interacting with the person heard on the tape. These effects may be a manifestation of uncertainty reduction about how one will communicate with the target person once the face-to-face meeting occurs.

We should point out that there may be circumstances under which observers might prefer to observe a given individual in a formal as opposed to an informal context. For example, a boss who is interviewing a prospective employee might place the prospective employee in a particular formal situation to see how he or she responds in the situation. Obviously, such a 'test' would tell the employer something about the ability of the prospective employee to cope with the situation, but we believe it would not tell the employer very much about the prospective employee as an *individual*. In some formal contexts, persons may find it necessary to misrepresent themselves or present themselves in ways which are at variance with their actual beliefs and preferences, e.g. misrepresent one's political opinions to agree with the boss so that one will win the favour of the boss. We would argue that formal situations are more likely to encourage such misrepresentations.

The above observational strategies tell us something about the conditions which persons feel will optimize their information gain about a target person. However, the above research does not tell us about *specific* characteristics or attributes about a person which might be important in reducing uncertainty about him or her. For example, the way in which a person is dressed may indicate something about the person's status. Certain facial features may be taken as evidence for a particular kind of personality. Even hair colour (redheads have hot tempers) might be used by some to infer something about a target person's temperament. A number of studies have linked such attributes as physical attractiveness (Berscheid and Walster 1974) to the desirability of persons. Obviously, the way persons dress may be more or less attractive to us; however, the critical question here is what inferences we make about a person given a certain form of dress; that is, what do persons' manners of dress tell us about them. Clearly, the links between various person attributes and the inferences observers make upon observing them is important; for it is on the basis of such inferences that we interact with the person being observed.

Active strategy I: asking others about the target person

The passive strategies outlined above do not require the observer to do any more than situate himself or herself in a particular context and observe the target person. By contrast, active strategies demand considerably more activity from the observer. In the present case, the observer tries to find persons who know the target person and to extract information about the target person from them. Notice that as in the case of the passive strategies there is no direct interaction between the observer and the target person; nevertheless, the observer reduces uncertainty about the target by asking others for information about the target.

This information acquisition strategy has not received research attention, but there are some important observations that can be made about it. First, the person who is gaining information by asking others about the target person must be concerned about the possibility that the persons being asked will tell the target person that the observer is asking questions about him or her. If the target person is so informed, considerable embarrassment might be experienced by the question-asking observer. Secondly, if the target person is informed that the observer is asking questions about him or her, the target person might take steps to modify his or her behaviour in such a way that he or she is able to effect an unrepresentative self-presentation. Thus, the observer will gain faulty information. Finally, observers must be concerned about the credibility of the information that informants give them about the target person. Such information may be either wittingly or unwittingly distorted, so that the second-hand view of the target person may contain a considerable amount of inaccurate information. An interesting issue here is how and to what extent observers attempt to verify the second-hand reports of informants. How many different informants' reports are sought before the observer is satisfied that he or she has obtained a reasonably accurate assessment of the target person? How does the observer handle conflicting reports from various informants? These issues seem to be worthy of some research attention.

Active strategy II: environmental structuring

In the case of the strategy of environmental structuring, the observer manipulates some aspect of the physical or social environment of the target person, observes the target person react to that physical or social environment, and uses the responses of the target to gain knowledge about the target. One of the best examples of this kind of knowledge gaining strategy is the way in which psychologists and other social scientists study social interaction in laboratory situations. Frequently, naive subjects are placed in particular circumstances and their responses to the circumstances are observed through a one-way mirror. The experimenter is usually interested in comparing the responses of subjects to different conditions to see if and how various conditions affect the subjects' responses. For example, in a classic study Schachter (1951) examined the effects of deviance from group opinions on communication to the deviant. In some discussion groups a confederate of the experimenter consistently disagreed with various solutions to problems being discussed by the group; while in other groups the experimenter's confederate consistently agreed with the consensus of the group. During the course of these discussions, the amount of communication directed toward the confederate was measured. This study revealed that the deviant received more communication than the conformer up to a point. However, if the deviant continued to disagree, the amount of communication he or she received began to decrease.

From the point of view of knowledge gaining strategies, we can say that in the Schachter experiment some aspect of the social environment was manipulated by introducing either a deviant or conforming confederate. Then, the responses of the naive group members to the confederate were observed and compared. The critical question is whether in our everyday lives we structure environments in ways to gain knowledge about persons whom we do not know. The answer to this question seems to be affirmative. First, in employment interviews, interviewers may arrange the interview situations in such a way that they obtain specific information about the person being interviewed. Staged incidents may be used to see how the person being interviewed reacts to stress. Second, there are occasions in which an observer might strategically arrange seating in order to be able to observe a target person. The target person might be seated next to a person whom the observer knows well so that the observer can ask his or her friend about the target person after the event is over. There are no doubt numerous other situations in which the observer structures either the physical or the social environment in such a way as to gain information about a target. It is important to keep in mind, however, that the notion of environmental structuring does not include direct contact between the observer and the target. The observer structures the environment and then observes the responses of the target person to these stimuli.

Interactive strategy I: interrogation

By contrast to the passive and active knowledge gaining strategies, the interactive strategies involve direct contact between the observer and the target. These strategies require that the observer become a participant–observer in the social situation. One great advantage of interactive strategies over passive and active strategies from the observer's point of view is that he or she can do more to probe the target person in order to clarify potential ambiguities that the observer may feel about the target person. However, this benefit comes at some cost. When the observer becomes a participant–observer, he or she must be concerned about his or her self-presentation and give at least some thought to these concerns. Some degree of preoccupation with self-presentation may detract from the amount of attention that the observer can give to the target. Thus, when the observer employs passive or active strategies, he or she may be able to devote almost all of his or her attention to observing the target. In the interactive mode, the observer must divide his or her attention between concerns for self-presentation and concerns for gaining information about the target person.

One of the most obvious ways of gaining information about a stranger is simply to ask the stranger questions about himself or herself. Berger (1973b) and Calabrese (1975) both found that the first few minutes of initial interactions between strangers were dominated by question asking. Most of these questions were concerned with requests for background information, for example, 'Where are you from?', 'What is your main subject?', 'Where do you live?', and so on. After the first two or three minutes, the rate at which questions were asked in these studies showed a marked decline. Part of the reason for this decline is the tendency for persons to spend some time dwelling upon conversation topics on which they have some degree of shared experience; thus, if two persons find that they are from the same home town or have both travelled to the same city, they may spend considerable time talking about matters related to these topics. However, initial questions may serve another function. The answers to them may give us hints about other attributes that the person possesses but which we have not yet observed. If we find out that a particular person is a college professor and that another person is a miner, we will most likely make quite different inferences about the preferences and opinions that these two persons have. Such inferences might determine whether or not we will continue to interact with this person.

The importance of information exchanged in the first few minutes of an interaction for the future of the relationship was demonstrated in a study by Berger (1975). In this experiment, students initially filled out an attitude questionnaire which measured their opinions on a variety of issues. In addition, students gave such information as their home town, major, and number of brothers and sisters in their family. This latter information is the type that is usually exchanged in initial encounters between college students. A few weeks later, students were given a questionnaire on which there was background information about another student. This information had been filled in by the experimenter in such a way that for half of the students the background information was very similar to their own background; for the other half of the students, the background information was very dissimilar. After reading the background information about the other person, the students were asked to guess how the student would fill out the rest of the questionnaire. The remainder of the questionnaire contained a large number of attitude items, some of which the students had filled out several weeks before. The students' own responses to the opinion items were then compared with the opinions they guessed for the other student. This study revealed that the degree of similarity between subjects' own attitudes and the attitudes they guessed for the other students was much higher when they believed that the student was from a similar background. Those students who received the dissimilar background information tended to guess attitudes which were quite discrepant from their own. This study clearly indicates that when we find that our backgrounds differ greatly from those of the persons with whom we are interacting, we are likely to assume, perhaps erroneously, that our opinions are very different from those of the person with whom we are interacting. By contrast, if we find we are from a similar background, we are likely to assume, perhaps erroneously, that our opinions are quite similar to those of the person with whom we are conversing.

While the questions that are asked and answered during an initial interaction between strangers may serve to reduce uncertainty and reveal common ground between interactants, there is most probably a limit to the number of questions which can be asked during such encounters. In formal interview situations, doctor–patient interactions, and other similar communication situations, we expect that one person will do most of the question asking and the other will do most of the answering. However, in an initial encounter between strangers in an informal social context, such asymmetries in question asking would not generally be tolerated. Moreover, it is probable that even if persons asked equal numbers of questions in an informal context, they would not continue to ask questions at a relatively high rate over time. Mutual interrogation is probably just as negatively viewed as unilateral interrogation after a certain point. At this time we cannot say at what point an initial encounter becomes an interrogation because of excess question asking, however, there appears to be such a point. Furthermore, it is evident that the kinds of questions which are asked change as the interaction progresses. Finally, we can ask what happens when one runs out of questions; that is, what other knowledge gaining strategies can be employed when one has asked the 'appropriate' number of questions?

Interactive strategy II: self-disclosure.

One possible alternative interactive knowledge gaining strategy to that of interrogation is self-disclosure. Gouldner (1960) and Jourard (1971) both suggest that a norm of reciprocity exists in social interaction situations such that persons of equal status are expected to exchange information about themselves in similar quantities and levels of intimacy. Jourard (1971) labelled this notion the 'dyadic effect' in his self-disclosure research. He found that persons who reported more willingness to disclose personal information about themselves to others also reported that they received more personal disclosures from others. By contrast, persons who were unwilling to disclose personal information about themselves reported that others were unwilling to disclose personal information to them. Other experiments have found evidence for the dyadic effect and the potential negative consequences of non-reciprocated self-disclosure (Worthy, Gary and Kahn 1969; Ehrlich and Graeven 1971; Sermat and Smyth, 1973). Generally these studies indicate that when persons demand disclosures from others and the others comply by giving the information, refusal to reciprocate these disclosures lowers the attractiveness of the nondiscloser. Persons who reciprocate disclosures are generally judged to be more attractive.

The norm of reciprocity and the dyadic effect can be used by the knowledge seeker to glean information from a target. The research cited above implies that when all other things are equal (of course they rarely are), persons will tend to reciprocate information that we are willing to disclose to them about ourselves. Thus, if you wish to find out whether the person with whom you are conversing is afraid of snakes, you might disclose to him or her that you are afraid of snakes and discuss a vivid instance in which you showed such fear. There is the chance that the person will reciprocate at the same level of intimacy but not in the same content category as your disclosure. Thus, the person might respond to your revelation by talking about his or her fear of rabbits or high places. Of course, once the target person begins such a disclosure process, it may be possible for you to interject a question about the specific item of information in which you are interested. For example, after the person describes his or her fear of high places, you might ask something like, 'How do you feel about snakes?'

Detecting deception

For the most part, our discussion of knowledge gaining strategies has thus far assumed that the target person does not engage in any kind of intentional deception. The possibility of deception is especially problematic when it comes to the interactive strategies. In the case of both interrogation and self-disclosure, the target person may both answer our questions and reciprocate our disclosures; however, it may also be the case that the target person is deliberately giving us false information. The question is how might such deception be detected. First, there is the possibility of changing one's opinion to see if the other person follows suit. For example, assume that you are conversing with a person whom you suspect is agreeing with you in order to ingratiate himself or herself with you. Every time you state a preference or an opinion, the person shows agreement. Once the target person has said that he or she agrees with your opinion on an issue, you might announce a change in your opinion sometime later in the conversation. If the person continues to agree with your 'changed' opinion, you might then assume that the person is simply engaging in indiscriminant agreement with you, probably for some ulterior motive like ingratiation.

There is a large literature on verbal and nonverbal cues that persons emit when they are engaging in deception (Ekman and Friesen 1969; Knapp, Hart and Dennis 1974; Bauchner, Kaplan and Miller 1980). However, while these studies show that when persons engage in deception their verbal and nonverbal behaviours change, these studies do not tell us what *strategies* persons use once they suspect that deception is taking place. In addition to the strategy of opinion change suggested above, sometimes persons very directly ask whether or not the target person is telling the truth. The success of this deception detection strategy depends upon the ability of the target person to 'lie with a straight face'.

On remaining unknown

A final issue to be considered here concerns the kinds of counterstrategies targets might use against observers who wish to gain information about them. There are a number of reasons which might induce a target to try to prevent a person from gaining knowledge about him or her. The target might simply dislike the knowledge seeker for some set of reasons and wish to avoid developing a relationship with the person. Some persons place extremely high values upon personal privacy and do not wish others to invade their personal lives unless those others are invited to do so. Finally, the target might have 'something to hide' in terms of his or her personal life and not wish to risk sharing the 'something' with another person. Obviously, in order for such counterstrategies to be employed, the target must be at least dimly aware that some observer or observers are trying to gain information about him or her. There are a number of possible ways in which persons can avoid being known by others. First, persons can isolate themselves. In a sense, the late American billionaire Howard Hughes employed this strategy for remaining unknown. Popular figures in sports and entertainment sometimes go to great lengths to avoid interaction with others. A second kind of counterstrategy for foiling knowledge gaining attempts is that of non-responsiveness. When persons are approached by others who attempt to engage in conversation, the persons might give minimal responses to questions and generally indicate that they do not wish to interact. A third possibility to avoid being known is to interact within the confines of role-determined action. In work situations, persons can do a very good job of fulfilling the demands of work related roles and essentially remain unknown to their co-workers. These persons limit their communication with co-workers to work related matters and do not discuss their 'personal lives' in the work situation. You may interact with the same person almost every day of your life, e.g., a newspaper man or a store clerk, and not get to know them as individuals because your communication with them is confined to role relation-ships.

One final possibility for remaining unknown to others is to talk with them but keep the focus of interaction away from one's self. This can be accomplished by chronic joke telling or talking about such topics as the weather or sports. Persons can communicate around such topics for long periods of time and learn little about each other. There may be a considerable volume of talk in such interactions but the type of talk is such that little is learned about the target person beyond their most superficial preferences. In this regard it is interesting to note that wives are often heard to complain about their husbands' unwillingness to talk about what they consider to be less superficial topics. This complaint may, however, have some basis in fact, since studies show that males are generally lower in self-disclosure than are females (Jourard 1971).

Three attribution approaches

Our discussion of knowledge gaining strategies emphasized specific techniques that persons might employ to find out things about others or to prevent others from gaining knowledge about them. In this section we will try to answer the question how persons process and combine social information once they have obtained it. This question is central to attribution theory. The general aim of the attribution approaches we will consider is to explain how persons arrive at confident estimates of others' dispositions and how persons evaluate the causes of their own and others' actions. By forming our individual accounts of others' dispositions and the causes of their behaviour, we make other persons more predictable and more understandable. This increased understanding enables us to communicate more effectively with others and to achieve our interaction goals – as long as our dispositional and causal attributions are reasonably correct. In everyday life, we generally base our communication behaviour on what we *believe* to be the case rather than upon what the case may actually be. The attribution approaches to be discussed below also consider the kinds of conditions which give rise to attributional biases which may in turn interfere with the smooth conduct of social interaction.

Heider's analysis of social action

In his book *The Psychology of Interpersonal Relations*, Heider (1958) considered a number of issues related to how persons perceive and evaluate the actions of others. Heider contended that while most persons may not have the sophisticated knowledge of human behaviour that a psychologist might have, in their everyday lives persons do try to make assessments of intentions, motives and dispositions so that they can predict the behaviour of others. Heider also recognized that persons are active perceivers of their environments and not merely passive recipients of experience. Persons actively seek to predict and explain the actions of others; however, Heider noted that it is impossible for persons to perceive social reality accurately. Our perception of social reality may be adversely affected by the presence of *distracting physical stimuli* in the social environment; moreover, our *prior experiences* may also determine how we perceive a person or group of persons. Heider noted that we can usually determine the accuracy with which we perceive physical objects by reference to some kind of physical measurement system; however, it is difficult to provide standards by which to assess the accuracy of our perceptions of others. In the case of social perception, we may rely upon the consensus judgements of a group of persons. The difficulty with this approach is that the group judgement may be totally inaccurate!

Heider pointed out that persons communicate their naive analyses of others' social actions in the form of statements that we hear every day. For example, if a person takes an examination and does well, we might attribute his or her performance to such personal forces as ability or motivation, or some combination of the two. It is also possible, however, that we might attribute the person's outstanding performance in the examination to environmental forces such as task ease or good fortune; that is, the person did well because the examination was easy or the person was lucky, or some of both. Personal or environmental forces could be invoked to explain a poor performance. A low examination score might be attributed to such personal factors as low ability or low motivation, or the same poor performance might be attributed to the inordinate difficulty of the task or to bad luck.

Personal or *internal* forces and environmental or *external* forces as explanations of actions may be viewed in terms of their *stability*. The internal force of ability is a relatively stable attribute of an individual, while the internal force of motivation shows more variation and is therefore less stable. With regard to external causes of action, task difficulty can be viewed as a relatively stable attribute and luck can be viewed as an unstable property of the environment. When we make causal attributions regarding the behaviour of others, stable internal attributions might be more difficult to change than unstable internal attributions. The same may hold true for external attributions.

Considerable research has examined how persons attribute causality in response to success and failure. For example, Johnson, Feigenbaum and Weibey (1964) found that teachers attributed the consistently poor performance of students to the *students*' low levels of motivation and ability. By contrast, when students showed improvement, teachers tended to attribute such improvements to the *teachers*' efforts. Streufert and Streufert (1969) found that persons who were successful at a task tended to attribute their success to internal factors;

persons who failed at tasks tended to attribute their failures externally. Feather (1969) found that when persons were initially confident of their ability to do a task, persons attributed success to their ability and failure to bad luck; however, persons who were initially unconfident attributed success to good luck and failure to their lack of ability. In a follow-up study, Feather and Simon (1971) reported that unexpected outcomes were attributed more to unstable environmental factors (luck). Berger (1973a) found that persons were more attracted to those who tended to agree with their attributions of causality for performance. When persons succeeded at a task and others attributed their success to a high level of ability or when persons failed and others attributed their failure to bad luck, the persons receiving the causal assessments from the others indicated that they liked those persons giving the assessment. However, when the others attributed success to good luck or failure to lack of ability, those persons receiving the assessments of the others liked them considerably less.

These studies indicate that when persons evaluate the causes of their own performance, they tend to attribute cause in ways which will enhance their self-esteem. Success is attributed to internal factors (ability/motivation) and failure is attributed to external factors (task difficulty/luck). Thus, there appears to be a kind of attribution bias in assessments of causes for success and failure. Obviously, in any given case of success or failure, one or more of the four possible causal attributions we have discussed might be used to explain performance; however, there is a distinct tendency to weight some factors over others when it comes to explaining our own successes or failures.

Correspondent inference theory

Jones and Davis (1965) extended Heider's (1958) initial thinking on attribution to the area of dispositional attributions. These investigators were interested in answering the question of what factors are responsible for our willingness to take persons' actions as reliable indicators of their underlying dispositions. For example, if a person behaves in a friendly way toward us, we might ask whether the person's behaviour is an indicator of a friendly disposition or whether the friendly behaviour might simply be a temporary state and not really indicative of the person's true disposition. What we as observers can see regarding other persons are their actions and the effects of their actions. By observing their actions and the effects of their actions we make inferences about their dispositions. When we take actions to be reliable indicators of dispositions, we have, according to Jones and Davis, made a *correspondent inference*. When we have low levels of confidence that persons' actions are true indicators of their dispositions, it is not possible to make correspondent inferences.

Before we can draw correspondent inferences from observing actions, we must first determine whether the person intended to produce a particular effect by his or her actions. For example, if you observe a person strike another person, you would need to know whether or not the person *intended* to strike the other before you would be willing to impute a hostile disposition to the person doing the striking. It could be that the person hit the other person by accident, and if you believed this to be the case, you would most probably not attribute the disposition of hostility to the person doing the striking. Even if you did believe that the striking behaviour was intended, you still might not be willing to attribute a disposition of hostility to the striker. Let us say that you found out that just before the striking incident occurred, the person who was struck had insulted the striker in some significant way. Given this piece of information, you might attribute the aggressive actions of the striker to external factors, rather than to some disposition of the striker. However, if you found out that the striker hit the other person without provocation, you would then be more likely to attribute a hostile disposition to the striker.

Once we have solved the intent problem, according to Jones and Davis (1965) there are four factors which determine whether or not we will draw correspondent inferences from observing actions and their effects. First, we can observe the *choices* that the person makes and the effects of these choices. For example, let us assume that a person is in the process of choosing between two jobs. Let us further assume that a number of effects of the person's choice would be similar for both of the two jobs. Perhaps both jobs are with large corporations which are located in warm climates. Additionally, the jobs might involve approximately equal levels of responsibility and authority. However, the one effect they do *not* hold in common might be that one job is located in a city where the job applicant's intimate friend is also located while the other job is in a city far away from the location of the intimate friend. In the terms of Jones and Davis (1965) the effect of being close to or far away from an intimate friend is a *non-common* effect of the choice. No matter which job the person chooses, we as observers of the choice and its effects will generally base our attributions concerning the disposition of the person making the choice upon the non-common effects of the choice. In our example, the non-common effect of relative proximity to the intimate friend gives us considerable information about the choice-maker's disposition. Jones and Davis (1965) argue that choices which have *few* non-common effects give rise to correspondent inferences, while choices which have a large number of non-common effects do not give rise to correspondent inferences. Thus, if the two jobs were dissimilar with respect to size of company, climate of the job location, levels of responsibility and authority as well as proximity to the intimate friend, it would be much more difficult for us as observers of the choice and its effects to confidently explain the job seeker's choice. There are too many plausible alternative explanations; however, when just one effect is 'non-common', we are more likely to assert confidently that the location of the intimate friend played the critical role in the person's choice.

A second factor which influences the confidence with which we will make dispositional attributions from observations of actions is that of *assumed desirability* of the actions and their effects. If a person behaves in a very friendly way toward us, if a political candidate advocates a position which is popular with the audience, or if a person compliments us on some achievement, there are a number of potential attributions which we can generate for those behaviours. In all of the above cases, the persons might be saying what they are saying or behaving the way they are in order to ingratiate themselves with us for some reason, e.g. getting our vote. However, it is also possible that the positive or agreeing actions might be sincere expressions of feelings and beliefs. By contrast, *socially undesirable* actions like criticizing, snubbing and taking an unpopular stand on an issue tend to have *fewer* plausible alternative explanations. When someone snubs us or criticizes us, we can eliminate ingratiation as a possibility and assume that these negative expressions are true indicators of the person's dispositions, that is, the person is a 'critical' person or a 'snob'. Furthermore, if a political candidate advocates a position which is unpopular with his audience, we are more likely to take his arguments as true expressions of his beliefs.

A study done by Schulman (1976) demonstrates this relationship quite nicely. Schulman (1976) constructed three bogus transcripts of an alleged conversation between a male and a female who had just met at a party for the first time. The conversations were identical except that one version contained no compliments, a second version contained two compliments, and a third version contained eight compliments. Persons read one of the three versions of the conversation and then rated the participants in the conversation on a number of scales. These ratings revealed that the compliment giver was judged to be most attractive when he gave two compliments and least attractive when he gave eight compliments. The attractiveness of the person in the no-compliment conversation was greater than the attractiveness of the person who gave eight compliments but less than the attractiveness of the person who gave just two compliments. Paralleling these results were uncertainty ratings. Persons who read the two-compliment transcript felt the least uncertain about the person who gave the two compliments. Those who read the other transcripts expressed the most uncertainty. These results suggest that very positive behaviour may make a person less attractive because the socially desirable behaviour makes observers of that behaviour less certain concerning the motives for the behaviour. Remember, uncertainty increases as the number of alternatives in the situation increase. Socially desirable behaviour may lead to more plausible alternative attributions than socially undesirable behaviour because of the possibility of ulterior motives like ingratiation.

A third factor which influences the extent to which we will judge a person's actions to be reliable indicators of their underlying dispositions is the *hedonic relevance* of the person's actions to us as observers. If we perceive that a person's actions have a direct bearing on whether we will or will not receive rewards or punishments in a given situation, the person's actions become hedonically relevant to us. According to Jones and Davis, as the hedonic relevance of the actor's behaviour increases, our tendency to attribute the actor's behaviour to his or her underlying dispositions also increases. Thus, for example, in an employment situation we would expect employees to make a large number of correspondent inferences about their bosses, since the bosses have the power to reward or punish the employees. By contrast, bosses would be less likely to make correspondent inferences on the basis of observing employee's actions, since the employees do not have much power to mediate rewards and punishments for their bosses.

A final factor which influences the making of correspondent inferences is that of *personalism*. Personalism refers to the belief on the part of the observer that the actor is adjusting his or her actions for the sake of the observer; that is, the actor is 'personalizing' his or her behaviour for the observer. When the observer is in the actor's presence, the actor behaves in one way; however, when the observer is not present, the actor behaves in another way. It is assumed that as personalism increases, the tendency to make correspondent inferences also increases. So, if you believe that a close friend of yours treats you in a 'special' way, you are more likely to take the person's actions as true indicators of his or her underlying dispositions.

Kelley's attribution approach

The final attribution approach we will consider here is that of Kelley (1967, 1971, 1972). In one sense, Kelley's attribution concerns are somewhat broader than those of correspondent inference theory. While correspondent inference theory seeks to explain the confidence with which persons will infer personality dispositions from observations of actions, Kelley's model is concerned with the broader issue of causal attribution in general. This causal attribution problem is best illustrated by a simple example. Let us say that you observe John watching a television variety show. A comedian appears on the screen and tells several jokes. By the end of the comedian's act, John is on the floor laughing. Now, as a naive scientist you are interested in answering the question, 'Why did John laugh so much?' According to Kelley's analysis, there are three possible explanations for John's behaviour. First, John may have laughed so much because of the comedian (a stimulus attribution). Second, John may have laughed so much because John has a sense of humour (a person attribution). Third, John's laughter may be explained by something about the circumstance in which John viewed the comedian (a circumstance attribution). Of course, there is the possibility that some combination of these factors may have produced John's laughter.

Kelley (1972) has advanced three basic principles of causal attribution which are relevant to the problem of establishing the basis of causality in our example. The first of these principles is that of *covariation*. The covariation principle simply states that effects are attributed to causes with which they covary over time. So, if John is a very serious person unless he is watching a comedian, as observers we are likely to attribute John's laughter to the presence of the comedian, since when the comedian is absent, John tends to be very serious. A second principle relevant to causal attribution is that of *discounting*. If we as observers perceive a *number* of causes for John's laughter rather than just one, we are less likely to see any one cause as having a great influence in producing John's laughter. The more potential causes we perceive for a given effect, the less we weigh the influence of each cause. Finally, the *augmentation* principle asserts that if a given cause must overcome countervailing influences in order to produce an effect, we are likely to see the cause as more influential. Thus, if John is watching television in a public place where loud laughter is perceived to be inappropriate but John laughs very loudly in spite of the normative proscription against loud laughter, we are more likely to judge the cause of John's laughter to be extremely powerful. By contrast, if we observed John watching television in the privacy of his own home where such social prohibitions against loud laughter would be fewer, and John laughed loudly, we would not judge the cause of his laughter to be as powerful, since the cause did not have to overcome countervailing influences of various kinds.

Although the covariation, discounting and augmentation principles tell us how causes are associated with effects and how causes, once established, are differentially weighted, the three principles do not directly address the issue of what factors are responsible for attributions to stimuli (the comedian), persons

(John) or circumstances (watching television). Kelley (1967) has provided an analysis which details what *patterns* of data will give rise to these three *loci* of attribution or combinations of them. It is to this analysis that we now turn.

According to Kelley (1967) there are three types of information which help us to determine whether to attribute a given effect to the stimulus, person, circumstance or a combination of the three. These three types of information are distinctiveness, consensus and consistency. *Distinctiveness* information refers to uniqueness of the response to the particular stimulus. In our example of John's response to the comedian, distinctiveness information would indicate to us how John responded to a number of other comedians. Does John generally laugh at all comedians, or does John only laugh at the comedian he is currently watching and no other? When John's responses are similar across a large number of comedians, his pattern of behaviour is displaying low distinctiveness. When John laughs at only one of many comedians, his behaviour is highly distinctive.

Consensus information refers to the way in which other persons respond to the stimulus. Again in our example, if most persons found the comedian very funny, there would be high consensus among observers. However, if most observers found the comedian to be relatively unfunny, there would be low consensus. *Consistency* information takes into account the interaction of the person with the stimulus over time and situations. If John laughs a great deal when he sees this particular comedian on different occasions and in different situations, for example on television and in person, John is exhibiting considerable consistency in his response to the comedian. By contrast, if John's response to the comedian varies over time and situations such that sometimes he finds the comedian funny and sometimes not, then John's responses to the comedian exhibit considerable inconsistency.

According to Kelley's analysis, it is combinations of distinctiveness, consensus and consistency information which determine whether attributions will be made to the stimulus, person or circumstance. The following table summarizes the various combinations of the three information factors and the attribution outcomes that they produce.

Table 2.1   Information patterns and the attributions they produce

	Type of information		
	Distinctiveness	Consensus	Consistency
Stimulus Attribution	High	High	High
Person Attribution	Low	Low	High
Circumstance Attribution	High	Low	Low

As the above table shows, when all three of the information factors are high, the observer is likely to attribute the person's response to the stimulus. Thus, when you as the observer find out that John laughs only at the comedian he is watching and at no other comedians (high distinctiveness), and that most persons who see this comedian laugh at him or her (high consensus) and that every time John encounters this comedian he has the same response (high consistency), you are likely to conclude that it is the comedian (stimulus) which is causing John's laughter.

The table also indicates, however, that when you as the observer of John's laughter learn that John laughs at all comedians (low distinctiveness), that almost no one laughs at this particular comedian that John is watching, (low consensus) and that John consistently laughs at this comedian (high consistency), then you are more likely to attribute John's laughter to something about John himself rather than to something about the comedian. Finally, if you find out that John laughs at only this comedian and no other (high distinctiveness), that most other persons do not laugh at this comedian (low consensus), and that sometimes John laughs at this particular comedian but at other times he does not (low consistency), you are likely to attribute John's behaviour to something about the situation.

The three information patterns shown in Table 2.1 can be thought of as basic schemata or mental templates that persons use to arrive at causal explanations for behaviour. It is also important to notice that each of the three patterns has *one* unique informational element. Looking down the columns of Table 2.1 notice that *low distinctiveness* is unique to the person attribution. *High consensus* is unique to a stimulus attribution, and *low consistency* is unique to a circumstance attribution. This property of these three causal schemata suggests that they can each be used when we have less than complete information on each of the three information dimensions. For example, if we find out that John laughs at all comedians in addition to the one he is watching (low distinctiveness), we are likely to conclude that John's response to the particular comedian we are observing him watching is the product of something about John, for example, his sense of humour. By contrast, if we only learn that almost all persons who view this particular comedian find him funny (high consensus), we are likely to attribute John's response to the 'funniness' of the comedian. Finally, on the basis of low consistency information alone (John sometimes finds this comedian funny), we are likely to conclude that John's reaction to the comedian is being produced by something about the situation. Thus, in order to make one of the three attributions it is not necessary to have complete information on the distinctiveness, consensus and consistency dimensions.

In an important test of Kelley's attribution model, Leslie McArthur (1972) constructed a number of situations similar to our John example, varied the three information dimensions, and asked persons to indicate whether the person's behaviour was caused by the stimulus, person, circumstance, person and stimulus together, or some other combination. For example, McArthur created situations such as, 'George translates the sentence incorrectly' or 'Professor Jones compliments student Smith'. Following each of these statements she gave the three types of information in differing patterns. After the sentence 'George translates the sentence incorrectly' persons might be told 'George always translates sentences like this incorrectly' (low distinctiveness), 'Most persons translate the sentence correctly' (low consensus) and 'George has not been able to translate this sentence correctly in the past' (high consistency). After reading the situation and the three pieces of information, McArthur's subjects were asked to indicate whether George's response (incorrectly translating the sentence) was due to the sentence, George, the situation, the sentence and George together, or some other combination. In this particular situation we would expect persons to attribute George's inability to translate the sentence to

George rather than to something about the sentence or something about the circumstance.

By varying the information patterns and situations, McArthur found support for Kelley's model; the predictions shown in Table 2.1 were generally confirmed. Two additional findings from the McArthur study are of importance. First, McArthur's results showed that subjects most frequently made *person* attributions, that is, they more frequently judged the person's behaviour to be a product of factors residing in the person than factors outside of the person (the stimulus or the circumstance). Second, she reported that of the three types of information, consensus had the least impact upon attributions. Distinctiveness and consistency information showed more influence in the making of the casual attributions.

Later studies have essentially confirmed McArthur's findings. Orvis, Cunningham and Kelley (1975) used situations similar to those employed by McArthur (1972) to determine whether the same effects that McArthur observed could be produced with more limited information. For example, in the situation in which George fails to translate the sentence, what kind of attribution would be made regarding George's performance if we learned only that George was never able to translate any sentence (low distinctiveness)? Given this one piece of distinctiveness information, we would most likely attribute George's failure to George himself; that is, he lacks ability, motivation or both. If we were only told, however, that along with George, most persons failed to translate the sentence (high consensus), we would be more likely to attribute George's failure to something about the sentence rather than to George himself. Orvis *et al.* (1975) generally found that just one critical piece of information would lead persons to the same attribution as would a complete set of information on all three dimensions. This finding led them to conclude that the three information patterns shown in Table 2.1 are fundamental and that persons first look for the critical information on each information dimension in order to make an attribution. So, if you encounter low distinctiveness information when you are trying to make a casual attribution, you are likely to make a person attribution as long as information on the other two dimensions does not contradict the information pattern for the person attribution. If, however, you first receive low distinctiveness information and then receive high consensus and low consistency information, a pattern which does not fit with a person attribution pattern, then you will make some kind of combination attribution; that is, the person's behaviour was caused by the person, the stimulus and the circumstance. Of course, it takes much less cognitive work to make the attribution based upon the low distinctiveness information itself.

Attribution biases

The three attribution approaches we have discussed appear to make persons quite rational decision-makers when they are interested in explaining others' actions and linking actions to dispositions. We did note, however, in our discussion of Heider's (1958) work, that several studies have revealed the tendency for persons to attribute their successes to internal sources like ability and motivation and to attribute failures outward to such factors as bad luck or inordinate task difficulty. This tendency can be thought of as a kind of ego-defensive attributional bias; that is, persons make these biased attributions in order to preserve a positive image of themselves.

In addition to the ego-defensive or self-serving attributional bias, other work has demonstrated additional biases which may interfere with the generation of accurate causal or dispositional attributions. Jones and Nisbett (1971) have noted that actors and observers tend to make differing attributions because of their different perspectives in interaction situations. They suggest that actors tend to see external factors as causes of their actions while observers of actors tend to perceive the actors' actions as internally caused. This bias arises because the perceptual fields of observers are flooded or engulfed by actors' actions. Actors are oriented outward toward the environment rather than to themselves. Thus, they tend to explain their own behaviour in terms of conditions they perceive in the environment. Storms (1973) has shown how videotape replays of interactions can be used to modify these actor-observer differences. By watching one's self on videotape, thus becoming an observer, environmental attributions for behaviour can be changed to internal or dispositional attributions for behaviour.

Given the predisposition of observers to attribute the actions of others to their internal dispositions, it should come as no surprise that a number of studies have shown that when persons engage in interpersonal conflict or experience the dissolution of their relationships, they frequently attribute their relational difficulties to some internal disposition of their relational partner rather than to themselves or to some aspect of the environment (Harvey, Wells and Alverez 1978; Kelley 1979; Orvis, Kelley and Butler 1976; Sillars 1980a). Kelley (1979) has noted that relational partners have great difficulty specifying relational problems in terms of specific behaviours, for example, 'I don't like him because he fails to greet me sometimes.' Rather, persons are more prone to couch complaints in terms of undesirable personal dispositions of the other, for example, 'I don't like her because she is just plain unfriendly.' Because of the tendency to see relational problems as a product of the other person's negative personality dispositions, it becomes difficult to modify specific behaviours in such relationships. Sillars (1980a) found that when persons attribute the causes of conflict to the undesirable personality characteristics of their partners, they are less likely to try to negotiate a solution to their problems. Instead, they are more likely to avoid their partners. This avoidance strategy makes some sense since if one assumes that it is a personality trait of the other that is causing the conflict, it might be difficult or impossible to change such a trait. Thus, the most efficient way to deal with the conflict is to avoid the person. Of course, the problem with this reasoning is that it is based upon the questionable assumption that the conflict is solely caused by some undesirable personality trait the other person possesses. It is probably the case that in most conflicts *both parties* share some responsibility for the difficulties experienced.

A final kind of bias we will consider here is one which has been labelled the *negativity effect* (Kanouse 1971; Kanouse and Hanson 1971). These researchers present evidence which suggests that when persons are presented with both positive and negative information about a person, the negative information assumes an inordinate weight in the formation of an overall impression of the person. Thus, one negative attribute in a sea of positive attributes will lower an overall impression to a greater extent than one positive attribute in a sea of negative attributes will improve an overall impression. Another way of looking at this effect is to say that equal amounts of positive and negative information about a person are likely to produce a somewhat negative overall impression of the person. Wegner and Vallacher (1977) have suggested two explanations for this effect. One of these states that since persons expect positive things to occur in their everyday lives, negative instances tend to stand out more. A second explanation asserts that persons are sensitive to potential threats in their environments for purposes of survival.

Regardless of the explanation for the negativity effect, it is important to note that it can exert considerable impact upon relationship development and change. When persons first meet, there may be conscious attempts to suppress negative behaviours in order to project a positive social self to the other person. When persons date they tend 'to put their best foot forward'. However, after relationships develop and persons become closer, some negative aspects of behaviour may no longer be masked. The unmasking of negative behaviours may have a very negative impact upon the relationship. These instances of unmasking lead persons to say such things as 'I never knew that he could be so nasty' or 'I can't believe how sloppy she is' and so on. The potential problems created by this attributional bias suggest that persons could try to counter-balance it by consciously thinking about positive attributes of their relational partners.

Other information processing biases have been discussed with reference to social judgement and decision making. Several of these shortcomings have been noted by Nisbett and Ross (1980). These authors suggest that frequently persons are willing to make inferences on the basis of incomplete information or biased samples of information. Furthermore, they note that persons may be unaware of factors which may have been responsible for their reaching a particular decision. Thus, even though we may strive to gain an understanding of another person, various biases and limitations in information processing capacity may interfere with our ability to gain an accurate explanation for his or her actions.

Limitations of attribution theories

Several recent studies have suggested some limits upon the generality of attribution principles. These studies do not totally refute correspondent inference theory or the Kelley model, but they do suggest that the theories may be somewhat more limited than first supposed. Enzle, Harvey and Wright (1980) tested what they argued is a contradiction between correspondent inference theory and the Kelley model. Specifically, as we saw earlier, Jones and Davis (1965) assert that the more an observer believes that an actor is varying his or her behaviour for the benefit of the observer (high personalism), the more likely the observer is to take the actor's actions as representative of the actor's underlying dispositions. High personalism leads to a person or dispositional attribution. By contrast, Kelley's model predicts that such variations in behaviour (high distinctiveness) do not lead to person attributions. It is when the response is similar across stimuli and distinctiveness is low that we tend to attribute the response to the person. These investigators confronted these conflicting predictions in a study which involved an interviewing situation. After an interview, the interviewee was given high or low distinctiveness information about the interviewer's past interviewing behaviour. Unknown to the interviewee, observers watched the interview and were given the same set of distinctiveness information that the interviewee received after participating in the interview. The findings of this study showed support for Kelley's prediction that low distinctiveness leads to person attributions and little support for Jones and Davis's personalism prediction. However, it is crucial to note that these findings held only for those persons who *observed* the interview. The interviewees themselves were not influenced one way or the other by the distinctiveness information about the interviewer. Persons who were *actively involved* in the communication situation did not behave in line with either of the theories. These findings suggest that not only is the personalism prediction of correspondent inference theory in need of revision, but more importantly that both of the attribution models may only hold for observers of social interaction rather than for participant–observers. This latter finding may not be as surprising as it might first appear, since the theories which were tested were developed by persons whose business it is to be keen *observers* of social interaction! It may be considerably more difficult for social scientists to develop theories of human action from the point of view of the *participant–observer*.

A second limitation of these attribution approaches is suggested by another study (Major 1980). In her experiments, Major allowed subjects to seek distinctiveness, consensus and consistency information rather than giving this information to subjects as had been done in the McArthur and Orvis *et al.* studies. Major (1980) found that when given the choice, persons acquired more consistency information than distinctiveness or consensus information in order to establish a causal attribution; however, persons utilized relatively little of the total information available to them to make their attributions. Persons were willing to make attributions on the basis of relatively limited samples of available information. These findings suggest that persons may not do as thorough a job of acquiring critical information as would scientists.

A third limitation of attribution models stems from the work of Pyszczynski and Greenberg (1981). These investigators led subjects to expect that another person would either give help or refuse to give help when asked to do a favour. For some subjects their expectations were confirmed; that is, the person did what they expected the person to do. Other subjects observed the person engage in behaviour which disconfirmed their expectations. Subjects were then given the opportunity to acquire additional information, some of which was relevant to their expectations and some of which was irrelevant to their expectations. Results showed that persons whose expectations were disconfirmed chose more information relevant to their expectations than did persons whose expectations were confirmed. These findings indicate that persons will become active information processors, seeking the causes of behaviour, when unexpected or unpredictable events occur. When the expected happens, persons may not process information the way that attribution theories suggest.

A final limitation to the generalizations of attribution theory has been suggested by Hewstone and Jaspars (in press). These authors point out that attribution models have a distinct 'individualistic' bias in that they focus upon the information processing strategies of isolated individuals. They assert that persons respond very differently when they perceive themselves to be connected with social groups than when they perceive themselves as individuals. One difference the individual versus group emphasis might make in terms of attribution is in the extent to which consensus information influences attributions of causality. In two studies, McArthur (1972, 1976) found that when compared with distinctiveness and consistency information, persons generally under-utilized consensus information. In these studies, however, persons responded to the various situations as individuals, that is, their memberships in social groups were not made salient to them. One implication of the Hewstone and Jaspars (in press) critique of attribution models is that if group memberships were made salient to individuals, consensus information might assume a much greater role in determining their attributions; in this case it would be the consensus of the group which would strongly influence the individual's attribution.

As we noted at the beginning of this discussion, the limitations to attribution models outlined above do not totally invalidate them; however, they do suggest that there are potentially significant limits to the conditions under which attribution theories are likely to work in terms of prediction and explanation. At present, we will have to wait and see whether attribution theories can be modified successfully to take into account these limitations or whether other theories will take their places. In the section which follows, we will examine some other approaches to the processing of social information which might at least partially supplant or significantly augment the attribution models we have considered.

Thought and talk: how aware are we?

Our examination of the various attribution approaches and knowledge gaining strategies carries with it the implication that persons are highly conscious and thoughtful when they prepare for and engage in social interactions with others. We did note in our discussion of attribution that recent research has shown that persons engage in attribution making only under a limited number of conditions. Also, it was suggested that persons become concerned with knowledge gaining strategies when they observe deviant actions, anticipate future interactions, and believe that others can reward or punish them. The question we will address in this section concerns the extent to which persons are aware of their communicative actions during social interactions. There are a number of research areas which suggest that for a variety of reasons, persons may be more or less conscious of what they are doing within the context of a particular social situation. We will examine four of these areas: (1) Scripts and mindlessness, (2) Objective self-awareness, (3) Self-consciousness, and (4) Self-monitoring.

Scripts and mindlessness

For most of us, our lives consist of a number of routine activities which vary little from day to day. Consider the sequence of actions involved in your getting up and preparing yourself to face yet another day at the academy; or consider the sequence of actions in which you must engage in order to purchase an article at a clothing store. While there may be minor variations from day to day in your 'getting up' sequence and some differences in the routine involved in buying clothing, these kinds of action sequences are generally routine. Not only do we participate in these kinds of routine sequences of actions, but we also observe others participating in them. Much of the entertainment fare on American television is written according to various 'formulas' or standard story lines. The same situation holds for movie plots. For example, there is the standard story consisting of male meets female; male and female are attracted to each other; adverse circumstances intervene in their relationship; the problems are solved; and male and female live happily ever after. Even conflict situations can become routine. Husband complains that wife doesn't keep house clean; wife complains that husband does not make enough money to support family; husband begins to drink heavily; wife accuses husband of ignoring her for the sake of drink; husband physically attacks. And so it goes.

The above examples are but a small sample of the kinds of routine action sequences which persons either actively participate in or observe in their everyday lives. There are two questions which we can ask about how persons deal with such routine sequences. First, how do persons *know* when they are involved in a particular kind of sequence? Second, once a person can identify the kind of situation that they are in, how do they know what to *do* or how to *act*? These two questions are answered, in part, by the notion of *scripts*. Abelson (1976) defines a cognitive script as 'a coherent sequence of events expected by the individual, involving him either as a participant or as an observer' (p. 33). According to Abelson (1976), scripts are cognitive structures which enable us to gain an understanding of the situation in which we find ourselves. Scripts also serve as guides to the actions that we should display in the situation. A cognitive script enables us to predict what will happen in a given situation. In this sense we can say that *scripts enable us to reduce uncertainty about the situation in which we find ourselves* – as long as we have an appropriate script for understanding and acting in the situation.

Abelson (1976) and Schank and Abelson (1977) point out that scripts are learned by direct participation in event sequences of various kinds or they may be acquired by observing others participate in various event sequences. For example, when we go to a restaurant, we may be seated by a host or a hostess, approached by a waiter or a waitress, given a menu, asked to order, be given our food, eat our food, leave a gratuity and pay the bill. This rather typical sequence may be learned by going to a number of restaurants for meals or by observing others go to restaurants, perhaps in plays or in television productions. In either case, repeated exposure to the sequence produces a cognitive structure or script which allows us to understand what to expect in future restaurant trips and allows us to know what to do when we are in a restaurant. Obviously, while there are similarities among restaurants, the routines which we go through from restaurant to restaurant may vary. For example, in some restaurants there may be no host or hostess to seat us. If we are in a so-called 'fast food' establishment, we will not be served at all and we will not leave a tip. These variations in routines are accounted for by the idea that any given script like a restaurant script may contain several tracks to account for these variations.

According to Abelson (1976) and Schank and Abelson (1977), by adulthood we have acquired thousands of scripts for the understanding of various routine action sequences: Once this large file of scripts is developed, the problem for the human understander facing a particular situation is: (1) to determine whether he or she has a script to fit the particular situation being faced, and (2) if there is a script, what role he or she will play in it. Once these issues are resolved in an affirmative way, the person can enact the sequence of behaviour involved in the routine without paying much attention to what he or she is doing. Thus, once a well formulated script is learned, the necessity for thinking about the details involved in the sequence decreases.

There is considerable research which demonstrates the role that scripts play in our abilities to recall action sequences. For example, Chiesi, Spilich and Voss (1979) found that persons who had high levels of knowledge about the principles and strategies of baseball were better than their low-knowledge counterparts at: (1) recognizing information changes in verbal descriptions of action sequences of baseball games and (2) recalling event sequences which followed a normal order. In a related study, Spilich, Vesonder, Chiesi and Voss (1979) found that when high and low baseball-knowledge persons were presented with a one-half-inning narrative of a baseball game, high knowledge-level persons were better able to: (1) recall information that was related to the goals of the game (scoring, runs, etc.), (2) integrate sequences of goal-related actions, and (3) recall more information in the appropriate order. Finally, Bower, Black and Turner (1979) conducted a series of experiments in which persons were asked to respond in a variety of ways to a number of different scripted sequences of actions. Their research revealed that when persons were asked to recall scripted sequences after reading them, they tended to fill in details which were *not* given to them in the original script. Thus, scripts can cause persons to 'recall' events of an action sequence they have observed when the events actually did not take place but are part of the cognitive script they use to process the action sequence. The Bower, Black and Turner (1979) study also demonstrated that persons were better at recalling actions which deviated from scripted expectations than they were at recalling actions that were consistent with the script. We are more likely to recall the waiter who spills his tray of food all over us than we are to remember the waiter whose actions are like those of all other waiters. A study by Graesser, Gordon and Sawyer (1979) also showed that script-deviant actions are better recalled than are script-congruent actions.

While the above research shows how scripts influence the recall of routine action sequences of various kinds, there is another important consequence of scripted activities. Langer (1978) has argued that when persons develop scripts for routine action sequences, they enact these sequences with little attention to the details of how they actually carry out the sequence. For example, when persons learn to brush their teeth, they pay little attention to the various angles and strokes they use to accomplish toothbrushing. When persons drive their cars over the same routes many times, they may end up at their destinations and not be aware of exactly how they arrived there. When action sequences become overlearned or scripted, persons tend to become *mindless* with respect to those activities according to Langer (1978). In this context, mindlessness can mean at least two things. First, mindlessness can refer to a situation in which a person is doing one thing but thinking about another, for example, thinking about a date while washing dishes. With respect to the actions involved in dish washing, one is mindless. In the second sense of mindlessness, the person is engaging in some kind of action but not thinking about anything. Watching television might be an example. According to Langer (1978) most of our daily social interactions are so routinized that we are generally mindless with respect to them; even though we may give the appearance of being actively involved in them. Persons may look like they are engaged in thoughtful conduct, but may in fact be mindless.

Langer, Blank and Chanowitz (1978) reported a series of experiments which demonstrate the operation of mindlessness. In one of them, individuals about to make copies on a xerox machine were approached by a confederate of the experimenter. The confederate asked the persons about to use the machine if they would allow him or her to make copies first. The confederate told half of the persons waiting that he or she had to make five copies (small favour), while the other half of those waiting were told that the confederate needed to make 20 copies (large favour). In addition, the request was followed by three kinds of justifications. Some of the waiting persons were given no justification for the request. A second group was told that the person needed to make copies because he or she was in a hurry (real justification). A final group was told that the person needed to use the xerox machine in order to make some copies (placebic justification). Obviously, the placebic justification is no justification at all. Langer *et al.* (1978) reasoned that the request for the small favour would induce little mindfulness in the receiver so that a placebic justification would be as effective as a real justification. However, in the large-favour situation, the person receiving the request would become more mindful and recognize the absurd nature of the placebic justification, thus reducing the effectiveness of the placebic justification. This study revealed that within the small-favour group, 93 per cent of those given the placebic justification allowed the confederate to make his or her copies first and 94 per cent of those given the real justification complied. Of those given no justification, 60 per cent granted the favour. Of those persons who were asked for a large favour, 42 per cent of those given the real justification complied with the request, while only 24 per cent of those given the placebic justification complied. For those given no justification for the request, 24 per cent complied.

The findings of the above study provide support for the operation of mindlessness. When a small favour was requested, an absurd justification was just as effective in gaining compliance as was a reasonable justification; however, when a large favour was involved, the placebic justification was no more effective in gaining compliance than was no justification. In the second experiment of their study, Langer *et al.* (1978) surveyed secretaries' wastepaper baskets to determine the general form of memos sent to the secretaries. Their survey revealed that the structure of these memos was generally an unsigned request as opposed to a signed demand. Armed with this knowledge of the structure of the typical memo, Langer *et al.* (1978) devised a memo which requested that the receiver of the memo return the memo to a non-existent room in the office building. The message was obviously silly; why would a person send a memo to someone and ask that they return the piece of paper to a particular room? Langer *et al.* devised four forms of the memo. In some cases the memo was written in a request form while in others it was written in a demand form. Some of the memos were signed by the sender and others were not signed. The researchers reasoned that memos of the typical form (unsigned request) would be processed in a mindless manner, and more of these memos would be returned; however, memos which were unusual in form, for example signed demands, would induce more mindfulness and the reader would become aware of the absurdity of the content of the memo, thus lowering compliance in the group. The results of this study supported these predictions. Of those secretaries who received the memos of the typical form (unsigned requests) 90 per cent returned them to the non-existent room. By contrast, only 60 per cent of those secretaries who received the most structurally deviant memos (signed demands) returned them.

It is interesting to speculate why the 60 per cent who received the memos of the most structurally deviant form still complied with the absurd request. Presumably, the form of the memos they received would make them more mindful, thus making them aware of the ridiculous nature of the content of the message. However, it is also possible that since the memo was both in the form of a demand and signed, some secretaries might have over estimated its importance and paid little attention to the content of the message. This latter possibility would suggest that some secretaries in the signed-demand group might have also been mindless with reference to the content of the message because their attention was drawn *away* from it by the message's structural characteristics.

Many of our everyday interactions with family, friends and co-workers are routine in nature. The findings of the above studies indicate that while scripts may aid us in getting through these conversations in a relatively smooth manner, Langer's research indicates that this increased efficiency may come at a price. Certainly there are situations in which misunderstandings develop between friends and family members because of mindlessness. On the basis of minimal cues, persons *assume* that the person providing the cues is beginning a particular kind of script (e.g. a conflict script). On the basis of this assumption, the person receiving the cues becomes angry or overreacts in some way and begins to 'run through' the script. The other person who innocently provided the 'wrong cues' is now offended and also 'gets into' the conflict script and a ritualized fight then ensues which neither party can stop until the script plays itself out. This approach explains why in some close relationships persons may wish to avoid conflicts but cannot.

Lest the preceding discussion lead the reader to believe that we are always mindless during social interactions, Langer (1978) has cited a number of conditions which are likely to make us more mindful of our actions in social situations. Increased mindfulness occurs when:

1. We encounter a novel situation for which we have no script.
2. The enactment of scripted behaviour becomes effortful for some reason.
3. The enactment of scripted behaviour is interrupted by external factors which prevent its completion.
4. We experience consequences which are discrepant with the consequences of prior enactments of the same script.
5. The situation does not permit sufficient involvement.

Any one or a combination of these factors will increase mindfulness in a given situation.

Scripts are functional in that they allow us to perform various action sequences without having to attend closely to what we are doing. This condition frees our mind to think about things that are more important than what we are doing. However, scripts can introduce distortion into recall such that we assume that events took place which actually did not. Moreover, scripts can cause us to become inattentive to nuances and details in interactions which may provide important cues to the understanding of the other person's feelings and emotions. In short, scripts are useful for dealing with mundane situations with 'prototypic' others. However, when we wish to deal with persons as *individuals*, scripts may become dysfunctional and counterproductive to achieving satisfaction with the relationship.

Objective self-awareness

Our discussions of knowledge acquisition strategies and attribution models painted a picture of persons as relatively self-conscious, rational information processors. The research on scripts and mindlessness indicated that the degree to which persons attend to what they are doing in social interaction situations varies as a function of the extent to which scripts are relied upon to process information. Another area of theory and research directly addresses the issue of self-awareness. Duval and Wicklund's (1972) theory of objective self-awareness states that persons experience two states of consciousness: objective self-awareness and subjective self-awareness. When in the objective state, the person's consciousness is dominated by his self or her self; that is, attention is focused inward on the self as an object of experience. In the subjective state, attention is focused outward, away from the self as an object. The self blends in with the surrounding environment. Duval and Wicklund (1972) argue that when persons are objectively self-aware, they experience discomfort and attempt to become subjectively self-aware. The discomfort produced by objective self-awareness is due to the fact that when attention is focused upon the self, persons become aware of the discrepancies between what they would ideally like to be (ideal self) and the way they actually are (real self). Awareness of these discrepancies produces discomfort and the desire to focus attention away from the self toward the environment. Duval and Wicklund (1972) also contend that the two states of consciousness are binary in nature: a person is either objectively or subjectively self-aware. Movement between these two states can be rapid, but at any point in time a person is either objectively or subjectively self-aware.

Objective self-awareness is induced by self-reflecting stimuli in the person's environment. Mirrors, tape recordings of one's own voice, watching videotapes of one's self and anticipating delivering a speech to an audience are some ways in which objective self-awareness can be created. It has also been suggested that when a person holds an opinion which is discrepant with those of other group members, the discrepant member is likely to feel objective self-awareness. Ickes and Wicklund (1971) found that persons who completed questionnaires designed to measure their self-esteem made more negative ratings of themselves when they listened to a tape recording of their own voice than did persons who completed the self-ratings when they heard the voice of another person. The difference between the two groups in their self-esteem ratings disappeared over time, most probably because persons who listened to their own voice devised ways in which to divert their attention away from themselves and become subjectively self-aware.

Another study which demonstrates the aversive nature of objective self-awareness was done by Duval, Wicklund and Fine (1971). These researchers informed some persons that they had performed poorly on a test relative to other students. Other research participants were told that they had done very well on the test compared with other students. All research participants were then asked to wait for another study to begin, but were told that after waiting for about five minutes, they should seek out the experimenter if he did not appear. Some subjects waited at a table facing a mirror, while other subjects waited at the same table with the mirror covered. When the lengths of time that subjects in the various groups were willing to wait were compared, it was found that subjects who had been informed that they had done poorly relative to others who were also seated in front of the mirror waited significantly less time than did those persons who did poorly but who did not see themselves in the mirror. For those subjects who had done well, there were no differences in waiting times between those persons who were exposed to the mirror and those who were not. These findings indicate that the mirror created more aversion for those who did poorly, presumably because of increased objective self-awareness. In a later discussion of objective self-awareness theory and research, Wicklund (1975) has asserted that objective self-awareness might not always produce aversive reactions. While it is probable that if we think about ourselves for a long enough period of time, we will become aware of various shortcomings, it is also true that sometimes we do better than we expected in various activities. Becoming aware of positive discrepancies should not be at all aversive.

Other research in this area has shown that when persons are made objectively self-aware they tend to react more extremely to stimuli which produce positive or negative emotional reactions (Scheier and Carver 1977). Persons who filled out questionnaires about themselves while objectively self-aware were more likely to behave in ways which were consistent with their questionnaire responses than were persons who completed the questionnaires while subjectively self-aware (Pryor, Gibbons, Wicklund, Fazio and Hood 1977). Finally Duval and Wicklund (1972) suggest that when persons receive information which they know they will have to pass on to others at some later time, they will do a better job of integrating that information than when they believe that they will not have to transmit the information to others. Thus, when persons are preparing to give a speech to an audience, they are likely to become more objectively self-aware; however, once involved in the process of actually giving the speech, the focus of attention will shift to the audience and subjective self-awareness will become more prevalent.

In general, objective self-awareness theory and research indicates that our attention to ourselves as objects in the environment can be influenced by a number of self-reflecting stimuli. When we become objectively self-aware we are likely to experience some discomfort. This discomfort can be reduced by turning our attention outward to the environment. When we prepare to communicate with others, we are likely to experience objective self-awareness; moreover, when we are in a communication situation, certain stimuli may induce objective self-awareness. Not only might the presence of mirrors make us objectively self-aware but remarks made about us in our presence might induce objective self-awareness. The frequently observed awkwardness that many persons display when they receive compliments from others may be the product of objective self-awareness induced by the compliments. In special communication situations, for example, psychotherapy, attentional focus upon one's self may be both easy and desirable; however, outside of such special situations, we can say that objective self-awareness may interfere with the smooth conduct of social interaction.

Self-consciousness

Objective self-awareness can be created by a variety of environmental stimuli; it is a more or less transient state. By contrast, self-consciousness is conceived as a relatively enduring personality characteristic which is relatively slow to change (Fenigstein, Scheier,and Buss 1975). According to Fenigstein *et al.* (1975), self-consciousness has at least two different components. First, *private* self-consciousness occurs when the self is focused upon as an object, much like objective self-awareness. Second *public* self-consciousness is created when we become aware that other persons are focusing their attention upon us. This type of self-consciousness might be experienced during some kind of public performance before an audience. A dimension related to these two self-consciousness factors is social anxiety. There have been a number of studies which have examined the impacts of these three dimensions upon various aspects of behaviour.

Scheier and Carver (1977) found that persons scoring high in private self-consciousness reacted more extremely to emotionally arousing stimuli than did persons who scored low in private self-consciousness. In this respect, the highly private self-conscious individuals reacted much like persons who were made objectively self-aware. Also similar to the objective self-awareness findings was the finding that persons high in private self-consciousness gave more accurate self-reports about their future behaviour than did persons low in private self-consciousness (Turner 1978). Fenigstein (1979) observed that females with high levels of public self-consciousness were more likely to react negatively to rejection by a group. These persons were also more likely to quit the group.

These research findings suggest that persons with high levels of private self-consciousness behave as if they were in a state of objective self-awareness with all of the attendant difficulties of being in that state. We can only speculate that persons who have high levels of private self-consciousness may feel less affiliative toward others than their low private self-consciousness counterparts. Unfortunately, we have no research which links private self-consciousness to communication behaviour. It does appear, however, that persons with high public self-consciousness are sensitive to the reactions of other persons to them. Persons with high levels of self-consciousness in the public sense might find face-to-face interactions difficult and communication with large audiences even more unnerving. Again, because of the relative youth of the self-consciousness research, it is difficult to talk about these links to communicative conduct with any degree of certainty. However, this area of theory and research suggests that persons may be chronically more or less aware of themselves and their conduct in social interaction situations, depending upon their levels of self-consciousness.

Self-monitoring

Like public and private self-consciousness, self-monitoring is conceived of as a relatively enduring personality disposition of an individual (Snyder 1974). According to Snyder (1974, 1979), high self-monitors are persons who are generally concerned with making favourable impressions on others. Because of this concern, they possess two general characteristics. First, they are sensitive to the behaviour of others for cues which will enable them to gain an understanding of the person with whom they are interacting. High self-monitors are more socially perceptive. Secondly, high self-monitors have better developed acting skills. They can affect a particular 'personality' when they wish to do so. This means that high self-monitors might not express their inner feelings or beliefs in order to avoid offending the person with whom they are interacting. By contrast, low self-monitors are persons who 'tell it the way they feel it'. They are less concerned with the impressions they make on others and because of this lowered concern for impression management, low self-monitors are not as sensitive to cues which others provide which might be used to guide their conduct.

Since Snyder (1974) created the self-monitoring construct, there have been numerous studies which have contrasted the behaviour of high and low self-monitors. Snyder (1974) developed a 25-item scale to measure self-monitoring and found that actors scored higher on self-monitoring than did college students, and college students scored higher than did mental patients. Snyder (1974) also found that high self-monitors were better able to enact different emotional states when requested to do so. When they thought that they would be interacting with a stranger, high self-monitors spent more time studying information about the stranger than did low self-monitors who also thought they would meet the stranger.

Subsequent research has generally supported the differences between high and low self-monitors. In the study described earlier, Bersheid, Graziano, Monson and Dermer (1976) asked students to agree to let the experimenter determine their dating choices for varying periods of time. The students were then given the opportunity to watch a videotaped discussion in which their prospective date was a participant. After watching the videotape, the students were asked to make various ratings of the persons in the tape. This study revealed that students who were high self-monitors: (1) recalled more details about their prospective dates, (2) made more confident trait ratings about their prospective dates, and (3) liked their prospective dates more than did students with low levels of self-monitoring. Elliott (1979) found that persons with high self-monitoring levels were willing to spend more money than lows to purchase information about a person to whom they were asked to misrepresent their opinions on an issue. Geizer, Rarick and Soldow (1977) reported that high self-monitors were better than lows at being able to pick out persons who misrepresented themselves within the context of a television game show. All of these studies provide support for the notion that high self-monitors are both more sensitive to the actions of others and are more concerned with uncertainty reduction when they know they will be interacting with a stranger who may determine whether or not they will reach their interaction goals – whatever these goals may be.

Other research supports the idea that high self-monitors are better able to change their behaviour in response to changes in situational demands. Snyder and Monson (1975) found that high self-monitors changed their levels of conformity in response to changes in situations to a greater extent than did low self-monitors. Lippa (1976) had high and low self-monitors enact the roles of introverted and extroverted teachers. This study revealed that the behaviour of the high self-monitors changed more when they shifted from one role to the other than did the behaviour of low self-monitors. In addition, persons who observed the role playing were better able to identify the intended personality style when it was played by high self-monitors. Thus, high self-monitors were not only more flexible across roles, but they did a more 'convincing' job of enacting the assigned role. In all likelihood, these differences stem from the kinds of social knowledge bases that high and low self-monitors use to guide their self-presentations. Research reported by Snyder and Cantor (1980) suggests that high self-monitors use prototypic conceptions of *others* as guides to their self-presentations in social interaction situations. Low self-monitors use their *self-images* as guides for their self-presentations. Since we generally see more variations in the behaviour of others and tend to see ourselves as less 'variable', it is not surprising that the range of potential self-presentations that the low self-monitor can display is more limited than the range that the high self-monitor can generate.

Summary

At the beginning of this chapter we raised the questions of how persons go about gaining information from others and how persons process that information in order to develop predictive and explanatory knowledge for the purpose of reducing their uncertainties about themselves and others. We also indicated that uncertainty reduction is a critical prerequisite for the exercise of control in social interactions. Finally we recognized that our discussion of knowledge acquisition strategies and attribution models was biased in the direction of assuming that persons engage in considerable thought and planning when they interact with others. We considered a number of different research areas which suggest that when persons enact routine sequences of action, they may be relatively inattentive to the details of their performances.

Our discussion of knowledge acquisition strategies revealed that persons may gather information about others by: (1) observing them unobtrusively, (2) studying their reactions to a set of conditions set up by the observer, or (3) engaging in interaction with them. Within each one of these general classes of strategies, we considered a number of more specific strategies which might be employed to gain knowledge. We considered the problem of assessing the veracity of information gleaned by these methods and counterstrategies that might be employed to foil knowledge gaining attempts.

We then turned to a discussion of various models of attribution. These models attempt to explain how persons arrive at characterizations of others' dispositions and how persons arrive at causal explanations for others' actions. These models are concerned with uncertainty reduction at the predictive and explanatory levels. We saw how a number of factors influence the extent to which we are willing to take a person's actions as representative of his or her dispositions (correspondent inference theory) and we indicated how different kinds of information influence the ways we attribute causality (Kelley's approach). We suggested several limitations of these attribution models.

We then considered some other approaches to social knowledge. Our discussion of scripts indicated that when persons engage in the same or similar patterns of interaction over time, they are likely to become less mindful of the details of their performances. We also found that stimuli in the immediate environment of the individual can make him or her more or less self-aware. Finally, we considered approaches to self-awareness and self-monitoring which conceive of these attributes as enduring traits which persons possess. We saw how various facets of social interaction and social judgement are influenced by these attributes.

Communication is not only something which we receive from others, it is a tool we use to gain knowledge. In the chapters which follow, we will examine how specific linguistic cues are associated with the impressions we form of others and how language is used to effect control in relationships. While we consider these issues, however, it is important to keep in mind that 'forming impressions' from linguistic stimuli is but another form of reducing uncertainty by gaining knowledge about the language user. Moreover, employing language to exert control in relationships may also be a way of reducing our uncertainties both about the other person in the relationship and ourselves.

3

Language and impression formation

The Diplomat sits in silence, watching the world with his ears.

Leon Samson

An important feature of the previous chapters is the argument that in some circumstances interactants are 'naive scientists' who attempt to reduce their mutual uncertainties by assigning causes to behaviour. Now we are ready to examine in detail the multifaceted role which *language* plays in uncertainty reduction and interpersonal interaction. This chapter will focus on language as an indicator of 'facts' which facilitate or inhibit uncertainty reduction. Generally here we view the person attempting to reduce uncertainty as employing the active and passive strategies of knowledge acquisition described in the previous chapter. In the next chapter we move on to the interactive mode where language is viewed as the primary instrument for prying information from sometimes reluctant others.

We will begin by discussing some important conceptual distinctions in the study of language, focusing on those which are most pertinent to the interpersonal context. We will then describe the kinds of information which language can reveal to information seekers in their attempts to reduce uncertainty. This will be followed by a brief inventory of specific language variables which have been shown to relate in important ways to the processes of impression formation and attribution. We argue for the importance of contextual information in these processes. Finally, we will discuss the validity of the knowledge which linguistic cues yield to uncertainty reducers in their interpersonal endeavours.

Conceptions of speech, language and communication

In everyday life we hear persons use the terms 'speech', 'language', and 'communication' as virtual synonyms, e.g., 'His speech was coarse', 'His language was obscene', 'His communication style raised eyebrows'. From a technical standpoint, however, these concepts can be usefully distinguished. We conceive of 'language' as an abstract system of phonological, syntactic, semantic and pragmatic rules (Bradac, Bowers and Courtright 1979). Normal adult members of a language community have a knowledge of this system which they acquire as children. This knowledge is used to produce utterances which are usually spoken. That is, abstract rules are 'translated' into various physical movements which yield acoustic stimuli for hearers. It is important to note that linguistic knowledge can be encoded in other, non-acoustic modes as well, e.g., visual ones as in the case of American Sign Language (Klima and Bellugi 1976). There is a distinction, then, between language and speech which has been referred to as the distinction between 'competence and performance' (Chomsky 1965), between '*la langue et la parole*' (de Saussure 1966). Communication is a more general concept involving the exchange of messages which may or may not be spoken and linguistic in form. As we mentioned in Chapter 1, such messages have as a primary function the reduction of uncertainty in interpersonal interactions.

When thinking about language and interpersonal communication, a useful distinction can be made between digital and analogical codes (Watzlawick, Beavin and Jackson 1967). The essential components of a digital code are arbitrary elements, e.g., phonemes of a language or numbers; and rules for combining these elements, e.g. rules of grammar, morphophonemic rules, or rules of addition, subtraction, and multiplication. Important properties of digital systems are potential transformation of elements without loss of meaning, e.g. $(1 + 2 = 3) = (2 + 1 = 3)$ or 'John is kind' = 'Kind is John' = 'Kind John is' but $\neq$ 'Is John kind?', and generativity or the capability of producing an infinite number of novel structures from a finite set of elements and rules, e.g. $1 + 1 = 2, 1 + 1 + 1 = 3, 1 + 1 + 1 + 1 = 4, 1 + 1 + 1 + 1 + 1$ . . .; 'John is kind', 'John is kind and nice', 'John, who is kind and who is nice, is . . .'; 'A rose is a rose is a . . .'. Digital codes are uniquely designed to convey propositional meanings, e.g. 'Man is a featherless biped' or 'I want you to go to the party with me'.

Analogic codes, on the other hand, are continuous signals which vary exclusively in terms of intensity and duration. Examples are human screams, the threat gestures of baboons, and (probably) the whistles of dolphins. It is difficult to think of an analogic code in terms of arbitrary elements, rules of combination, transformation and generativity. It has been suggested that analogic codes are highly iconic, i.e. they resemble the phenomenon they are attempting to respresent (CAT versus 🐱 ; Watzlawick, Beavin and Jackson, 1967) but this seems misleading to us, in some cases at least. What does a scream look or sound like? Does the threat gesture of a baboon really look like a punch in the nose? At any rate analogic codes are uniquely designed to convey intensity, strength, magnitude, distance, length, and so forth. In both non-human and human communication, analogic signals convey information about strength of affect and nature of the relationship between the sender and the receiver of the signal (Watzlawick, Beavin and Jackson 1967).

It is probably clear by now that speech (or performed language) is both an analogic and a digital system. The elements are phonemes (or categories of sound) which are combined according to rules into meaningful structures. The major continuous features, i.e. aspects of speech which cannot be decomposed easily into discrete units, are rate, volume, duration, non-segmental pitch (mean fundamental frequency) and intonation (pitch variation). Importantly from our standpoint, both the analogic and the digital aspects of speech convey information about communicators which is used by the 'naive scientist' to form hypotheses about their attitudes, background, and so forth.

When we discussed the propositional aspect of digital codes and the relationship-signaling aspect of analogic codes, we were describing the *functions* which these codes serve. It will now be useful to examine the functions of speech in more detail. There are three primary functions of speech in social interaction, and we will label these 'referential', 'instrumental' and 'expressive' (cf. Jakobson 1972). Words are invented to refer to objects, actions, events etc., or more accurately, they are invented to refer to *concepts* which have some correspondance to the social and physical reality of the members of a speech community. We can discourse about 'vegetables' because this term indexes a class of objects which we understand to be more or less 'vegetably'. This sort of class of objects has been characterized as a 'fuzzy set' (Brown 1978; Rosch 1973) which implies that at the centre of the set we will have a prototype (peas or carrots) and at the edges we will have marginal cases (nasturtium petals? capers?). When we link words ('carrots', 'vegetables') to various logical connectors ('are', 'are not'), we can discourse about our conceptual world in referential propositions ('carrots are vegetables'). Obviously, we can do this sort of thing in the presence of others or alone, out loud or in silence. We are engaging in propositional thought in any case. The referential function of language will be very important to the issues broached in our discussion of relational communication in Chapter 5.

By the instrumental function of speech we mean that performed language is a tool for getting people to do things. On the one hand, we have orders ('Halt!'), utterances which, in appropriate circumstances, e.g., military combat, are highly likely to produce the effects intended by speakers. On the other hand, we have requests, petitions and hints, where the speaker is largely at the mercy of his or her hearer. Pertinent here also are speaker intentions such as persuading, intimidating, impressing and threatening. Ordering and impressing are examples of speech acts which have been labelled 'illocutionary' and 'perlocutionary', respectively (Searle 1969). These types of speech acts and the various instrumental functions of speech are crucially important to relationship development and to the interactive knowledge gaining strategies discussed in the next chapters.

By the expressive function of speech we mean to suggest that performed language conveys information to hearers, often quite apart from the intentions of speakers. Some information is 'given off' by speech (Goffman 1959). We could just as well refer to the 'attributional' or 'diagnostic' function of spoken language in this context. The term 'speech marker' has also been used to indicate that performed language is an index of various biological, sociological and psychological states (Giles, Scherer and Taylor 1979). The remainder of this chapter focuses on the ways in which speech conveys information about speakers.

What does speech express?

A commonplace of human information processing theory is that stimulus *variation* is essential to perception and cognition (cf. Chapter 2). We notice *change*. In a static, timeless world we would neither see nor think. More realistically, 'naive scientists' appear to assume that that which does not vary in their environment need not be noticed. Language can be discussed in terms of both variance and invariance. That is, some aspects of language change as speakers and situations change. Other aspects are constant across speakers and even across cultures. For example, all languages are organized on the same basic principles, using a limited stock of phonemes to form words which are combined according to syntactic rules to form sentences (Hockett 1960). Similarly, all languages seem to prohibit certain kinds of syntactic constructions, e.g. violation of the Complex Noun Phrase Constraint is never permissible ('Some drivers hit pets which children often play in streets which are crowded with frequently;' Martin, Bradac and Elliott 1977; Ross 1967). Invariance points to the biological underpinnings of language (Lenneberg 1967). The invariant aspects of language make verbal communication possible. They constitute the system which humans exploit to exchange messages.

By contrast, many linguistic features are highly variable, and it is these which yield or 'give off' information to receivers. These variable features are used for the purpose of knowledge gaining in interpersonal interaction. In the next major section we will inventory some of these features. Before we do this, however, we should discuss the kinds of information which linguistic variations can convey to hearers.

Variation which occurs within speakers, as opposed to between speakers, potentially signals changes in affect or mood. As a person's speech moves from neutrality to extreme obscenity, we will probably infer a change in his or her psychological state. We may also relate within-speaker language variation to changes in the situation, as when a teacher enters a room and students' speech becomes quiet and mild. Between-speaker variation, on the other hand, yields information about psychological traits. If two speakers are consistently distinguished in terms of the power of their speech styles (see pages 60–1 below), we are likely to attribute this to a personality difference – 'Tom is a strong person, but Bill is a milksop'.

A recent letter to Ann Landers (1981), the American newspaper columnist, shows that more complex language assessments are possible:

> Dear Ann: I have a problem I have never seen mentioned in your column as yet. It is ruining my marriage.
> It seems like whenever Ernie is angry, he starts to cuss me out. . . .
> Ernie calls me every foul name he can think of, and sometimes when he really wants to hurt my feelings, he will say something like, 'Ha, ha, your mother is dead.' My mom and I were extremely close. She died six months ago, and I miss her terribly.
> I am very much offended by his foul mouth, and he knows it. Whenever he is frustrated by some simple thing, like not knowing how to put up the weather-stripping or not being able to open the door, or when the car won't start, he swears at me.
> Last week the commuter train broke down. Ernie didn't get to work until noon. He called me the minute he got to the shop, and for nearly 10 minutes he swore a blue streak. I just stood there on the other end and didn't say one word. It is not unusual for him to call me at my part-time job to swear and hang up on me.
> This is not a very pleasant household in which to bring up two precious little girls . . . . – Lee.

> Dear Lee: Ernie is operating at the emotional level of a 10-year-old; in fact, he sounds like a case of arrested development.
> The man is in dire need of professional help. . . .

In this case the writer and Ann are using both within- and between-speaker variation to infer that (1) Ernie's obscenity is produced by various frustrators, including Lee; (2) Ernie's use of obscenity is extremely deviant compared to other speakers; and (3) Ernie's personality is 'arrested' and pathological. Or in the terminology of Jones and Davis (1965), Kelley (1967), and McArthur (1972), the writer and Ann are making a dispositional inference about Ernie's obscenity primarily on the basis of the low distinctiveness of Ernie's cussing and, at least implicitly, on the basis of low consensus and high consistency – Ernie swears in the presence of frustrators more than other people do and he does this consistently across situations.

Between-person variation is also a very important source of inferences about a speaker's many social group memberships. The paradigm case in this regard is the dialectologist's hypothesis about a speaker's birthplace which is formed on the basis of language cues, as in *Pgymalion* (Shaw 1946). Often less highly trained persons, i.e. 'naive scientists', will make more global judgements on the basis of speech. For example, many normal midwestern Americans believe they can distinguish speakers born in the southwest from those born in Boston. (The *validity* of such judgements is an issue which we will address below.) Many other types of group membership are potentially revealed through language: age (Helfrich 1979), gender (Mulac and Lundell 1980), profession (Lakoff 1975), race (Labov 1969c), ethnicity (Giles 1979a), and others. Even small and highly specialized groups may become known for their speech style. In southern California, a person uttering the following sentence would almost certainly be labelled 'surfer': 'Some toadster on a disco chip orned me on that last set and put gnarly snackle in my rhino chaser' (Barnes 1980).

So, within- and between-speaker variation conveys information about psychological traits and states and about group membership. Or in the terminology of Chapter 1, speech variation constitutes psychological, sociological and cultural data. An implication is that even in initial encounters a person's speech style may allow us to relate to him or her at a psychological level. But note that in such a situation we are just 'scratching the surface' of the person's psychological make-up. We are taking widely disseminated knowledge about psychological types and applying it (perhaps hazardously) to this particular case, ignoring this person's psychological idiosyncracies.

Our linguistically based judgements of a speaker's psychological make-up and affiliations allow us to reduce uncertainty. There are four models of this process, each of which is probably valid in particular circumstances (Figure 3.1). Generally, the models assume that hearers use spoken language to categorize speakers along various social psychological dimensions (McKirnan and Hamayan 1980). Further, the models suggest that hearers' judgements of speaker similarity constitute a crucial mediating variable, and there is some support for the claim that speech allows hearers to make similarity judgements (Bishop 1979; Bradac, Desmond and Murdock 1977; Delia 1972).

The first model indicates that on the basis of language cues, a hearer forms a hypothesis about a speaker's group affiliations. This hypothesis leads in turn to a judgement of the extent to which a speaker is similar to the hearer, and when similarity is high uncertainty is reduced. Model 2 indicates a similar process except that a judgement of a psychological trait or state mediates uncertainty reduction. Model 3 is the most complex representation. Language yields a hypothesis about group membership. This is associated (via social stereotypes)

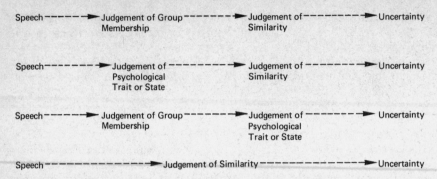

Figure 3.1

with particular psychological traits which leads in turn to an estimate of speaker similarity, and the similarity assessment culminates in a feeling of certainty or uncertainty about the speaker. By contrast, Model 4 is the simplest. It suggests that language variation can produce *directly* a judgement of speaker similarity which results in increased or decreased uncertainty. The implication here is that in some cases cultural, sociological and psychological stereotypes do *not* mediate language variation and similarity judgements, that particular language forms may simply seem odd or familiar without calling up a specific cognitive category (cf. Sebastian, Ryan, Keogh and Schmidt 1980; Mulac and Lundell 1980).

A final issue is under what circumstances language cues which produce hearer judgements of similarity or dissimilarity will serve to reduce or to increase uncertainty. Generally, it seems clear that language which elicits a similarity judgement will facilitate uncertainty reduction. On the other hand, language which elicits a judgement of dissimilarity will probably increase uncertainty when (1) the hearer does not have a full-blown stereotype into which he or she can fit the speaker and (2) even if a stereotype is suggested, when a script for dealing with the stereotyped speaker is not available. Conversely, language which triggers a stereotype and an appropriate script while eliciting a judgement of dissimilarity should facilitate uncertainty reduction.

An experience of one of the authors in Iowa City, Iowa, provides a relevant concrete example. He was sitting with two friends at a table in a restaurant during a period when many tables were available. Suddenly a middle-aged woman sat down next to him, without an invitation. She began to speak in an exaggerated style and with great volume about a Communist conspiracy to take over the radio stations of this university town. She gesticulated wildly. The author immediately assimilated her communicative behaviour to the category 'paranoid' and then, with less certainty, he extended this to 'escapee from a local institution'. A judgement of great dissimilarity was also made. And in this case the author experienced uncertainty to the point of paralysis because he had nothing resembling a script for dealing with a 'paranoid escapee'. Fortunately, the author and his friends had already paid for the lunch which they had finished, so it was relatively easy simply to escape from the situation. All this is represented by Model 3.

Attributionally rich language variables

We have thus far suggested that performed language 'gives off' information which is used by 'naive scientists' in the process of uncertainty reduction. Now we will briefly describe and discuss several specific aspects of speech which have been shown to produce attributions of a social and psychological sort. This will be a quick inventory of the major language variables.

Familiarity and goodness

Some words are more or less familiar to hearers, whereas others are completely known or unknown to them. The use of unfamiliar terms should serve to increase the hearer's perception of the speaker's dissimilarity which should heighten the hearer's uncertainty, unless the hearer has a stereotype for a person who uses baffling words. Words which are known to be unfamiliar to the hearer, e.g., slang or argot, may be used by a speaker to 'mystify' the hearer (Duncan 1962) or to increase the speaker's sense of personal identity as in the case of a person from Wales speaking Welsh to a conservative British schoolmaster (cf. Bourhis and Giles 1977; Drake 1980). Familiarity is related to lexical 'goodness' in that words which are familiar or predictable will tend to be rated positively by hearers (Zajonc 1968). Goodness is a more general construct, however, in that there are many reasons why particular words may be rated positively or negatively. There are 'linguistic taboos' (Hudson 1980), words or phrases which denote excretory and sexual processes, profanation of sacred objects, and death or decay. Conversely, there are 'linguistic charms', lexical items which typically produce very positive evaluations. Other things being equal, we should be more attracted to the charmer than to the defiler (Cohen and Saine 1977). Persons who use these positively valued words may also be rather persuasive (Eiser and Pancer 1979).

In many initial encounters, a heavy use of obscenity will probably increase our uncertainty about a communicator. Of course if *we* are habitually highly obscene, the use of obscenity by another person may produce a judgement of high similarity and a sense of high certainty.

Immediacy and intensity

Both of these variables reflect speakers' affect or feelings about the referents of their discourse. The immediacy concept indicates that speakers approach or avoid the topics or referents of their messages linguistically (Wiener and Mehrabian 1967). Speakers 'leak' their true feelings to hearers through their lexical choices. Highly immediate language has been shown to produce preceptions of high liking; that is, if a speaker talks about Richard Nixon in highly immediate terms, we will infer that he or she *likes* Nixon, quite apart from the manifest content of the speaker's utterance (Hess and Gossett 1974; Wiener and Mehrabian 1967). Linguistic immediacy is increased by the use of: (1) greater specificity ('that person' versus 'his mistress'), (2) spatial or temporal indicators of proximity ('there's John' versus 'here's John'), (3) forms of inclusion and mutuality ('we' versus 'you and I'), (4) implied voluntarism ('I want' versus 'I must'), (5) sequencing ('John, Bill, Jean and Joe are my friends' – John is best liked), and (6) probability ('I will' versus 'I may').

Intensity, on the other hand, does not signal direction of affect (like versus dislike), rather it indicates *magnitude* of feeling whether positive or negative. Speakers using highly intense language are perceived as deviating from attitudinal neutrality (Bowers 1963). Within a culture certain linguistic forms will be judged by most members as indicating high or low intensity or, on the other hand, neutrality. For example, most people would probably agree that 'It was an extremely devastating earthquake' is more intense than 'It was a sort of nasty shake', unless the speaker is being clearly ironic.

Speakers using high intensity and high immediacy should be perceived as quite similar to their hearers when they are talking about someone or something the hearers like. Conversely, in this kind of situation low intensity and low immediacy should decrease perceptions of similarity because we do not like persons to damn our favourite persons and ideas with 'linguistically faint praise' (Bradac, Bowers and Courtright 1979, p. 261). In the former case uncertainty should be relatively low, in the latter case relatively high. Of course, in a first-impression context extremely high intensity or immediacy might be perceived as unusual, regardless of attitudinal congruence, and in this case our uncertainty might be heightened – 'This guy comes on strong; I had better *watch out*'.

Elaboration, restriction and verbal fluency

Some speakers exhibit a highly diversified vocabulary, whereas others appear comparatively lexically impoverished. Bernstein has argued that British speakers of the lower class will tend to be of the latter sort, whereas speakers of the upper and middle classes will tend to be of the former (1971). More generally, as a result of the presumably homogenizing effect of ghetto experiences, most importantly rigid family communication patterns, lower-class persons may fail to develop the ability to take their listener's role linguistically. For example, this failure would cause the lower-class speaker to use pronouns whose referents are unclear to others who do not share his or her experiences. This 'elaboration–restriction hypothesis' has been hotly debated (Labov 1969c; Sankoff and Lessard 1975). One of the difficulties with the theory is the claim that social status is inversely related to homogeneous experience. Some middle- and upper-class environments appear rather homo-geneous along particular dimensions (race, gender, dress style, and so forth). It is not clear that socioeconomic status is a covariant of linguistic elaboration. But perhaps where we do find speakers with rather homogeneous communication experiences, for whatever reasons, we will discover that they perform in a linguistically restricted manner.

Regardless of the determinants of degree of elaboration or verbal fluency, it is clear that this variable has consequences for communicators. In a series of studies, Bradac, Davies, Courtright, Desmond and Murdock (1977) constructed messages which exhibited high or low lexical diversity. The low-diversity messages exhibited a high level of repetition, whereas those of high diversity used synonyms wherever possible. The messages were presented to respondents via audiotape or transcript, and after hearing or reading them respondents evaluated speakers and messages on several semantic-differential-type evaluative scales, e.g., 'The speaker seemed:

_____:_____:_____:_____:_____:_____:_____',.
incompetent   competent

Consistently, high diversity produced judgements of high communicator competence and effectiveness, low anxiety, and high socioeconomic status. One study showed that extremely low diversity led respondents to disagree with the statement: 'The speaker thinks like me' (Bradac, Desmond and Murdock 1977). This suggests that a speaker exhibiting low diversity will be seen as dissimilar by most hearers and therefore unpredictable (cf. Bradac, Courtright and Bowers 1980).

However, it is probably not all as clear cut as we implied in the last paragraph. For one thing, Giles, Wilson and Conway (1981) found that persons may react more favourably to low diversity than to high in terms of judgements of *sociability*, a dimension not examined in the studies cited above. This suggests that persons may view a speaker exhibiting low diversity as relatively cooperative and friendly, attributes evaluated positively in most interpersonal encounters. Further, Scherer (1979b) reports that in the context of a simulated jury discussion diversity level was *inversely* related to judgements of the amount of influence exerted by jurors. Also, propagandists, rhetoricians and advertisers have long assumed that repetition of lexical items is *directly* associated with persuasion. Finally, the 'mere exposure' hypothesis (Zajonc 1968), which asserts that persons become increasingly favourable to stimuli simply as a function of increased exposure to them, also tends to call into question the claim of a simple positive relationship between diversity and favourableness of evaluations. The obvious conclusion is that particular kinds of repetition in particular contexts will increase a communicator's persuasiveness and attractiveness, while other kinds of repetition will have the opposite effect.

'Good' and 'bad' grammar

Some combinations of words, some lexical constructions, are evaluated as acceptable, appropriate or correct, whereas others are judged unacceptable, inappropriate or incorrect. An important question at this point is: acceptable etc. to whom? Teachers of English and of other languages have learned traditional models of grammar which they use to evaluate discourse. Linguists have special grammatical theories which admit certain lexical strings to the office of sentencehood while excluding others. On the other hand, non-specialists have tacit, unarticulated models which are used to scrutinize discourse. Persons of the latter sort have been labelled 'naive grammarians' (Bradac, Martin, Elliott and Tardy 1980). Language teachers, linguists, and 'naive grammarians' may or may not agree on the acceptability or correctness of a particular utterance. It seems that the naive grammatical models which most untutored persons use in everyday life are the most important for attributional purposes in interpersonal communication.

There is some evidence that 'bad' grammar, a lexical construction which deviates from the naive model of acceptability, is a potent factor in person perception. For example, Triandis, Loh and Levin (1966) exposed respondents to a message which varied in terms of grammar and opinions expressed about civil rights. The communicator was black or white, well or poorly dressed, and of a high or low ascribed status. On the dimension of 'interpersonal distance', a measure of respondents' willingness to affiliate with the communicator in various contexts, grammar was overwhelmingly the variable with the greatest predictive power; the college student respondents were rather disinclined to affiliate with the speaker exhibiting 'bad' grammar. Much depends on the grammatical model which persons have internalized. A particular person may habitually use certain forms which his or her internalized model prohibits, but this person (1) may notice deviant performances of other speakers but not of self ('What an uneducated boor he are.'), (2) may notice deviations in self-performance only which may in turn lead to self derogation ('I sounds stupid and uneducated.'), or (3) may notice deviations in the performance of both self and other ('We is boorish birds of the same feather.'). Clearly in some cases 'bad' grammar is used intentionally to produce perceptions of increased similarity and solidarity, whereas in others it is used to produce perceptions of *dis*similarity and fracture. When adolescent males try to sound 'bad' in front of their teachers, they are exploiting grammar for both purposes. Sounding 'bad' signals the teacher to beware and it shows that the speaker is 'just one of the boys'.

Powerful and powerless speech

Some words or phrases are associated with powerful persons, whereas others are associated with those who are weak. Here, of course, we are talking about social, as opposed to physical, power. Lakoff (1975) has argued that there is a 'female register', a style of talking like a powerless woman. Supposedly, women are more inclined to use hedges ('well, . . .'), intensifiers, ('It really is.'), 'empty adjectives' ('glorious, divine'), and tag questions ('It is, isn't it?'). The behavioural evidence in support of the 'female register hypothesis' is inconclusive at this point (Brouwer, Gerritsen and De Haan 1979; Fishman 1980; Smith 1979). O'Barr and his associates argue that there is a style associated with socially powerful and powerless persons, quite apart from gender (Erickson, Lind, Johnson and O'Barr 1978). Powerless persons have learned to hedge, to be polite, etc. It seems to us that a speaker's self-perception ('I am in control here.') is the basis for this dimension of speech style, not necessarily his or her objectively determinable social power (judge versus defendant). This implies that a given speaker may sound powerful in one situation and powerless in another as his or her self-perceptions vary (cf. Brown and Fraser 1979; Fishman 1980).

Regardless of the causes of these style differences, there is evidence that in courtroom contexts, at least, power of style is directly associated with judgements of communicator credibility and attractiveness (Erickson, Lind, Johnson and O'Barr 1978; Bradac, Hemphill and Tardy 1981). Also, the powerful style is in fact judged by naive respondents as indicating a more powerful and assertive speaker than is the powerless style (Bradac, Hemphill and Tardy 1981; Newcombe and Arnkoff 1979). Although powerful communicators may generally be seen as competent and attractive, if we feel powerless in a particular situation we may see a powerless communicator as being more similar to us and therefore more predictable. Our powerlessness may incline us toward the safety of predictability, so we may actually prefer to affiliate with this unattractive and incompetent other. In fact there is some evidence that persons with low self-esteem may prefer to associate with relatively unattractive partners (Berscheid, Dion, Walster and Walster 1971).

Talk, silence, and interruptions

The previously discussed variables reflect the semantic and syntactic components of language. Now we turn to variables which are phonological or, more broadly, paralinguistic. The most basic of these is the variable 'talk/silence states'. Given two persons interacting, regardless of *what* they are saying, there are four basic ways they can 'make noises' as a dyad: (1) person A can be talking while person B is silent; (2) B can be talking while A is silent; (3) A and B can both be silent; (4) A and B can both be talking (cf. Cappella 1979, 1980; Siegman and Feldstein 1979). These state differences are objective and are literally detectable by a machine. But each of these states can take on different *meanings*, and when we talk of meaning we can no longer rely upon mechanized detection. For example, in state (1), A can be talking to B who is inattentive; A can be talking to himself in B's presence; or A can be talking to B who is attending closely. Under (3), A and B may be merely in each other's presence; they may be switching speaking turns with one of the parties having not yet picked up the conversational ball; or they may both just have run out of things to say. Under (4), A may have the floor while B is attempting to gain it by interrupting or A may have the floor while B is engaging in 'back-channel' behaviours ('yes', 'I see', etc.) (Duncan, Jr, 1973). We attribute different *intentions* to a person who is interrupting as opposed to producing back-channel behaviours or who is talking to herself in the other's presence as opposed to talking to the other directly (cf. Badzinski 1982).

From another standpoint, there are different ways of distributing talk and silence in conversations. For example, A and B can both produce about the same amount of talk during a given period; A can talk a lot while B is mostly silent; or both persons may talk infrequently. Observing the dyad, we will form different impressions of the personalities or moods of each interactant based upon the way in which talk and silence are distributed. Where both persons are frequently silent we may infer that they are both angry, uncomfortable, relaxed or shy. In this case we can become more certain about the probable cause of the silence only by searching for additional clues. On the other hand, there is much evidence that a person who talks a great deal compared to another will be seen as having a disposition which we can label dominant, aggressive, controlling, etc. (Sorrentino and Boutillier 1975). Of course, if we have reason to believe that this high level of talk is unusual or 'inconsistent' (Kelley 1967), perhaps because we have seen this person being silent upon other occasions, we will probably attribute this verbal outpouring to a state induced by a large intake of ale, to the person being talked to, or to other temporary causes. The implication is that a speaker's talk/silence ratio is viewed from the standpoint of various baselines including the speaker's performance in other situations, other speakers' levels of talk/silence in the present situation, and the observer's own tendencies to talk or remain silent. The talk/silence ratio is compared to this baseline information and an attribution of causality results.

Pitch and intonation

These variables are extremely rich sources of information about speakers' meanings, moods, personality, gender, and even ethnic background. Typically, the 'naive scientist' will view pitch as a relatively enduring characteristic of a speaker which is largely outside of the speaker's control ('He has a squeaky voice'), whereas intonation will be seen as more controllable and transitory (cf. Laver and Trudgill 1979). Thus, we would expect pitch to be associated stereotypically with attributes like personality and group affiliation, whereas intonation should be linked primarily to characteristics like mood and affect. And there is evidence consistent with this claim.

Not surprisingly, average pitch level is strongly associated with gender, which is typically not transitory. Schwarz and Rine (1968) found that untrained persons were capable of correctly assigning very small samples of speech – as small as single phonemes – to correct gender categories based upon pitch distinctions. Thus, a male with a high-pitched voice may be seen as having an effeminate or androgynous personality. Generally it seems that pitch is directly related to judgements of smallness, weakness, frailty, etc. In addition to gender, age attributions are probably related to pitch. Here we seem to get a curvilinear relationship, at least for male speakers, such that young and old persons are thought to speak at a higher pitch, whereas a lower pitch is expected of those in their middle years (cf. Helfrich 1979).

Intonation yields information about how angry, interested, bored or fearful a speaker is, among other things. For example, there is some evidence that depressed persons exhibit a narrow, unvariegated intonation (Newman and Mather 1938). Angry or frightened persons may exhibit an extremely wide variation in intonation (Pronovost and Fairbanks 1939). It seems reasonable to hypothesize that aroused persons exhibit much intonational variation, whereas those who are non-aroused exhibit little such variation. Here we are referring to basic physiological arousal – heightened heart beat, pupillary dilation, etc. Observers of this vocal activity produced by high or low arousal attribute specific emotional states to the speaker on the basis of various situational cues: wide intonational contour + smile = enthusiasm, + shaking fist = anger; narrow contour + smile + lax posture = mellowness, etc. This is a reversed version of Schachter's labelling theory of emotion (1964).

For the sake of accuracy it should be noted that in some cases intonation may be used to make attributions about permanent conditions (psychological traits and group membership); for example, women may tend to use a greater variety of intonational patterns than do men (Smith 1979). And conversely pitch may be used to make attributions regarding transitory states; for example, a relatively high level of pitch (in conjunction with much intonational variation and situational cues) may be associated with the emotional state of anger (Pronovost and Fairbanks 1939).

Phonetic variation

Between-speaker variation in speech sounds is a powerful indicator of membership in particular social groups. There are many social stereotypes of specific sound patterns. In America, for example, gay males are stereotypically associated with a frontal lisp. The substitution of a voiced alveolar stop (/d/) for a voiced dental fricative (/ð/) is likely to call up a cluster of group affiliations, the most specific being 'street gang in Brooklyn, New York,' the most general being 'lower class'. And it will not surprise you that there is evidence showing that social class membership covaries with the use of certain speech sounds. A classic study in this regard was conducted by Labov (1969b). This researcher had confederates ask salespersons a question which was designed to elicit the response 'fourth floor'. The questions were asked in three stores in New York city which differed in the average amount of money spent per customer. The inference was made that this average was an indicator of socioeconomic status of both customers and salespersons. Labov found that speakers in the 'lower class' environment were less likely to produce *r* sounds in medial and final positions in words than were those in the 'upper-class' store. The 'middle-class' speakers were more variable in their responses, more likely to include the *r* when asked the stimulus question a second time than were the 'lower-class' speakers.

More generally, mispronunciations or speech errors may lead to the attribution, 'This speaker is a foreigner', or under some circumstances, 'This speaker is a child'. These attributions have in common the assumption that the speakers have not yet learned the correct model. To make these inferences 'naive scientists' will have to have a reasonably large sample of speech, i.e. more than a word or two. This is because a single error may be attributed to a slip of the tongue or to an isolated case of incorrect learning. A *pattern* of errors is used to attribute foreignness or childishness to speakers.

It seems to us that persons rarely gain a great deal of psychological information directly from phonetic variation. Particular speech errors, e.g. spoonerisms ('Bring ice' becomes 'Bing rice') may cause hearers to attribute the states of fatigue or anxiety to speakers. Spoonerisms in the form of Freudian slips may yield clues about a speaker's real intentions or feelings, as in the case of the person introduced to his competitor who says, 'Very glad to beat you' (Motley, Camden and Baars 1979, p. 195). Repetitions of initial syllables ('pi . . . pi . . . pirate') may also produce judgements of fatigue or anxiety (Kasl and Mahl 1965) or, of course, the judgement that the speaker is a stutterer. The latter attribution would again demand a pattern of repetitions. But it should be noted that *in*direct information about psychological traits is readily available to hearers once they have assimilated a particular phonetic pattern to a social stereotype: 'He is from Brooklyn and therefore he is unintelligent.'

Finally, a hearer's judgement of a speaker's *reason* for using particular phonetic forms influences the information value of those forms. If, for example, the hearer believes (1) that the speaker believes that the hearer is from Brooklyn and can therefore use the 'low-class' *r* only, (2) that the speaker has the ability to use both 'high-class' and 'low-class' *r* sounds, and (3) that the speaker *chooses* to use the 'high-class' *r* when talking to the hearer, then the hearer will probably evaluate the speaker negatively, assigning to him or her the trait of snobbishness (cf. Simard, Taylor and Giles 1976).

Volume and rate

Both of these paralinguistic variables can be related to the construct 'intensity'.

A combination of high volume of voice and fast speech rate should produce an impression of high intensity, and, conversely, a low volume combined with a slow rate should lead to a judgement of low intensity (cf. Markel, Phillis, Vargas and Howard 1972). Another way of saying this is that an increased expenditure of physical energy is associated with perceptions of increased stimulus intensity.

Some evidence indicates that loudness is associated with the attribution of introversion–extroversion; the louder the speaker, the more extroverted he or she is perceived to be (Allport and Cantril 1934). The trait of deafness may be associated with a high level of loudness in circumstances where loudness seems inappropriate, e.g. a theatre or a funeral home. Rather obviously, particular psychological states are associated with increased volume also: enthusiasm, excitement, communicator's sense of the importance of the communication topic, etc.

There is some evidence that speech rate, like loudness, is directly related to perceptions of extroversion (Scherer 1979a). Several studies by Brown and associates (Brown 1980) have shown that rate is directly related to judgements of communicator competence. On the other hand, rate and perceived communicator benevolence have an inverted U-shape relationship such that both low and high speech rates produce judgements of low benevolence, whereas relatively high benevolence is attributed to a moderate rate. There is also some evidence that speech rate is positively related to a communicator's persuasiveness (Miller, Maruyama, Beaber and Valone 1976). As in the case of loudness, an increased rate is associated with various transitory states as well, e.g. enthusiasm and anxiety (Siegman and Pope 1972).

These variables, like several of the others discussed previously, will produce judgements of permanent traits *or* transitory states depending upon the availability of multiple speech samples. The 'naive scientist' perceiving a communicator for the first time may be uncertain about the permanence of a high level of rate and volume and, therefore, uncertain of the permanence of the psychological characteristics these variables may indicate. Uncertainty will be reduced with multiple exposures. If high levels of rate and volume persist across situations these levels will probably be taken as signals of a 'manic' personality or a competent personality, etc.

Pragmatic deviation and normalcy

This final variable potentially embraces semantics, syntax and phonology. There are rules for engaging in certain communicative routines, which are learned by normal members of a cultural group. For example, Nofsinger (1974) characterizes the rules underlying the use of 'demand tickets' – devices for getting the floor to transmit information to another person. A normal 'demand ticket' exchange would be:

John: You know what?
Mary: What?
John: I heard the pub burned down last night.

or:

Mary: John?
John: Yes?
Mary: I need a loan of five pounds. Can you spare it for a week?

Presumably, assuming two serious interactants, the following exchange should not occur:

John: You know what?
Mary: What?
John: What.

nor should:

Mary: John?
John: Yes?
Mary: (silence)
John: Yes?
Mary: (silence)
John: Yes?!
Mary: (silence)

The third and fourth exchanges violate rules governing the use of 'demand tickets' (cf. Nofsinger 1974). For example, after initiating the exchanges, both Mary and John are *obligated* to transmit information which they believe that the other does not possess following the other's acknowledgement of their request for attention. In both cases they do not live up to this obligation.

Although little research has been done on the attributional consequences of violating pragmatic rules, it has been suggested that such violations will lead to a judgement of violator 'madness' or 'badness' (Watzlawick, Beavin and Jackson 1967). That is, we will judge the violator as 'crazy', maladjusted or odd, or we will judge him or her as perversely exploiting the rules, perhaps for the sake of fun. Also, the intentions of a speaker who violates a pragmatic rule may be misunderstood, as when a directive is understood as a question (Ervin-Tripp 1980; Tannen 1979). It seems likely that in some cases we may attribute foreignness or childishness to the violator. We may assume that the violator simply has not yet learned the rules. Whether we attribute maladjustment or foreignness to the rule violator, pragmatic deviations seem highly likely to increase our uncertainty about this person. It seems that we have few readily available scripts for dealing with something as potentially disruptive of the social fabric as violations of the rules which constitute and regulate our many social games (cf. Searle 1969).

Dialects, idiolects and 'linguistic items'

Several of the language variables described above can be thought of in terms of the concept 'dialect'. That is, dialectal variation includes variations in lexical, syntactic and phonological patterns. Dialects are clusters of linguistic features which are traditionally associated with geographically dispersed groups. Thus, dialect varies with group membership which varies with region of country. Dialectal variations are strongly associated with hearer judgements of status (Giles and Powesland 1975) and sociability (Ryan 1979). Recently the concept of dialect has been extended to groups which are geographically coterminous but sociologically distinct, e.g. males versus females (Mulac and Lundell 1980). To account for the systematic quirks of individual speakers within dialect groups, the concept of 'idiolect' was invented. Idiolectal variation suggests that some speakers may be marginal members of their dialect groups while others are prototypical. Thus, dialect groups may be thought of as 'fuzzy sets', the boundaries of which are extremely difficult to determine.

This fuzziness of boundaries and the many non-geographical determinants of language variation have led one theorist to abandon the historically space-bound concept of dialect altogether. Hudson (1980) wants to substitute for dialect the notion of 'linguistic item'. 'Linguistic items' are 'not only lexical items but also syntactic constructions and morphological and phonological patterns of any type . . . simply a pattern which may be identified, at any level of abstraction, in the structure of the sentence (p. 189).' These are 'bundles' of linguistic phenomena which vary with speakers and occasions. Hudson revels in the fact that there are many and diverse social psychological causes of language variation. From our standpoint, the research wave of the future will include investigation of the ways in which many of these yet to be discovered linguistic 'bundles' are used attributionally by 'naive scientists' in their quest for interpersonal certainty.

Language in context

As indicated several times in the preceding section, language variation does not occur in a social vacuum. It is contextualized. There are many linguistic and extra-linguistic components of context which determine or influence the forms which language assumes. Most importantly from our standpoint, these contextual components affect the hypotheses formed by 'naive scientists' on the basis of a communicator's speech style.

When we use the term 'context' we imply that speech is embedded temporally and spatially – events occur before and after an utterance and this same utterance is 'surrounded' by a physical setting and by participants, spectators and inattentive others. These attributes of context are 'objective' in that most observers could probably agree more or less on conclusions like, 'They were talking in an auditorium; he spoke for ten minutes and then she responded to his remarks; there was an audience, etc.' More important than these 'objective' components of context are those which are *salient* to speakers and hearers. Persons construe events differently; they impose dissimilar sometimes highly idiosyncratic 'construct systems' upon persons and messages (Delia 1977; Kelly 1955). The subjective interpretations of communication events – in a sense the meaning of the events – are probably the most important factors affecting language performance and perceptions of this performance (Bradac, in press). When we examine the meanings which speech has for interactants in their subjective environments, we are viewing language as a social psychological phenomenon (Giles, Hewstone and St Clair, in press).

Until recently, the last 10 years or so, much of the research on consequences of language variation largely ignored the role of context. This was especially true of experimental studies. There is now evidence that this was a serious omission because various contextual features have been shown to intensify, minimize or even reverse particular effects of language (Bradac, Bowers and Courtright 1979, 1980). We will now discuss some contextual influences on speech and the judgements of hearers.

Prior message context

Typically in human interaction messages are exchanged serially. (Of course monologues and simultaneous messages occur also.) Some research shows that a person's perception of a prior message can affect the way in which he or she responds to a subsequent one. Bradac, Davies and Courtright (1977) obtained 'contrast effects' for high- and low-diversity messages. When a second speaker's lexically redundant message followed the lexically diverse message of an initial speaker, it produced stronger judgements of communicator incompetence and unclarity than did the same redundant message in the initial position. Conversely, a highly diverse message which followed a message of low diversity produced stronger judgements of communicator competence and clarity than did the same diverse message in the initial position.

Another kind of outcome has been labelled 'optimal convergence' (Giles and Smith 1979). Given a message by an initial speaker, a second speaker can converge to the style or content of this message or she or he can diverge from it. In other words communicators can attempt to appear linguistically similar or they can accentuate linguistic differences. The question is how will persons react to a second speaker's convergence or divergence? Two studies suggest that partial convergence, as opposed to total convergence or divergence, produces the most favourable evaluations of a second speaker. Giles and Smith found that a speaker who converged to the content and speech rate of a second speaker but not to the second speaker's pronunciation was rated more favourably by listeners who rated his performance than was a speaker who converged on all three dimensions. Bradac, Hosman and Tardy (1978) discovered that the personality of a second speaker who converged to an initial speaker's low level of language intensity but diverged from the first speaker's low-intimacy self-disclosure was rated more favourably by respondents than was a speaker who converged to both low intensity and low intimacy.

Message topic

There is evidence that the *substance* of a communicator's discourse interacts with speech style in the production of attributions. Specifically, the communicator's *expressed attitude* toward the referents of his or her message and the *form* in which this attitude is encoded function together to produce hearer judgements of increased or decreased similarity. For example, when hearers initially agree with a speaker's expressed attitude (speaker and hearers are pro-Bristol), the use of high-intensity language will produce greater attitude reinforcement in hearers than will the use of low-intensity language ('I love the marvellous and radiant port city of Bristol!'). Conversely, in the case of hearer *dis*agreement, speakers' use of high intensity may cause a 'boomerang effect' or in other words drastically reduce their persuasiveness (cf. McEwen and Greenberg 1970; Mehrley and McCroskey 1970). These outcomes may be mediated by hearer judgements of speaker similarity. Bradac, Bowers and Courtright (1980) argue that '[l]anguage intensity and initial agreement with the proposition of the message interact in the production of receiver attributions in such a way that intensity in congruent messages enhances, but in discrepant messages inhibits, attributions of source similarity' (p. 202). This proposition is supported by Miller and Basehart's (1969) study which showed that an initially trusted source encoding a discrepant message in highly intense language reduced receivers' ratings of trustworthiness more than he did encoding this message in low-intensity language. And perceptions of reduced trustworthiness should correlate with perceptions of reduced similarity (Bourhis, Giles and Tajfel 1973; Wheeless 1978).

Other language variables seem likely to interact with message topic in the production of hearers' judgements. For example, a person speaking rapidly will probably be judged as relatively low in trustworthiness (Brown 1980) and perhaps high in enthusiasm. If in this case the rapid speech rate is linked to attitudinally discrepant content, hearers should attribute great dissimilarity to the speaker. Or, a communicator employing Mexican American accented English may be viewed as lower in status by Mexican American respondents when talking about school-related topics than when talking about topics related to family life (Ryan and Carranza 1975).

Communicator role

Social groups cast actors in different roles. Roles are essentially expectations about behaviours which are appropriate for particular kinds of persons. There is evidence that roles interact with speech styles in the production of hearers' judgements of speakers. In one study by Bradac, Courtright, Schmidt and Davies (1976), respondents were told initially that a speaker they were about to hear was either high or low in status. This perception of status differences was produced by telling half of the respondents that the speaker was a gifted graduate student whose parents were professors and the other half that the speaker was an academically deficient freshman whose parents were partially supported by welfare checks. Half of the respondents heard a highly diverse message and half heard a message which was low in diversity. Results showed that the high-status speaker was evaluated very favourably when he exhibited high diversity and very unfavourably when he exhibited low diversity. Evaluations of the low-status speaker were not affected by diversity level. High- and low-diversity messages produced equal ratings in the low-status condition, and in this case the ratings fell right between the very positive and very negative ratings given to the high-status speaker.

Speaker gender has also been related to speech style and attributions in interesting ways. Bradley (1981) had male and female confederates interact with other persons in small discussion groups. The confederates manipulated three communication variables during discussions: support for statements (evidence) versus no support; the use of tag questions versus no use of tag questions; and the use of disclaimers ('I'm no expert but . . .') versus no use of disclaimers. After discussions each group member rated all other members (including confederates) on a number of dimensions. Most interesting from our standpoint was the finding that females using disclaimers were judged less intelligent and less knowledgeable than were males using these forms; in fact, apparently it simply did not matter whether or not males used disclaimers – they tended to be judged as relatively intelligent and informed in any case. This rather dismaying finding suggests that women had better avoid 'powerless' forms if they choose to be perceived as credible. This implication is consistent with the results of a study by Erickson, Lind, Johnson and O'Barr (1978) who found that both male and female speakers achieved higher credibility ratings when they used powerful speech styles.

Situation type

This is the most global of the contextual variables, potentially incorporating all of those described above, and in many ways it is the most interesting. We are sure that interactants' construals of the nature of the interaction situation are crucially important to the uncertainty reduction process. But there is little research linking situational construals to the speech styles and attributions of interactants, because this is a very new area. Still, there are a few studies which provide room for speculation.

At the most general level, we suggest that there are some situations which persons are very certain about – that they can label these as being a such-and-such situation (a party, a cricket match, a fight, etc.) – and that there are other situations which are ambiguous for one reason or another. Scotton (1976) demonstrates that speakers may adopt 'strategies of neutrality' when situational uncertainty is high. For instance, where the ethnic background of our inter-locuter is unclear and where it is unclear for this reason how favourably he or she will view *our* ethnic background, we may adopt a linguistic strategy which will mask our ethnic identity, perhaps using a *lingua franca* instead of our native tongue.

More generally, where the definition of the situation is vague we may use linguistic strategies which attempt to prevent others from perceiving us as being committed to a particular situational definition (Scotton 1980). Probably the clearest strategy of this type is keeping one's mouth closed until one has gained sufficient information through observations of others' behaviours. This is cautious. But it is also not very creative. In some cases it might be much more useful for a speaker to gain control of the situation by being the first to define it linguistically. In this case speech can function as an independent variable which determines or influences the situation's shape and flow (cf. Giles, Hewstone and St Clair, in press).

All of this suggests some possible attributional consequences: (1) in an uncertain situation if we commit ourselves to a particular definition which is *incorrect* from the standpoint of the other person, we may be perceived as foolish, boorish, incompetent, etc.; (2) if we commit ourselves initially and cause the other to accept our definition, we may be perceived as dominant and aggressive; and (3) if we adopt a linguistic strategy of neutrality (Scotton 1976) the other will be relatively uncertain about us, at least when linguistic cues are especially salient, and we may appear intriguing, mysterious, enigmatic, and so forth.

But often situational definitions are perfectly clear to all parties. Everyone is certain about the sort of situation it is. What are some criteria which are used to distinguish such situations? In Chapter 2 we suggested that persons prefer situations which are relatively unstructured for gaining knowledge about others. This suggests a situational distinction which can be labelled 'con-strained/unconstrained' or 'formal/informal'. Joos (1967) argues that there are styles of speech which are appropriate in informal situations and other styles which are suited to formal events. There are many clear examples of this: use title and last name when meeting your professor for the first time; avoid lacing your Sunday sermons with obscenities; do not crack jokes at funerals, etc. Common sense suggests that a person will be judged an effective communicator if he or she exhibits casual speech in informal situations and 'frozen' speech (Joos 1967) in formal ones. Yet one study suggests this may not always be the case. Bradac, Konsky and Davies (1976) found that a speaker exhibiting a highly diverse vocabulary was perceived as more effective in an *in*formal situation than in a formal one.

A related distinction is 'non-intimate/intimate' or 'public/private'. Many cultures clearly distinguish activities which may be performed safely in the 'privacy of one's own home' from those which are permissible in a place like Kensington Gardens. This distinction affects speech as well as other sorts of behaviours. Richard Nixon attempted to prevent the private use of obscene language from spilling over into a public arena by deleting expletives from the Presidential Transcripts (Nixon and the Staff of the *Washington Post* 1974). Jimmy Carter caused a strongly negative reaction by publicly disclosing that he had 'committed adultery in his heart many times' (*Playboy* 1976). Apparently some persons felt that this private feeling should not have been revealed in a public situation (cf. Bradac, Hosman and Tardy 1978).

Forgas (1976) found the distinction between intimate and non-intimate situations to be subjectively important, i.e. salient, to British housewives and female college students. These persons also discriminated between situations in which they know how to behave and those in which they do not. This could be described as a 'familiar/unfamiliar' dimension. Other situational dimensions which have been shown to be important to various groups are: 'evaluative/non-evaluative', 'interpersonal orientation/task orientation' and 'anxiety producing/anxiety reducing' (Forgas 1978a). It will be useful for future researchers to investigate antecedents and consequences of speech in terms of these subjectively important situational dimensions. We should hypothesize, for example, that where the situation is highly evaluative and where the orientation is decidedly interpersonal, communicators will use flattery, they will be polite, and they will discuss non-intimate topics.

Effectiveness and expectations

When persons characterize a communicator's performance by saying, 'He put his foot in his mouth', or, 'She made a telling comment', they are making a judgement of *effectiveness* of an utterance in a particular context. When they say, 'Her remark caught me completely off guard', or, 'He talked right from the book', they are judging the extent to which an utterance was *expected*. These are two basic kinds of reactions to contextualized speech. Virtually all of the particular judgemental outcomes described in the preceding sections can be assimilated to one or both of these concepts.

It seems to us that effectiveness and expectancy judgements are independent or 'orthogonal'. For instance, if Mary is always polite and the situation demands tact, her expected performance will be an effective one. In the same situation, John who is always rude will perform ineffectively, as expected. Similarly some unexpected performances are effective while others are not. In films when the milksop finally stands up to his aggressive boss and manages to shout him down, the audience always applauds. When the brilliant actor forgets his lines repeatedly, the audience boos.

The case of the military general who orders his subordinates to pass him salt at the dinner table ('Salt!') is interesting to think about in terms of expectancy and effectiveness. An observer of this event might judge the general's performance as effective (he got the salt) and expected (generals are always giving orders), but still the observer may have a negative reaction to the general. This suggests that in some cases persons will distinguish between the *instrumental* success or failure of utterances and the *character* of the utterer – 'He gets what he wants but he's a *#!**!.*' In a sense the effectiveness construct may bifurcate. We can sometimes talk of effectiveness of actions and effectiveness of character. This sort of distinction appears frequently in the literature of communication research in various guises: 'logos/ethos' (Aristotle 1932), 'expertness/trustworthiness' (Hovland, Janis and Kelley 1953), 'competence/benevolence' (Brown 1980), 'status stressing/solidarity stressing' (Ryan 1979; cf. Hosman 1978).

The concept of expectation can be discussed somewhat more formally. As we suggested in our discussion of 'pragmatic normalcy' above, in many situations there are rules for utterances (Searle 1969). These assume two basic forms: 'In context X, Y counts as a Z', and 'Do/do not do Y'. In everyday language we can say, 'In a theatre, the utterance "Fire!" counts as a warning', and 'Do say "Fire!" when you see flames and smell smoke'; 'Do not say "Fire!" just for the fun of it.' Or 'For a firing squad, "Fire!" counts as a command.' 'Do not say "Fire!" if the squad is in disarray.' etc. These 'counts as' and 'do/do not' rules have been labelled 'constitutive' and 'regulative', respectively (Searle 1969; Sanders and Martin 1975).

In many situations, say a casual conversation at a party, we expect communicators to know and obey many rules simultaneously: string words together in such a way that they are recognized as English sentences (unless you are in Paris); relate one sentence to another to form coherent patterns; 'You are a foolish nitwit' counts as an insult in this context if seriously intended; do not insult people; talk; smile; do not depart five minutes after arriving, etc.

When we discuss rules or socially mandated expectations, we must be careful not to impute to them total authority over interaction. We are not 'sociolinguistic automatons' who slavishly and mechanistically follow every rule in the book (Giles 1977). There is room for idiosyncracy. Sometimes we invent our own rules. Sometimes we negotiate rules with other interactants (Pearce 1976). Some rules have more force than others – there are *rules!* and 'variable rules' (Kay and McDaniel 1979; Labov 1969a). Some rules are never followed. And so on.

The concept of expected or unexpected language performance can be related directly to matters covered in Chapter 2. We would suggest that where a speaker's language performance is expected or rule-following, hearers will react to him or her mindlessly (Langer 1978). When a speaker's verbal response to us is low in distinctiveness and when the form of this response is highly consensual (everybody would respond in this way), we will not notice the response (Kelley 1967). We will not use it for attributional purposes. It takes only a moment's worth of introspection to realize that *often* we do not consciously attend to speech characteristics. English teachers, linguists and phoneticians may be highly aware of the details of language performance, but most of us are not most of the time. Carroll, Bever and Pollack (1981, p. 170) make a similar point:

> Speaker/hearers are subjectively preoccupied; they are not ordinarily aware of unacceptabilities, presuppositions and ambiguities in their own utterances, or in the speech of others. In order to have intuitions about acceptability, linguists must almost cease to be behaving speakers/hearers. They must pause and reflect; in the terms of Duval and Wicklund 1972, linguists objectify the sentence from all the specific potential functional contexts of its utterance.

Of course even linguists may respond like normal humans in some contexts; we must not forget this. Also, many stimuli which we are completely unaware of can influence our behaviour in important ways, and this is almost certainly true of linguistic stimuli as well as of their non-linguistic counterparts, e.g. the molecules which stimulate olefactory receptors.

On the other hand, the 'naive scientist' will be energized by rule violating or unexpected speech. When we meet for the first time a person who has a non-local accent, who is highly intense, highly obscene and frequently insulting, we will probably attend closely to her communicative behaviour, especially if we are high self-monitors anticipating future interaction with her. This tendency should increase if we discover she is our new boss. We will search for clues regarding the extent to which her speech is situationally coerced on the one hand or a product of a basically abusive personality on the other. In such a case there may be an attributional bias toward discovering a situational cause for this behaviour. (Of course this bias may be reduced if we realize that we are a prominent part of the situation.)

There is some research evidence that unexpected language performance is used by respondents to make situational or dispositional inferences and judgements of degree of uncertainty about the performer. Bradac, Courtright, Schmidt and Davies (1976) interpreted their finding that persons did not discriminate between high and low diversity in the case of a low-status speaker as indicating that they saw his performance in both cases as externally controlled, not as a sign of ability or capacity. Conversely, Bradac, Hemphill and Tardy (1981) found that when one speaker used powerless language and a second speaker used powerful forms, the powerful speaker was judged as having a highly 'internal' personality, i.e., a strong tendency to perceive himself as controlling his environment and destiny (cf. Rotter 1966). Unexpectedly intense language also produces judgements of high internality (Bradac, Hosman and Tardy 1978). Finally, Bradac, Schneider, Hemphill and Tardy (1980) found that a male who used very low-intensity language in an initial, friendly heterosexual encounter was judged as less predictable than his counterpart who used high-intensity language. Presumably, respondents view a highly intense male as more predictable in this situation; they are more certain about his motives. Results of a study by Burgoon, Jones and Stewart (1975) also suggest that male communicators are expected to be relatively intense.

Generally, we suggest that if John's speech is consistent across situations, if it is not distinctively related to a specific hearer, and if others do not talk the way John does, the judgement will be made that 'John talks this way'. If John is consistent, if his speech is distinctively related to a specific hearer, and if others talk the way John does to this hearer, the judgement will be made that the hearer is responsible for John's style of speech. If John is inconsistent, if his speech is distinctive, and if others do not talk like John, the judgement will be made that 'John talks this way in this situation'. Observers appear to have a general bias toward the first sort of attribution when they respond to a single sample of behaviour – they are apparently likely to infer situational consistency. This has been labelled the 'fundamental attribution error' (Nisbett and Ross 1980). This sort of error can have very unfortunate consequences in observers' judgements of speakers. A case in point is Labov's (1969c) description of black children who have been labelled linguistically or mentally deficient on the basis of their verbal performance in uniquely inhibiting situations. This observation leads us to the last issue to be broached in this chapter.

The validity of linguistically based impressions

When we judge John to be an extrovert on the basis of his rapid speech rate and loudness or, conversely, when we judge him to be enthusiastic about his particular interlocutor, Mary, how much confidence can we have in our judgements? This is a very important and a very complex question which we can only touch upon in this section. In fact this question is essentially the same as 'What is truth?', so there are clearly some difficulties here.

Nevertheless, it may be useful to distinguish between 'sophisticated' and 'naive' forms of knowledge at this point. Language scientists invent special constructs, logics and instruments to explore the phenomena which interest them. For example, phonologists use sound spectrographs and frequency statistics in attempting to explain human articulatory processes. The knowledge claims of phonologists and other scientists are scrutinized and, according to one philosophical position (Popper 1963), attacked mercilessly. Peculiar standards admit relatively few data to the status of 'evidence'. The distinctions which 'sophisticates' make when describing language are likely to be special ones derived from an explicit theory. Particular observations and even observational instruments are suggested by such a theory. 'Naive' linguistic knowledge, contrarily, is a body of claims which emerges from untutored observations of speech (Bradac, Martin, Elliott and Tardy 1980). The constructs of this knowledge are rendered in an everyday vocabulary and the logics used to connect constructs are 'practical' ones, such as the *enthymeme* or truncated syllogism (Aristotle 1932). Theories are usually implicit and observations unaided, typically involving nothing more than naked eyes and ears.

Although 'naive' and 'sophisticated' knowledge represent separate forms of mentation, they do have intercourse. The various current versions of attribution theory which we have referred to throughout this book have as their *exclusive* subject naive thinking. In this case the 'sophisticated' model *necessarily* employs distinctions contained in the 'naive' model (internal versus external causality etc.). An assumption of attribution theory and other cognitive theories is that persons' beliefs are often powerful predictors of their actions. A valid predictive theory of behaviour will *have* to incorporate naive beliefs if this assumption is true. And indeed there is reason to believe that 'thinking makes it so' (cf. Rosenthal and Jacobson 1968). Thus, if Mary believes John to be interested in her because he is talking rapidly and loudly in her presence, John may *become* interested, if he is not now, as a result of Mary's behaviour toward him which reflects her belief. 'Sophisticated' knowledge feeds into 'naive' knowledge as well (cf. Robinson 1979). Versions of the Skinnerian reinforcement model are now incorporated in parents' explanations of their child's language development (alas). A speech writer who worked for Richard Nixon employed the construct 'cognitive dissonance' when explaining reactions to an event which transpired during the Nixon administration (Safire 1975; Festinger 1957). The implication of this mixing of models is that many constructs will be common to 'naive' and 'sophisticated' discussions of language and social behaviour.

Perhaps the major difference between the two forms of knowledge is in the procedures used to test hypotheses. 'Sophisticates' use random sampling of respondents, random assignment to conditions, and special devices and instruments. At the other extreme, the 'naive scientist' may rely upon simple hearsay. 'Naive' scientists may trust stereotypes, whereas their 'sophisticated' counterparts trust only statistical generalizations. Also, the modes of expressing 'naive' and 'sophisticated' social knowledge will often differ. At one extreme we have the fully developed axiomatic theory of interpersonal communication (Berger and Calabrese 1975); at the other extreme we have the simple maxim: 'You can catch more flies with honey than with vinegar.'

Regardless of whether a generalization about speech and personality or about speech and social group membership is statistical or stereotypical, derived from a theory or embodied in a maxim, there is a *danger* in applying it to a particular speaker. The danger is that the generalization will be *wrong* in the particular case. Nevertheless we will all probably continue to apply generalizations to particular speakers and this will have consequences for our behaviour and for theirs. At least we should periodically 'catch ourselves' and willfully attempt to *refute* the generalization in the best Popperian manner (Popper 1963). This would be very rational of us.

More usefully, there are some generalizations which have greater force than others. The application of these to particular cases is less hazardous, although the risk never approaches zero. In the terminology of Giles, Scherer and Taylor (1979), there are strong and weak 'speech markers'. That is, there are some linguistic and paralinguistic features which are highly reliable indicators of traits and states, and there are others which are highly unreliable indicators. For example, there is evidence of a clear correspondence between biological gender and pitch level, probably as a result of both social learning and physiology (Smith 1979). If one's purpose is to detect gender accurately, then pitch is one reasonably valid measure. But it will not be 100 per cent valid. Some transvestites skillfully employ both high and low pitch levels. Less exotically, the statistical distributions of pitch levels in male and female populations overlap considerably at the high and low ends of the distributions, respectively.

Generally, those features of performed language which are less controllable by the speaker are likely to be more valid indicators than are those which are more controllable (Laver and Trudgill 1979). This will be the case especially when the traits or states which are indicated are also less controllable. Phonological aspects of language are probably less controllable than syntactic or semantic ones because of their connection with motor performance. States related to arousal, e.g. anger or fear, are probably relatively difficult to control, as are traits such as ethnic group membership. Thus, rapid repetition of initial syllables of a word (stuttering) when coupled with shaking hands and dilated pupils may be taken as a *relatively* reliable indicator of genuine nervousness. This complex of features should be rather difficult to fake convincingly. Conversely, highly controllable linguistic features which indicate controllable traits or states are more likely to be invalid, less likely to reflect a speaker's actual condition. Thus, true direction (as opposed to intensity) of affect may be easily masked with lexical choices, as in: 'I really like you, Boss'.

Summary

In the beginning of this chapter we discussed some technical distinctions which are useful in conceptualizing language and social phenomena. It was suggested that language is an analogical and a digital system which yields information to 'naive scientists' as they attempt to reduce uncertainty in initial encounters. We suggested also that language reveals 'facts' about speakers' psychological states and traits and about their group affiliations. These 'facts' produce judgements of increased or decreased similarity and feelings of increased or decreased certainty depending upon the availability of stereotypes and scripts. We inventoried several language variables which have been shown to produce hearer attributions regarding various states and traits; these were: familiarity and goodness; immediacy and intensity; elaboration, restriction, and fluency; 'good' and 'bad' grammar; powerful and powerless speech; talk, silence, and interruption; pitch and intonation; phonetic variation; volume and rate; and pragmatic deviation and normalcy. It was suggested that contextual features such as prior messages, message topic, communicator roles, and situational definitions will crucially affect the ways in which hearers react to language variation. We argued that effectiveness and expectancy judgements are basic to contextualized speech. Our consideration of expectancy judgements led to a discussion of awareness of speech and 'mindlessness'. Finally, we discussed the thorny issue of the validity of impressions based upon speech variation.

As we indicated earlier, language does not only 'give off' information. Interactants use language to refer to themselves and to their relationships. And they use language to get other people to do things. Language is used to 'woo' others, to seduce them, to impress them and to help them. It seems fair to say that language is the primary instrument of interpersonal progress. We turn to these interesting matters and to others in the next chapters.

4

Language and social interaction

But when I tell him he hates flatterers, he says he does, being then most flattered.

Shakespeàre

Who would succeed in the world should be wise in the use of . . . pronouns. Utter the You twenty times, where you once utter the I.

John Hay

Some relationships between language and passive/active knowledge gaining strategies were examined in the previous chapter. In this chapter we focus upon *interactive* strategies, examining in some detail the role which language plays in interrogation and self-disclosure. We will initially discuss at some length particular problems associated with the concept of 'self'. We will do this because this concept is *crucial* to the interactive strategies. Quite simply, both interrogation and self-disclosure cannot be understood clearly unless we are clear about their exclusive source of sustenance – the self. In a world without selves, interrogation and disclosure would not exist. We will then discuss specifics of these interactive strategies, examining their nature, antecedents, and consequences, going well beyond the preliminary comments we offered in Chapter Two.

The problematic self

When we are interrogated by another person, we can choose to reveal or conceal our 'true self'. We can lie or we can distort somewhat or we can be utterly candid. Similarly, when another person discloses personal information to us we can reciprocate, disclosing personal information which more or less accurately represents our feelings, opinions, etc. That is, reciprocal self-disclosures may be honest or dishonest (cf. Chapter 2). Both of these interactive strategies of knowledge acquisition entail the conscious revelation of self. Of course, in some circumstances some persons 'blurt out' things about self with a low degree of intentionality as in the case of the woman who recently wrote to Ann Landers (1979):

Dear Ann: This morning I am asking myself why did I talk the ear off a man I know only slightly? I went on and on about my children, their lives, etc. That poor guy must have been bored to death and glad when the dinner ended. . . . If . . . I'm asked a question, off I go, telling more than I should, certainly more than anyone wants to hear.

Usually, however, persons consciously control what they reveal to others, especially in initial encounters.

The construct of 'self' and the parallel construct of 'self-awareness' are interestingly problematic. There are several issues to consider when we attempt to conceptualize self-disclosing communication. It seems to us that until recently communication researchers have been rather unanalytic about the self and its various entailments. The research on self-disclosure has often reflected (and sometimes continues to reflect) this 'quick-and-dirty', unanalytic conceptualization. For example, the extremely important early research of Jourard and Lasakow (1958) viewed the self as a grab-bag collection of attitudes, tastes and interests, and feelings about work, money, personality, and body. Some items from the Jourard–Lasakow Self-Disclosure Questionnaire are: 'My views on communism'; 'The style of house and the kinds of furnishings I like best'; 'What I feel are my special strong points and qualifications for my work'; and 'My past record of illness and treatment' (p. 92). Respondents are supposed to indicate the extent to which they have talked about these items (and others) to various disclosure targets. There is nothing clearly incorrect about the items or the conceptualization of self which they reflect, but some of the items may have no *salience* for particular respondents – they may not be a part of these respondents phenomenal selves. Also, there is no suggestion about how these components of self are interrelated. Further, the assumption is made that respondents can validly report on the extent to which they have talked about these topics to specific targets, that respondents were aware of their communicative behaviours when they performed them and can remember them accurately. This assumption is questionable (cf. Chapter 2). Finally, it may be the case that the topics suggested by the Jourard–Lasakow Questionnaire are not the ones people talk about in most interpersonal exchanges (cf. Emler & Fisher 1981).

Flexible selves

To begin with, it may be incorrect even to attempt designing an instrument which purports to measure *the* self, as the Jourard–Lasakow instrument does. Some theorists and researchers argue that normal persons have flexible selves which vary with situations. In other words, across situations there may be sharp discontinuities in a person's feelings and behaviours (James 1892; Magnussen and Endler 1977; Mischel 1973). The notion of invariant personality traits may be more of a social fiction than an objective reality (Nisbett 1980). For example, Hewes and Haight (1979) tested the hypothesis that various communicative behaviours of individuals would be consistent across several communication situations and that these behaviours would correlate with self-reports of predispositions toward verbal behaviour and reticence. Thus, if persons who report low reticence also report tendencies to verbalize highly and if these persons in fact talk a lot in several dissimilar situations, we could take this as evidence of a highly verbal personality. Contrarily, if there is little correlation among self-report measures and actual verbal behaviours in the several situations, this would not support the notion of a single, enduring personality characteristic. Rather, this negative evidence would be consistent with the notion of multiple selves. In fact, Hewes and Haight found only three statistically significant relationships among fifteen possible correlations. Given the reliability of their individual measures, they interpreted their results as providing little support for the hypothesis of cross-situational consistency of communicative behaviours and, more generally, as providing little support for the notion of stable personalities.

This 'flexible self' theory is not without its critics (Bowers 1973), but if it is even partially true it suggests a problem for the would-be self-discloser: 'If my behaviours vary across situations and if this variation does not even correspond highly to my self-perceptions, what do I truly report to my interrogator?' Or, 'Which self should I tell her about?' Especially interesting and problematic is the apparent fact that this problem of accuracy becomes more difficult as we move away from superficial readily available information about persons to the more subtle and important information about feelings, tendencies, inter-personal habits, etc. In other words, the problem intensifies as we move through cultural and sociological knowledge to knowledge of a psychological sort (Miller and Steinberg 1975). To illustrate, typically there is really no problem accurately reporting our place of birth. This is a fact about self which does not vary at all, except in cases of brainwashing or pathological delusion. But there may be a severe problem in accurately describing our behaviours performed in the presence of the opposite sex. In this case we may have to invoke the flexible self notion: 'With shy and retiring types I come on strong, but in the presence of tigresses (or tigers) I become a pussycat.'

The stratified self

The last example suggests that in addition to flexibility we can talk of stratification. That is, some aspects of our self or selves are 'on the surface', whereas others are at 'the very core'. In other words, we can say that some personal facts are readily available to almost everyone whereas others are unknown to all but one or two of our most intimate friends. Some facts are unknown to *all* other persons. Some facts are probably unknown to all others and to oneself as well – a mysterious realm to be sure, but one which does not enter directly into revelations about self (Luft 1969). Altman and Taylor (1973) offer an 'onion' model which captures the idea of the layered self. Social penetration is the process of mutually discovering information at deeper and deeper layers.

To some extent within a given culture there will be similarity among persons with regard to what is at the surface of self and what is at the lower layers. In many western countries, for example, sexual fantasies are typically revealed only to one or two intimates, whereas other matters, favourite foods or occupation, are revealed to multitudes. There is a degree of cultural consensus on what is intimate or sensitive and what is not (Norton, Feldman and Tafoya 1974). But there is idiosyncracy as well. A possible case in point involved one of the authors who was riding on a bus from Iowa City, Iowa, to Chicago. A young woman sitting next to him with a child in her arms at one point began describing in graphic detail the sexual problems which she felt were ruining her marriage – this despite the fact that she and the author were total strangers. This may be a case of the strangers-passing-in-the-night phenomenon, where very personal revelations are made with impunity because it is virtually certain that the strangers will never meet again. Or it may be that for this woman sexual problems were very much on the surface and other problems were at the core.

In some sense the core of self is that information which is most personal. Here 'personal' refers both to intimacy and to uniqueness, constructs which are potentially independent in that a characteristic of self can be very unique but also non-intimate. Like intimacy, the uniqueness dimension is an interesting and important one. What uniquely distinguishes one person from another? There is, of course, no single answer to this, but certainly one's 'personal construct system' (Kelly 1955; Duck 1973) is an important distinguishing feature. One can think of a personal construct as a kind of template which one imposes upon the world when construing events. Thus, for some persons the dimension of intelligence is all-important when evaluating communicators, whereas for others trustworthiness overrides everything else (Bradac, Sandell and Wenner 1979; Delia 1976). Or there are probably persons for whom the qualities of the communicator's facial appearance, height, hair colour, or body shape are especially salient. When all of the constructs a person uses to apprehend the world are taken into account, we have a highly individuated entity. There is evidence that the degree of overlap between two persons' personal construct systems is a significant predictor of long-term friendships (Duck 1973). Complete overlap or construct identity takes us into the realm of science fiction where one mind *is* the other one, etc. But, more realistically, a recent case of twin sisters, which captured the attention of the media, may be an instance of a high degree of construct similarity:

> Unkind people in York, England, call them 'the mental twins', British slang for crazy. Greta and Freda Chaplin, 37, are identical twins who dress alike, walk in step, take two-hour baths together and frequently talk – and sometimes swear – in unison. . . . The Chaplins wear identical gray coats, but one originally came with green buttons and the other with gray. So they cut two buttons off each, and now both coats have two green and two gray. . . .
>
> The Chaplins eat in unison, slowly raising forks and spoons almost simultaneously and finishing up one item on the plate before starting on the next. When they argue they sometimes swat each other lightly with identical handbags, then sit down and sulk together. When they talk in unison, the words of one come a split-second late, creating an effect like that of stereo speakers slightly out of synch. . . .
>
> Says psychologist David Lykken: 'Here are two extraordinarily similar persons who are responding to identical stimuli in identical ways. You don't have to invoke anything spooky. Their mental reactions are just similar.'
> (*Time*, 1981, p. 45).

The two major aspects of self discussed thus far, namely, flexibility and stratification, are summarized in the model on page 80. The self is represented as two intersecting cylinders each of which is composed of layers (Version 1). Each cylinder represents a situated self. There are potentially many of these, depending upon the number of situations which are distinguished by a particular person. As the layers of each cylinder become darker, they encompass increasingly personal matters. The cylinders intersect at one point, and this represents the most stable and enduring aspect of self – that which transcends the situation. The intersection of the 'cores' is the darkest point which is the closest thing imaginable to the 'true self'. Version 2 – the fat version – depicts a self which is comparatively stable across situations; this is represented by a high

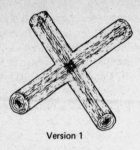

Version 1

Version 2

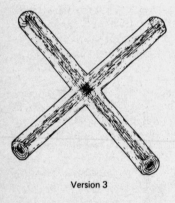

Version 3

Figure 4.1

degree of intersection. Version 3 – the skinny version – shows a self which is relatively compartmentalized, highly variable from situation to situation.

Awareness

A final issue involves the extent to which we are aware of self. Clearly this is related to matters discussed in Chapter 2. It would appear that we cannot self-disclose when we are in a state of mindlessness and subjective self-awareness (Langer 1978; Duval and Wicklund 1972). It is only when we are mindfully attending to ourselves as objects that we can consciously describe our traits and states. But talking about simple awareness is not enough. The picture is more complex than this. First of all, awareness of self has an evaluative aspect. We are more or less aware of parts of ourselves which we like or dislike to varying extents. Next, especially interesting and difficult from a research standpoint is the notion of 'meta awareness' or awareness of awareness. The possibilities here are dizzying: We can be aware of our awareness of self; we can be aware of another person's awareness of our self; we can be aware of another person's unawareness of our self; we can be aware of our awareness of another person's unawareness of our awareness of our self; and so forth. Each of these awareness states, and many others not listed, are highly usual and each has consequences for our communicative behaviour (Bowers and Bradac, forthcoming; Laing, Phillipson and Lee 1966). To illustrate, if we are aware of another person's awareness of our awareness of self, as when we see someone watching us watching ourselves in a mirror, we may feel we have to account for or justify our self-awareness. In the case of the mirror we might quickly produce signs that we are inspecting our suit for dust or wrinkles or, if we are close to the mirror, that we are inspecting our eye for a speck of dust. These are problems which justify a degree of self-awareness.

When we talk of John's flexible, stratified self which may be aware of the awareness of Mary's flexible, stratified self's awareness of John's flexible, stratified self's awareness of John's flexible, stratified self, we have jumped to a universe rather different from that of Jourard and Lasakow (1958). This complexity embodies the research wave of the future, and it may well turn out to be a *tidal* wave which will capsize many unwary research teams before breaking on the beach of our knowledge of self.

Modes of interrogation

Now, in a situation, say a party, John has a self which Mary wishes to discover. John has other non-party selves which Mary may or may not wish to discover also. As suggested in Chapter 2, Mary can interrogate John for this purpose. Interrogation is a legitimate social penetration strategy. But there are constraints on this instrumental use of language which we will now discuss.

The social context of interrogation

Within social groups and across social groups within cultures, there are expectations about how persons will ask other persons questions about themselves. We might say that these expectations are manifested in various scripts for interrogation. (Of course an individual's interrogatory scripts may be highly idiosyncratic and highly likely to violate others' expectations). A few common scripts come to mind readily.[1] These are scripts for two persons who are newly acquainted:

1. *John*: How are you?
   Mary: Fine, how are you?
2. *John*: Are you a relative of Bill's?
   Mary: Yes, he's my cousin.
   John: I thought there was a resemblance.

[1]In this chapter and in the next one, we will offer examples of various communication episodes. For the sake of focus, these will reflect an evolving heterosexual relationship. But the reader should realize that our discussion pertains to virtually any kind of interpersonal relationship involving human adults. This is not to say that the details of *type* of relationship will not affect the particular manifestations of the processes we describe.

3. *John*: Are you enjoying the party?
   Mary: Yes, I'm especially fond of the gin punch.
   John: It is good, isn't it.
4. *John*: Are you a movie star?
   Mary: Yes.
   John: Really?

The fourth example is offered flippantly, because in the USA, at least, this form of interrogation is known to be an 'opening line', an obvious ploy designed to flatter the other and thus elicit self-revelation. The first example is the minimal interrogative strategy imaginable; it is the baseline from which the others depart. In fact, in many cases the intent of the interrogator here is not to produce self-revelation but rather merely to signal acknowledgement of the other. There is an old and never funny joke which persons make by replying to 'How are you?' with 'I have bursitis; my nose is itching; I worry about my future; and my uncle is wearing a dress these days.' This illustrates that we expect very little real self-revelation when we ask someone how they are. The second and third examples strike us as very usual interrogative forms.

The following examples seem deviant to us:

5. *John*: Do you thoroughly enjoy sex?
   Mary: What?!
   John: Sex. S.E.X. Do you enjoy it utterly or only so-so.
   Mary: Help.
6. *John*: Do you like me a lot?
   Mary: What?
   John: Are you really attracted to the way my face looks?
   Mary: I think you are very strange.

Comparing the normal and deviant examples, it appears that interrogative strategies which are impersonal, i.e. non-intimate and de-individuated, are more acceptable initially than are highly personal strategies. Also the acceptable forms forcus upon matters external to the dyad (a role relationship and the party in examples 2 and 3, respectively), whereas the unacceptable forms focus upon one or another of the partners (Mary and John in examples 5 and 6, respectively). Thus, it appears that impersonal, externally focused strategies are likely to facilitate self-revelation when the interactants are newly acquainted and that highly personal internally focused strategies are likely to inhibit self-revelation. Most of us do not like to be stared at verbally by new acquaintances (cf. Cline and Johnson 1976), But we must *insist* that there are some persons who want to be asked *immediately* about their innermost desires. Also, there are some situations where new acquaintances are relatively free to become personal very quickly. A lot depends on the context, as usual. But this impersonal–external/personal–internal distinction strikes us as potentially useful in thinking about interrogative strategies.

Of course, once a relationship has been formed virtually anything is askable. However, in enduring relationships there may be a few topics which are forbidden and therefore there may be particular inquiries which cannot be made. For instance, if one partner is dying of a rare disease, if he or she is extremely frightened by this, and if both partners are aware of these facts, the healthy partner will typically not be free to interrogate the terminally ill partner about the details of her or his disease. Or, less grimly, if one partner is concerned about ageing, the other partner may not be free to ask: 'How does it feel to be getting up there?' Apart from these forbidden areas, as relationships endure and grow, the interrogative process becomes much more open and flexible, a key point of Altman and Taylor's social penetration theory (1973). With relational advancement, we move away from culturally mandated interrogative forms to dyad-specific forms which which are negotiated by the relational partners (Pearce 1976).

Rules and strategies for interrogation

In the preceding chapter we introduced the constructs of rules and speech acts, and these can be usefully invoked in this discussion of interrogation. A simple constitutive rule for the interrogative strategy is: You (verb) X? X refers to a state or trait of the person being interrogated. Here word order is optional, although the 'X' will typically be the last item uttered with rising intonation. 'You' and the verb can be deleted in some cases, i.e., 'X' can sometimes stand alone. This rule generates structures like: 'You are a monk?'; 'Are you a monk?'; 'Are you tired?'; 'Tired?' 'You drink martinis?'. These are all requests for information, a particular kind of illocutionary speech act (Searle 1969). It seems to us that in initial encounters there is a regulative rule which says: interrogate others by requesting information. Orders, another type of illocutionary speech act, are forbidden if seriously intended: 'I order you to reveal your feelings!' (In non-interpersonal contexts interrogative orders may be permissable). The interrogate-others-by-requesting-information regulative rule is not sufficient, however. We probably should add the notions of appropriateness and politeness: 'Interrogate others by requesting information in a polite style'; 'Do not repeatedly seek a particular item of information from a reluctant revealer'. This suggests a general model which describes the interrogative process as well as processes involving other strategies (cf. Schneider 1979). The model indicates that an intention exists initially and an attempt is made to fulfill this by deciding upon a strategy, choosing a particular speech act to implement the strategy and choosing particular language forms to express the strategy. The interrogator's speech produces a receiver response which feeds back to the interrogator and potentially affects his or her future strategic choices, choices of speech acts, and stylistic choices. Probably rarely the interrogator's intentions may even be affected as when a request for information

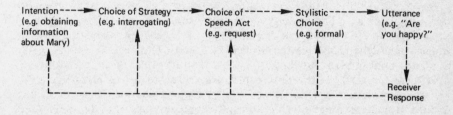

Figure 4.2

produces an unexpectedly negative response: 'I will never again *try* to get information about a person in this sort of situation.' The model implies conscious choices, but we all learn interrogative routines which often allow us to proceed mindlessly. (See Schneider 1979, for a greatly expanded discussion of intentions, strategies, and messages.)

The consequences of encoding speech acts, e.g., requests, in one style as opposed to another have been little researched, although a few studies have recently appeared. Cantor (1979) examined the effects of four forms of request upon contributions to door-to-door collectors representing the American Cancer Society. She found that for female collectors polite imperatives ('Please contribute to our fund') were more effective than agreement questions ('Won't you contribute to our fund?'), information questions ('Would you like to contribute to our fund?'), and statements ('We are asking you to contribute to our fund'); information questions were the least effective form. In an identical context, Cialdini and Schroeder (1976) found that the phrase 'even a penny will help' when added to the request, 'Would you be willing to help by giving a donation?', increased contributions. Presumably this phrase legitimized small favours.

No research of which we are aware has examined language choices in the context of requesting information about another person. But there is no reason to believe that this kind of request is essentially different from the type examined by Cantor (1979) and Cialdini and Schroeder (1976). If this is correct, the inter-personal interrogator would be advised to render his or her interpersonal request in the following way: 'Please tell me something about yourself – even something innocuous would help.'

Often perlocutionary speech acts are used to obtain information from other persons. Perlocutions demand a response from one's hearer for successful performance in a way that illocutions do not. Perlocutions are speech acts which are *necessarily* bound to the response of others. For example, if one says, 'I order you to march in step', this is a correctly performed order regardless of how the order's recipient behaves. An illocutionary speech act can be correct but also ineffective. Contrarily, one *cannot* say, 'I impress you with my majestic appearance', with the intention of impressing the hearer and necessarily success-fully *fulfill* the intention simply by completing the utterance. The success of this perlocutionary act is completely dependent upon the hearer. An impressive speech act is one which impresses the hearer; there is no rule for successful impressing. Some common perlocutionary speech acts are: threatening, persuading, intimidating, impressing, cajoling, and teasing.

In the context of interrogation, it appears that persuading is a commonly used perlocutionary act. The underlying form of such an act is: 'Tell me about yourself and I will reward you.' Compliance, in this case giving information, is induced through the offer, often implicit, of a contingent reward. In fact, rarely are contingent rewards (or threats for that matter) *explicitly* stated (Murdock 1978). The recipient of the inducement must feel free to give information about self or not to give it (Bowers 1974). Other compliance-gaining forms commonly used in the interpersonal interrogative context are impressing and flattering. In a multidimensional scaling analysis of how people get their way, Falbo (1977) obtained a simple two-dimensional representation for subjects' responses, and she labelled the poles of the dimensions 'direct/indirect' and 'rational/

emotional'. A speaker using a direct/rational appeal would employ references to his or her superior knowledge or skill, whereas a speaker using an indirect/emotional appeal would employ attempts to alter the feelings of the target. These correspond to impressing and flattering, respectively, or, in the terminology of Bradac, Schneider, Hemphill and Tardy (1980), to 'expert' and 'ingratiating' forms of inducement. Bradac and associates found that an ingra-tiating approach was judged by respondents as more likely to induce compliance than an expert approach in a heterosexual interpersonal context. This was true for both male and female would-be compliance gainers. Also, female subjects judged a male communicator as especially *in*competent when he clothed his expertise in highly intense language. We should note that an extremely high level of flattery might inhibit compliance gaining in initial encounters, especially if the would-be compliance gainer is of a lower status than is his or her target (Berger, *et al.* 1976; Jones 1964).

In addition to persuading, flattering and impressing, there are probably many other perlocutionary speech acts which persons use in their attempts to gain information about others for the purpose of reducing uncertainty and anti-cipating rewards and costs. For example, Sillars (1980b) found that in an inter-personal situation 'positive altercasting' and 'positive esteem' were appeals which respondents thought they would use to gain compliance. These are both 'impersonal commitment strategies with positive connotations' (p. 267). That is, persons who comply for these reasons see themselves as living up to an abstract ideal. The general form of positive altercasting strategies is: 'A person with positive attributes would comply'. Positive esteem strategies have as their underlying form: 'People who are important to you will think well of you if you comply.'

In our interrogative situation, examples would be: 'A friendly person would tell me something about himself' (positive altercasting) and 'Normal people tend to think highly of others who tell them something about themselves' (positive esteem).

Modes of self-disclosure

When interrogated about self, what does Mary say? What does John reveal about himself to elicit self-disclosure from Mary? In this section we examine the ways in which people disclose personal information and we discuss some con-sequences of these personal revelations. But first we need to think a bit more carefully about what disclosure entails.

Conceptualizing self-disclosure

Some theorists argue that self-disclosure is best conceptualized as the voluntary and intentional revelation of personal information which cannot be obtained from other sources (Pearce and Sharp 1973). This seems reasonable to us. It dis-tinguishes this mode of revelation from information gained through coercive means (drugs, torture, etc.) and from information leaked or revealed uninten-tionally. From the standpoint of the receiver of personal information, there should be a great difference between a personal revelation given freely by a communicator *to* the receiver and a revelation overheard *by* the receiver.

Imagine yourself in these two types of situations. In the first case, you will feel individualized, unless the communicator reveals personal information to everyone, in which case you will probably judge the communicator to be a highly disclosive personality (Kelley 1967). You may also feel trusted (Wheeless and Grotz 1977), and the feeling of being singled out for your trustworthiness may be rewarding. However, less positively, you may also question the revealer's motives – you may wonder whether he or she is attempting to manipulate you with a possibly false self-report. On the other hand, you will not feel rewarded by the overheard disclosure but you will not feel manipulated either because the discloser is involuntarily implicating you in the disclosive act.

Self-disclosure rules

We cannot think of a simple syntactic rule which will generate self-disclosures, because *any* statement in a specified context may be taken as an intentional revelation about self. Here are some examples, with Mary as discloser in each case:

1. *John*: Do you like punk rock?
   Mary: Yes.
2. *John*: What do you like?
   Mary: Punk rock, it is oddly sexy.
3. *John*: I saw *Hamlet* yesterday.
   Mary: Punk rock is terrific! It really turns me on!

Each of Mary's responses looks like a self-disclosure, according to our judgement. Each disclosure differs from the others syntactically and semantically. Also, as we move from the first through the third example, we infer higher voluntarism on Mary's part and a stronger attitude toward punk rock. Even though we cannot offer a generative rule for self-disclosing acts, we can identify some presuppositions or 'felicity conditions' which must exist for a self-disclosure to occur – these are contextual requisites, not syntactic demands:

1. The speaker's remarks are understood to pertain to the speaker; there is an implicit or explicit reference to self.
2. The speaker is sincere or is at least perceived as such by the hearer.
3. The speaker's remarks are addressed to a hearer – not to himself or herself or a tape recorder, for example.
4. The speaker believes that the hearer does not possess the information which is being revealed.
5. The speaker believes that the hearer believes that the speaker is free to reveal or withhold the information.

We can offer some regulative rules for self-disclosure, which seem likely to have force in much of the USA and the UK:

1. Do not disclose intimate information to new acquaintances.
2. Do disclose non-intimate information to new acquaintances.
3. Do disclose intimate information to intimate friends.
4. Do not disclose non-intimate information to intimates.

First of all, rule (4) is not in fact a viable regulative rule for self-disclosure. We put it in to complete the logical set; we thus illustrate that rules for communication do not necessarily fit together in perfectly logical ways. The Altman–Taylor social penetration model explicitly contradicts (4) by indicating that intimates discuss a wide range of non-intimate topics as well as some very intimate ones. Rule (3) may or may not be a rule. We cannot be sure at this point. It is probably a useful and good thing to disclose intimately to close friends, but is it necessary? Will a person who does not disclose intimately to close friends be negatively sanctioned? Maybe it is impossible to have 'intimate' friends with whom we are not intimate communicatively. Yet 'one-way' intimacies may be possible. Rules (1) and (2) are clearly viable. There is a good deal of supportive empirical research in both cases (Berger, Gardner, Clatterbuck and Schulman, 1976; Chaikin and Derlega 1974).

Two other regulative rules are:

5. Disclose positively valenced (non-intimate) information to new acquaintances.
6. Do not disclose negatively valenced information to new acquaintances.

The upshot of these is that there is a prohibition against revealing 'bad' things about oneself; conversely, we are encouraged to reveal 'good' things. For example, when chatting with Mary for the first time John should not say: 'I frequently have stomach aches.' He should say: 'I've been feeling very energetic lately.' There is some research which suggests that these are viable (Gilbert and Horenstein 1975).

The seventh and eighth rules are:

7. Do not disclose excessively.
8. Do disclose moderately.

These simply indicate that one should talk about oneself occasionally, but not constantly. Persons who always talk about themselves are boring. They are also frustrating, becasue they deny us the opportunity to talk about *our*selves. Of course, the meanings of moderately and excessively are unspecifiable in any general sense, probably depending upon the judgements of the persons in the relationship, the discloser and the disclosure target. To an outsider, persons in a relationship may have said very little in a given encounter, but from the standpoint of the persons themselves volumes of personal information may have been exchanged by the use of 'code words' – private symbols charged with meaning.

The ninth and last rule is:

9. Disclose honestly and accurately.

One should not be caught in a lie when discussing personal opinions or feelings. Of course people are dishonest and inaccurate occasionally, and these 'inauthentic' disclosures may be difficult to detect (Miller and Steinberg, 1975). Moreover, this is a weak rule, easily overridden by other regulative rules, e.g. be polite: 'Yes, I really adore your new green hairstyle.'

What happens to the rule breaker in self-disclosure? She or he is perceived as relatively unlikable (Chaikin and Derlega 1974) and incompetent (Bradac, Hosman and Tardy 1978). It is very likely that we will attend closely to the behaviour of the rule breaker and that we will view the self-disclosure as an indicant of an enduring trait (Jones and Davis 1965; Bradac, Hosman and Tardy 1978). If we do not have a stereotype into which we can fit the deviant discloser or if we do not have a script for dealing with this sort of person, our uncertainty will probably be high. Conversely, the behaviour of the person who adheres to the rules for disclosure will not be monitored closely. Perhaps in this case we will attend more to the substance of disclosure, to what the disclosure tells us about the person, for the purpose of predicting future rewards and costs.

The nine rules listed above incorporate four dimensions of self-disclosure: amount or quantity, intimacy or depth, valence, and honesty/accuracy. These correspond to four *factors* of self-reported disclosure tendencies empirically derived by Wheeless (1976) and replicated by Bradac, Tardy and Hosman (1980). A fifth factor is 'intended disclosure', the extent to which persons are aware that they are revealing personal information. But this is not implicated in any regulative rule that we can think of.

Encoding self-disclosures

Whether rule-violating or rule-conforming, self-disclosures are encoded. That is, information about self is expressed in some form. This simple statement raises some interesting and complex issues. It seems to us that self-disclosures can be encoded digitally or analogically. Obviously, digitally *and* analogically encoded disclosures are the most familiar ones. Persons *talk* about their feelings and opinions. But sometimes people reveal their attitudes about themselves or others through touch, posture, gaze and other analogic modes. For example, we infer that someone likes us because he or she strokes our hand or we infer that someone dislikes us because she stares at us without smiling and then spits. The first instance, the more pleasant one, is rather unambiguous because a stroke is a kind of touch where hand–body contact is of relatively long duration and this touch is usually repeated. The second instance is more ambiguous in that the discloser can always say, 'I wasn't thinking of you when I spat.' This may even be true. Generally, purely analogic self-disclosures are likely to be ambiguous. Also, there is a limited range of personal information which can be expressed analogically. Basically the analogic code restricts us to revelations about our feelings regarding self and others. A digital code is needed to express opinions and beliefs. It is also needed to express personal information of any sort with high precision: 'I like you 9.8 on a scale of 10. The only thing I don't like about you is the freckle on your ring finger.'

The language of the self

Regarding self-disclosive talk, the question arises: What do people talk *about*? There are two aspects of self which are traditionally and familiarly labelled *psyche* and *soma*. We can talk of enduring and transitory aspects of mind and body, and this is the 'stuff' of self-disclosure. The interesting question for us is: What sort or lexicon exists for talking about our mental and physical traits and states? It seems to us that most of us have a rather limited lexical repertoire for talking about our bodies. When a medical doctor asks, 'Where does it hurt?', most of us are likely to answer, 'My side', instead of 'The intercostal region on the left just below the pectoral muscle'. The thousands of distinctions codified in *Grey's Anatomy* are not available to most of us. Or, when someone is stroking our back and asks us, 'How does it feel?', we will probably answer, 'Good', or 'Nice', instead of 'Slightly ticklish with a degree of pressure detectable cutaneously and subcutaneously'. It really might be useful for us to expand our vocabulary for somatic self-disclosure. It might allow more effective treatment by doctors and friends. It might also produce the attribution, 'What a pedant!'

The lexicon of a particular bodily state, namely, the sensation of odour, has received some attention from researchers recently (Cain 1981). Various specialized groups, e.g. beer and wine tasters, have developed elaborate terminologies for olefactory distinctions. For example, a beeer may be estery, floral, hoppy, grassy, yeasty, catty, leathery or phenolic. Some evidence indicates that correct labels for odours initially provided by experimenters to respondents can facilitate greatly the respondents' identification of these odours on later trials compared to incorrect self-generated labels or to no labels at all (Cain 1981). The communication of one's experience of odours will be effective to the extent that speakers use correct labels which are understood by hearers who have also experienced the odours in question. This should hold true for other bodily states as well, although in some cases it may be difficult to find objectively correct labels.

With regard to bodily traits, important questions are: How do people talk about their faces? How do people talk about their body structure? And how do people talk about their deficiencies, handicaps, deformities and other physical stigmata? Our impression is that a rich lexicon exists for describing one's face, but that most persons rarely talk about their faces even to intimate friends. Persons are more likely to describe and talk about *other* persons' faces. Or they may talk about their face to medical doctors with a clinical interest. At any rate, the following words are commonly used to refer to faces or to parts of faces: shifty eyes, beady eyes, bulbous nose, acquiline nose, ski nose, pursed lips, buck teeth, prominent chin, weak chin, ruddy complexion, paleface, freckleface, Dumbo ears, handsome, ugly, plain, attractive and cute. (Many others could of course be offered.) If we are correct in suggesting that there is a relatively rich lexicon for the face, there may be several interrelated causes of this: (1) the face is controlled by a larger area of cerebral cortex than are other regions of the body; (2) facial muscles are highly manipulable; (3) the face has important signalling value in all human cultures (Ekman 1975); and (4) in many cultures the face is revealed while many other bodily parts are concealed. In other words the face is important so we have developed many words for talking about it. Similarly, we have a rich vocabulary for referring to sexual areas of the body. (To preserve our decorous posture we will not give examples.) One study suggests that a possible source of interpersonal difficulty for couples is the sometimes dissimilar lexicon which males and females use when describing sexual areas (Walsh and Leonard 1974). Contrarily, it is no secret that long-term sexual partners may develop their own terminology for sexual areas, and this personalization may facilitate communication and cooperation. Other parts of the body are talked about in less variegated and detailed ways. To describe the lower extremities, a comparatively large part of the body, we have: toes, toe nails, sole, heel, ankle, calf, shin, knee and thigh. We are hard pressed to think of other commom terms for this region.

To describe body structure we have: fat, obese, overweight, portly, skinny, tiny, shrimpy, gargantuan, muscle-bound, athletic, tall, short, etc. Rather clearly, these labels can have important consequences for self-perception. The labels that significant others use to describe our bodies can importantly affect our body image. Some advertisers believe that persons who would be labelled 'fat' by many others in everyday talk prefer labels such as 'large' as in 'large person's shop'. Similarly, emaciated persons may prefer the label 'slim'. There is a good deal of idiosyncracy here, apparently, because some persons view labels such as 'large' and 'slim' as condescending euphemisms; these persons willfully refer to themselves as 'fat' or 'skinny'. Probably the important thing to do is to surround yourself with others who use the body labels you prefer.

When we talk about severe obesity or emaciation, we are talking about a socially stigmatized body trait. Anything viewed as a deformity by members of society will be stigmatized. Thompson and Seibold (1978) define a stigma as 'any discrediting attribute which does not fit the perceiver's stereotype of what a "normal" individual is or does and is consistent with what the perceiver's reference group(s) would find stigmatizing' (p. 231). There is evidence that physical stigmata differ in perceived severity. For example, a third degree facial burn is judged more severe than is a swollen nose (Aamot, 1978). A question for us is: What happens when persons talk about their stigmatized body features to others? This question was examined by Thompson and Seibold (1978) who hypothesized that self-disclosure about a stigma would increase a hearer's acceptance of the discloser and that such disclosure would decrease the hearer's uncertainty about the discloser. They operationalized the concept of physical stigma by having a confederate sit in a wheelchair. This person either talked about his stigma to research subjects or he did not. Results indicated that disclosure about the stigma did not affect acceptance, but it did reduce uncertainty as measured by the number of references subjects made to the stigmatized attribute and the total amount of time the subject spend talking. The researchers conclude that 'disclosing personal information about one's stigmatized attribute is a tricky matter. . . . Future research . . . will need to vary valence, personalness, timing, and appropriateness of disclosures if realistic statements are to be made about disclosure as a stigma management strategy' (p. 239).

When self-disclosing we also talk about our moods or feelings and, to a lesser extent, our personalities. There is a rich lexicon for describing our emotional states. This lexicon comprises antinomous adjectival pairs such as good/bad, up/down, strong/weak, etc. Mehrabian (1980) has offered a three-factor theory of emotion which reflects these antinomies and which seems to us quite plausible. It is based upon Osgood, Suci and Tannenbaum's theory of connotative meaning (1957). Each of the three factors, which Mehrabian has derived empirically through factor analysis, suggests adjectives which persons can use when describing their feelings. The first factor is labelled *Pleasure* and this comprises bi-polar adjectives such as: happy/unhappy, pleased/annoyed, satisfied/unsatisfied, contented/melancholic, hopeful/despairing, relaxed/bored, comfortable/uncomfortable, excited/irritated, free/restrained, and secure/insecure. The second factor is *Arousal* and this comprises:

stimulated/relaxed, excited/calm, frenzied/sluggish, jittery/dull, wide-awake/sleepy, and aroused/unaroused. The third factor, *Dominance*, comprises controlling/controlled, dominant/submissive, influential/influenced, important/awed, autonomous/guided, in control/cared for, and powerful/overpowered. These experimenter-imposed semantic distinctions were meaningful to naive subjects who were asked to rate their probable feelings in hypothetical situations. Of course, some of these words may not be very frequently generated by naive persons themselves when describing their feelings. It seems to us that persons rarely say they are feeling 'melancholic' or 'autonomous' when describing the way they feel.

Mehrabian (1980) offers an expanded list of words which constitutes a 'preliminary dictionary of emotional terms' (p. 40); this was generated in a rather large study of University of California undergraduates. We will not list the 151 words which were rated in terms of the three factors of emotion. Rather we will suggest that the results of this study call attention to the fact that some emotional descriptors reflect two or three aspects of emotion simultaneously. For example, 'lonely' is negatively associated with the factors of pleasure, arousal, and dominance. 'Rejected' is negatively associated with pleasure and dominance. 'Terrified' is negatively associated with pleasure but positively associated with arousal. 'Sexually excited' is positively associated with both pleasure and arousal. And 'admired' is positively associated with all three factors. An implication of Mehrabian's theory is that emotion can be represented as a cubic space with three dimensions which intersect at a zero-point, and that when we describe our feelings to someone we decide where in the cubic space our feeling 'falls' and we find a word which best represents this geometric point. Probably the similarity of the 'semantic spaces' of the discloser and the disclosure target will determine the effectiveness of communication of emotion – the more similar, the more effective (Vick and Wood 1969; Wood, Yamauchi and Bradac 1971). For example, if for Mary 'lousy' refers to a state which is low in pleasure, low in arousal, and low in dominance, communication with John will be less effective if for him this term refers to a point which is low in pleasure, *high* in arousal, and low in dominance than if it refers to the same point in semantic space. Futher, we would expect that the more the semantic spaces for emotion differ between interactants, the less certainty they will have about each other. Probably most of us would be baffled by a person who uses the term 'ecstatic' to describe his or her state in a situation which *should* induce low pleasure, low arousal, and low dominance. There is an intriguing issue here: Does the person feel the same as we do in a particular situation but simply have an 'incorrect' label for the feeling? Or does the person label events in the way we do but have a very dissimilar emotional response to the situation? It may take a good deal of interaction in various situations before we can begin to guess at the correct answer. And guessing is all we can ever do, because there is no way to share *directly* experiences of emotion-inducing phenomena (alas). (But see the fascinating novel by D.G.Compton, *Synthajoy* 1968).

As we suggested above, self-disclosures about personality traits occur much less frequently than do descriptions of mood or feeling. It would seem to take a *very* high degree of objective self-awareness (Duval and Wicklund 1972) to say: 'I am an obsessive, moody, but basically unselfish person who is highly achievement oriented and afraid of ridicule.' There are very few situations which invite this kind of overt description of the result of a high degree of objective self-awareness. It is even fashionable for therapists and counsellors, those officially designated targets of self-disclosure, to respond to a statement like 'I'm an obsessive etc. person' with, 'But how do you *feel*? Tell me about your *feelings*.' There is, however, a rich lexicon of personality traits, but this is used primarily for talking about *other* persons. The situation is interestingly similar to talking about one's face or body. This suggests a general hypothesis: Persons are freer to talk about transitory states than about enduring traits because talk about traits implies a very high degree of objective self-awareness which is to some extent unacceptable in social exchanges. As we suggested earlier, one does not like to be caught looking closely at one's face in a mirror even by intimate friends.

Bromley (1977) has done an extensive analysis of the personality descriptions of ordinary speakers. He has looked closely at the language which 'naive scientists' use to characterize the psychological traits of others or of themselves. He suggests that the syntax of such descriptions is basically subject (a noun or noun phrase, the other person or the self; 'he', 'I'), verb (usually 'to be' or 'to have' with verbal auxiliary), object (an attribute), and qualifying words or phrases. This is essentially the syntax of any declarative sentence in English. Perhaps the most important aspects are the use of 'to be' or 'to have' and the specification of a person and an attribute. The syntactic form of a personality description essentially allows the linkage of a person with a trait or traits. This is done in both convoluted and straightforward ways.

The semantic analysis of personality attributes is more revealing. Bromley content analyses personality descriptions in terms of three general categories: internal, external and social personality. Under internal personality there are nine more specific categories: general trait ('awkward'), specific trait ('goes to church regularly'), ability and attainment ('well informed'), motivation and arousal ('is afraid to try'), orientation and feeling or attitude ('is confused'), object of an attitude ('is fond of animals'), expressive behaviour ('dresses well'), principles and moral values or character ('narrow-minded'), and self-concept ('self-pitying'). External personality includes identity ('middle-aged'), physical appearance ('dark hair'), physical and mental health ('poor eyesight'), life-history ('has suffered'), contemporary situation ('is fortunate'), prospects ('will enjoy life'), routine activities ('goes to bed late'), material circumstances and possessions ('seems well off'), and actual incidents ('I once heard her defending an acquaintance'). The social personality includes: social position ('head-master'), family and kin ('has two very good parents'), friendship and loyalties ('has only one friend'), person's response to others ('expects to be supported by his family'), others' response to person ('he is reputed'), comparison with others ('brighter than John'), person's response to subject ('he is kind to me'), subject's response to person ('I confided in her often'), joint action with the subject ('no real conflict between us'), comparison with the subject ('we hold equal rank'), evaluation ('good'), and collateral or irrelevant information ('her parents are very nice'). Although Bromley's categories may not be exhaustive, they constitute a useful typology of things people talk about when they talk about the personalities of themselves or of others. The distinctions represented by the typology are expressed by thousands of specific lexical items. If a given distinction is understood by both discloser and discloser target, and if the lexical items used to refer to the distinction are meaningful to both persons, self-disclosure about personality traits should reduce uncertainty about the discloser, unless the disclosure target has no routine for dealing with the trait described.

The last several pages have been devoted to the 'substance' of self-disclosure – the kinds of things people talk about and the words they use to refer to these things. We will now briefly discuss another aspect of talk about self which has been labelled 'disclosure style' (Bradac, Hosman and Tardy 1978). The essential notion here is that people differ in the *ways* in which they talk about themselves. Unfortunately, very little research has been done on this topic. One study uncovered a kind of self-discloser which the researchers labelled *Parent Cryptic* and another kind which they labelled *Parentally Open/Friend Cryptic* (Bradac, Tardy and Hosman 1980). The former type of person tended to be a male who reported disclosing positive information to parents with a high degree of control and low frequency; there was some evidence that he saw himself as dishonest and inaccurate when he did so. The latter type of person tended to be a female who reported being accurate, honest and relatively uncontrolled in disclosures to parents but comparatively guarded in disclosures to best same-sex friend.

More generally, Norton (1978) provides evidence that the following dimensions discriminate among persons in terms of self-perceptions of their communication styles: dominant, dramatic, contentious, impression leaving, relaxed, open, animated, friendly and attentive. Although these dimensions have not been linked to self-disclosure specifically, there is no reason to expect that they would not be useful in characterizing disclosure styles. On the contrary, it seems reasonable to suggest that there is a type of self-discloser who is open, relaxed and friendly, at least when talking to particular disclosure targets. There may be another type who is animated, dramatic and dominant; this kind of person might attempt to control attention by embedding self-disclosures in a dramatic narrative structure. A highly attentive and contentious person may reveal little personal information, focusing on the other person's self, disagreeing with and questioning the other's personal revelations. It would be useful in future research to relate the types of self-disclosers discovered by Bradac, Tardy and Hosman (1980) to the communicator style dimensions discovered by Norton (1978).

Consequences of disclosure

A final question in this section is: What are the effects or consequences of self-disclosure? Most importantly from our standpoint, messages about self allow persons to reduce their uncertainty about disclosers. Of course, in some cases self-disclosures can increase uncertainty as well – we may discover that the discloser's self is mysterious, very unlike other selves that we know. And self-disclosures allow us to predict how rewarding or costly future interactions with the discloser are likely to be. Both of these consequences indicate that self-disclosures provide psychological information about the discloser. Self-disclosive messages allow us to evaluate the discloser's personality in terms of similarity, likeability, competence, etc. (Bradac, Hosman and Tardy 1978; Chaikin and Derlega 1974.)

More particularly, messages about self will often have a particular 'command' function as well as the function of 'reporting' on the contents of self (Watzlawick, Beavin and Jackson 1967). The command is: 'See me as this type of person', or, more complexly, 'See me as the kind of person who sees herself in this way'. The second type of command suggests that an *evaluation* of self may be communicated with facts about self, and the target of disclosure may be asked to accept the discloser's self-evaluation: 'I am a quiet, intellectual person, and I *like* this aspect of myself.' This 'command' to accept an evaluaton of self will often be issued analogically, e.g. in facial expressions which accompany the self-disclosure. Probably only rarely do persons explicitly evaluate facts about self in the presence of others, especially in initial encounters. This would imply a very high degree of objective self-awareness (Duval and Wicklund 1972). Various therapy and encounter-type groups encourage persons to offer explicit self-evaluations, but these are exceptional communication contexts. Confessional situations, whether religious or secular, also invite this sort of communicative behaviour.

Summary

We began by discussing the multifaceted self, offering along the way a somewhat complex model. 'Self' was related to the interactive knowledge gaining strategies of interrogation and disclosure, and these strategies were examined in detail. A major point in this connection was that interrogations and disclosures can be characterized in terms of regulative rules and constitutive rules or felicity conditions. There are cultural constraints on these forms of knowledge acquisition which wane with relational advancement – cultural constraints give way to idiosyncratic ones. We spent some time considering the things people talk about when they talk about self, namely, physical and psychological states and traits or *psyche* and *soma*. Finally, we suggested that persons vary in the ways they self-disclose and that such variations have consequences for disclosers. In the next chapter we discuss a possible *result* of social knowledge-gaining strategies, namely, relational escalation. As usual, we focus upon the role of verbal communication in this process.

5

Language and relational development

Lovers never get tired of each other, because they are always talking about themselves.

La Rochefoucauld

Now we go beyond initial interaction to examine the role of performed language in the formation, maintenance and dissolution of interpersonal relationships. As in the preceding chapters we are concerned with uncertainty, but when we focus upon relational communication we are concerned with uncertainty about the *relationship* in addition to uncertainty about individuals. That is, at some point John's uncertainty about Mary becomes John's uncertainty about Mary and John as a unit. Here we scrutinize the ways in which speech maintains relationships and facilitates their growth. We also discuss the little broached topic of 'fractural' communication, examining what happens when a relationship 'breaks up'. At the outset we assume that two persons have observed and interacted with each other to the point that (1) they have gained some degree of mutual knowledge and (2) they have predicted more rewards than costs in future interactions. In other words a relationship has formed. This last statement sounds simple enough, but it masks many complexities which invite a discussion of the nature of relationships.

Defining relationships

There is a remarkable short story by Thomas Hardy entitled 'On the Western Circuit'. The title gives no clue to the fact that the story is about a peculiar kind of triangle involving two women and a man. The man, Charles Rae, is initially attracted to Anna, a pretty young woman who is, alas, illiterate and insensitive. Anna has a protectoress, Edith Harnham, who agrees to correspond with Charles in Anna's guise when he returns to his home in London. Edith is a very talented writer and a sensitive soul (as well as a kind of monster of deception) and after many rounds of correspondence, Charles comes to believe that he is in love with Anna because of her sensitivity and charm which transcend her lack of schooling. Of course, Charles is really in love with Edith, but deluded he marries Anna. Immediately following the wedding, which Edith attends as Anna's friend, the truth outs when Anna fails miserably at the simple task of writing a letter to Charles's sister. Edith confesses her duplicity. Charles realizes his dreadful mistake but stoically vows to remain in his married state. Edith returns to her husband who is a boring sort of fellow who has long been in the background of Edith's life. All of the characters anticipate a bleak future.

This outline masks the great artistry of Hardy's presentation. But it begins to call attention to the difficulty of saying what a relationship is and when one exists. As a first stab, we can distinguish between nominal and social psychological relationships (Cartwright and Zander 1968). Edith's relationship with her husband and Charles's relationship with Anna fall into the nominal category, whereas Charles's relationship with Edith is social psychological. Outsiders might view Edith and her husband and Charles and Anna as related by virtue of their marriages – and of course legally they are related – whereas persons privy to the attitudes and feelings of the characters might see the Edith/Charles association as the only 'true' relationship. These latter persons, romantics like the authors of this book, are discriminating between relationships and non-relationships on social psychological grounds. Of course, the peculiar and oddly fascinating thing about the one 'true' relationship in this story is that it is totally epistolary. We expect this does not happen often in real life. This nominal/social psychological distinction resembles the formal group/informal group distinction which pervades sociological literature on the small group (Homans 1950).

As outsiders, i.e. persons who observe others without a Thomas Hardy to give us access to their internal states, we are constantly making inferences about who is related and who is not. We say things like: 'I think Mary and John are now a team.', 'Do you think something is going on between Mary and John?', or 'I think Mary and John are on the rocks.' What cues do people offer to tell us about their relational state? There are some obvious bonding signals which need little discussion here: wearing the same wedding ring, kissing, one person sitting on another's lap, and walking hand-in-hand. It is worth pointing out that these signals are culturally bound to some extent. For example, in the USA two males walking hand-in-hand or arm-in-arm will be perceived by many observers as having a sexual relationship, whereas in various European countries this is likely to denote nothing more than a state of friendship.

More generally, there are two major kinds of cues which we use to make inferences about the extent to which two persons are related: nonverbal behaviours and explicit descriptive labels produced by the two persons or applied to these persons by others. Forgas (1978b) compared the influence of these two types of information upon observers' judgements of the degree of intimacy, warmth, etc. exhibited by two persons. Half of Forgas's subjects saw a videotape depicting a male and a female who were smiling at each other, gazing infrequently, and sitting in close proximity; the other half saw the same male and female but in this case they were not smiling or gazing and they were farther apart. Prior to viewing the tape, half of each group were *told* that the two persons were a young married couple and half were told that they were research assistants meeting for the first time. Thus there were two concordant conditions (nonintimate behaviours, nonintimate label; intimate behaviours, intimate label) and two discordant conditions (nonintimate behaviours, intimate label; intimate behaviours, nonintimate label). Forgas's results indicated that subjects were more strongly affected by the nonverbal cues than by the labels designating the type of relationship. But the defining labels did affect subjects' perceptions, especially in the discordant conditions. Interestingly, in the case of distant behaviour exhibited by putative intimates, subjects were likely to offer an 'external' explanation (something in the situation is precluding intimacy), whereas in the case of intimate behaviour exhibited by putative nonintimates, subjects were inclined to provide an 'internal' explanation (they are friendly and have a strong interest in each other).

The labels which persons use to describe their relationship or the relationships of others are especially interesting to us. Both Forgas's study and everyday experience suggest that they have an impact upon our perceptions and behaviours. One of the partners of an escalating relationship performs a crucially important act when he or she says: 'We will always be *just* friends.' An explicit relational definition implies a range of permissable and impermissable behaviours.

There has been some interesting descriptive research on the kinds of relationships which people have and the kinds of labels which are used to refer to them. Knapp, Ellis and Williams (1980) had a large sample of subjects rate 62 relational terms for perceived intimacy. The most intimate terms denote a sexual relationship: husband, wife, lover, fiancé(e), mate, intimate and spouse. High intimacy ratings were also assigned to terms denoting non-spousal kinship or, more specifically, relationships in the nuclear family: mother, daughter, sister and father. (Cousins, uncles and aunts received neutral ratings). Best friend, close friend and confidant also received moderately high intimacy ratings. At the other extreme, the lowest intimacy ratings were given to employer, acquaintance, neighbour, co-worker, aide, fellow, associate and colleague.

Some of these terms imply highly specific contracts between partners, whereas others do not. The husband/wife relationship is highly and intricately contractual in many cultures. In the USA, for example, husbands and wives are legally obligated to each other. There are also non-legal obligations associated with social customs, although these are rapidly changing: one person will be the provider, the other will be the caretaker; one will fix the plumbing, one will do the cooking, etc. Increasingly, couples are developing explicit idiosyncratic contracts which spell out the obligations and rights of each partner. Employer/employee relationships are also contractual in both the legal and non-legal senses: some mutual obligations have the force of law while others are informally negotiated by the two parties. Thus, relational contracts cut across the intimacy spectrum. But it seems to us that some relational types rarely employ explicit contracts, e.g. best same-sex friends. It is worth nothing that an explicit relational contract *demands* language for its creation. Contracts are constituted by definitions and propositions, essential products of a digital system.

Another approach to relational definition has been taken by Fitzpatrick and Best (1979). These researchers have developed an empirical typology of long-term heterosexual relationships by having dyadic partners respond to a questionnaire which includes items such as: 'We tell each other how much we love or care about each other (agree/disagree)'; 'A woman should take her husband's last name when she marries'; 'We are likely to argue in front of friends or in public places'; 'The ideal relationship is one which is marked by novelty, humour, and spontaneity'; and 'If I can avoid arguing about some problems, they will disappear'. Analysis of partners' responses has consistently yielded four basic types of relationships:

1. *Independents* are committed to an ideology of uncertainty and change. They are high in autonomy but also high in sharing.
2. *Separates* are high in avoidance of conflict and they engage in relatively little sharing. Their use of space is differentiated, yet they do not feel highly autonomous. They are not ideologically committed to either traditional or change-oriented values.
3. *Traditionals* exhibit low autonomy and low differentiation of space. They share a good deal and engage in conflict instead of avoiding it. They strongly oppose an ideology of uncertainty and change.
4. *Separate/Traditionals* are a mixed pair. In this kind of relationship the husband classifies himself as a Separate, whereas the wife defines herself as a Traditional.

Fitzpatrick and Best have also obtained evidence of some differences between the relational types on the dimension of dyadic adjustment. For example, Traditionals are higher than the other types on consensus, cohesion, and relational satisfaction. Separates are comparatively low on dyadic satisfaction and on cohesiveness.

From our standpoint, the interesting implication of the Fitzpatrick and Best (1979) research is that the label 'intimate relationship' or 'marriage' may be an inadequate descriptor. They have demonstrated that 'marriage' has multiple referents, each of which is rather unique. Of course, their four-fold typology has not been incorporated in everyday talk about relationships, but perhaps it will be if 'naive scientists' become aware of this sophisticated research.

A third approach to relational definition has been taken by researchers attempting to characterize the qualities or attributes associated with various relationship types. Encouragingly, there has been some consistency of results across researchers. Dickson-Markman and Wheeless (1980) had persons describe four relationship types: acquaintance, casual friend, best friend and intimate friend. In terms of intimacy ratings, there were basically two types of relationship: acquaintance/casual friend and best friend/intimate friend. Terms frequently used to describe acquaintances and casual friends referred to distance ('not close', 'impersonal', 'superficial'), rationale for interaction ('we only talk at club meetings', 'have mutual friends'), and frequency and type of interaction ('we only talk at parties', 'I see them often'). Terms used to describe best friends and intimates referred to closeness ('We share secrets', 'I can be open with them'), empathy and loving ('concerned', 'kind', 'loving'), reduction of uncertainty ('dependable', 'predictable'), and character ('dependable', 'honest', 'trustworthy'). Affect positivity was common to both types of relationship ('pleasant', 'fun', 'happy').

Using a similar approach, Wiemann and Krueger (1980) had persons describe three types of long-term relationship: best liked opposite sex, best liked same sex, and least liked other. Terms which were used to describe the two 'best' relationships reflected a supportiveness dimension (comfort, dependability, care, and sympathy), an affect dimension (primarily positive intimacy, positive evaluation, affection), an approach or approach-avoid dimension (movement toward or away, differentiation or unitization), and a dimension of structuring (spatial constraints, temporal constraints and shared control). The least liked other was talked about in terms of negative affect, avoidance, structure (in this case control struggle and demands), and incongruity ('a felt discrepancy between the way *S* thinks his/her partner feels or behaves, and the way the partner says he/she feels or behaves in the relationship' (p. 9)).

Berger, Weber, Munley and Dixon (1980) had persons respond to 36 questions for each of five relationship levels: formal role (e.g. doctor), acquaintance, friend, close friend, lover. A few of the questions were: 'To what extent does this person like you?' 'How friendly and pleasant is this person's personality?' 'To what extent are the attitudes and opinions of the person similar to yours?' and 'To what extent is the person easy-going, relaxed and spontaneous?' A factor analysis of subjects' responses yielded a three-factor solution: supportiveness, character and sociability. The five relationship types were compared in terms of these three factors and some interesting patterns emerged. On the supportiveness dimension, those in a formal position, acquaintances and friends were rated lower than were close friends and lovers. Close friends, lovers and those in a formal position were rated higher on the character dimension than were acquaintances and friends. For sociability, friends were rated lower than those in a formal role, close friends and lovers; acquaintances were rated lower than close friends and lovers. One conclusion of this study is that 'perceptions of supportiveness may be more important than perceptions of character or sociability in determining the extent to which a relationship will escalate in terms of intimacy' (p. 147)'.

These studies suggest that intimacy, affect, character, supportiveness, predictability and degree of structuring are salient dimensions for people when they are asked to talk about their relationships. A lengthy verbal description using terms which reflect all of these dimensions should be much more accurately informative about the nature of a relationship than the single-word designator 'friend', 'spouse', or 'lover'.

When persons talk about their relationships, they are engaging in a kind of 'meta-talk' or 'meta-communication' (Watzlawick, Beavin and Jackson 1967). This is communication about communication (talk about talk). The clearest example of this is when John says to Mary, 'We don't communicate enough anymore and I perceive this as a threat to our intimacy.' Meta-talk is a uniquely human mode of communication. Other animals communicate but there is no evidence that they communicate about communication.

An important function of talking about relationships is uncertainty reduction, but here uncertainty about the *relationship* is reduced (or increased). Whereas previously John attempted to reduce his uncertainty about Mary, now he attempts to reduce his uncertainty about Mary and John as a unit. This is an important shift, because relational uncertainty is of a different 'logical type' (Bateson 1979) than is uncertainty about individuals. For one thing, whereas a host of cultural, sociological and psychological stereotypes exist for categorizing individuals, it seems to us that comparatively few stereotypes exist for categorizing relationships (but see Emler and Fisher 1981). A relationship is a higher-order abstraction than is one's conception of an individual. Accordingly, relational uncertainty reduction should be comparatively difficult.

Our guess is that the major cognitive schemata most of us use when assessing our relationships in attempts to reduce uncertainty are learned in childhood through observations of our parents or other important relationship models (Krueger, in press; Laing 1969). If we feel that the relationship that we are in is increasingly at odds with the schematized relationship 'in our heads', uncertainty about the relationship should increase correspondingly. Conversely, if there is a good fit between the schematized relationship and our view of the relationship we are in, uncertainty should be low.

Probably many persons are unaware of their relationship schemata, and even those who are aware of them may have difficulty rendering them in verbal form. We are speculating here that these schemata exist as a set of extra-verbal images, literally mental pictures which guide our behaviours and our judgements of others' behaviours. At any rate, people do talk about their relationships, although often imprecisely and with great diffculty. Perhaps relational talk could be improved with increased awareness of relational schemata.

Implicit relational communication

There is another kind of relational communication, which is equally important. We have been discussing *explicit* relational communication, and now we will discuss communication which is *implicit*. Here we move to an examination of the unconscious 'statements' that people make about their relationships to their relational partner. Earlier we distinguished between 'report' and 'command' functions of communication, and this distinction is important here also (Watzlawick, Beavin and Jackson 1967). When persons talk to their partners about everyday events, they are simultaneously talking about the relationship. As Rogers, Courtright and Millar (1980) suggest,

> The relational approach to the study of communicative behaviours . . . is not primarily concerned with the content or 'report' aspects of interaction, but rather with the shape or form of the 'command' aspects as they evolve over time. A relational orientation assumes that the 'facticity' of a social relationship is its form rather than its content, that form is observable while content is inferred. (p. 201)

The implication is that Mary 'commands' John to accept her view of the relationship every time she produces an utterance. For example, if Mary constantly offers assertions, especially if these interrupt John's utterances, she is exhibiting the trait of relational 'domineeringness' (Courtright, Millar and Rogers-Millar 1979). She is 'commanding' John to see her as the dominant person in the relationship:

Mary: I say it was a great dinner party.
John: Yes, that's true. The caviar . . .
Mary: The caviar was excellent.
John: The beef . . .
Mary: The beef was perfect, could not have been better.
John: The . . .
Mary: The whole party was a brilliant success.

Of course, John may not accept Mary's attempts at control:

Mary: I say it was a great dinner party.
John: It was great – a great fiasco.
Mary: The caviar was perfect.
John: The caviar was perfectly atrocious.

Mary: The beef was marvelous.
John: My only beef about the beef is that it was actually a roasted boot.

Here both persons are exhibiting domineeringness. Neither will allow the other to achieve 'dominance'. Thus domineeringness refers to the individual behaviours of interactants, whereas dominance refers to a relational state which necessarily incorporates both persons, one who attempts to dominate, the other who accepts domination. Arguing for a connection between interpersonal attraction and social power, Kelvin (1977) criticizes approaches which focus exclusively upon the powerful or powerless behaviours of individuals instead of focusing upon behaviours in the context of a relationship:

It is . . . symptomatic of the stimulus-oriented approach to attraction that when power has been discussed . . . it has been considered not as a form of *relationship* but rather as a *property* of the attractive. Yet fundamentally the attractive has no such property – and that fact, and its consequences, is the core of the problem, (p. 359)

Kelvin seems to be calling for more studies of variables such as dominance, as opposed to studies of domineeringness and other variables of this sort.

Research on the command aspects of relational communication has by-and-large used a particular research procedure which is nicely summarized by Courtright, Millar and Rogers-Millar (1979):

The relational control coding system involves three progressive steps. First, each message in an ongoing interaction is assigned a three-digit code to indicate the speaker, the grammatical form of the message and the response mode relative to the previous message. The *grammatical* codes are: (1) assertion, (2) question, (3) talk-over, (4) noncomplete, and (5) other. The *response* modes are: (1) support, (2) nonsupport, (3) extension, (4) answer, (5) instruction, (6) order, (7) disconfirmation, (8) topic change, (9) initiation–termination, and (10) other. Using these codes, comunicative exchanges are represented by a series of sequentially ordered numerical codes.

The next step translates the numerical codes, according to a set of rules, into control directions. Messages attempting to assert definitional rights are coded one-up (↑); requests or acceptances of the other's definition of the relationship, one-down (↓); and non-demanding, non-accepting, levelling movements, one-across (→).

In the third step of the coding procedure, control directions of each pair of sequentially ordered messages are combined to form nine transactional types: one-up, one-down complementarity (↑↓,↓↑); competitive, submissive, and neutralized symmetry (↑↑,↓↓,→→); one-up transitory (↑→,→↑) and one-down transitory ↓→,→↓.

So, the first John/Mary exchange would be coded: Mary↑, John↓; Mary↑, John↓; etc. The second exchange would be: Mary↑, John↑; Mary↑, John↑; etc. In the first case there is dominance, in the second mutual domineeringness.

Research on communication and control has attempted to relate interaction patterns to various outcomes. For example, there is some evidence that domineeringness is negatively related to marital satisfaction, whereas dominance is not (Courtright, Millar and Rogers-Millar 1979).

Parks (1979) offers 15 'axioms' of communication and control which are based upon empirical research or previous theory. The axioms which are most interesting to us can be summarized in the following statements:

1. Low external threat and high role discrepancy produce competitive symmetry in a relationship; competitive symmetry is directly related to frequency of unilateral action, open conflict, threat messages, and messages of rejection; competitive symmetry is inversely related to satisfaction and (paradoxically) probability of relationship termination. Role discrepancy refers to the 'difference between actual role definitions or performances within a relationship and what members of that relationship believe each other's role definitions or behaviours ought to be.
2. Complementarity is directly related to role specialization, mutual envy and disconfirming messages; complementarity is inversely related to empathy. A disconfirming message 'is a metacommunication which says in effect: "The role you are playing does not exist."'

Both statements indicate, to us at least, that the states of complementarity and competitive symmetry are associated with undesirable outcomes. Persons in a competitively symmetrical relationship fight a lot, are mutually abusive and rejecting, but they 'tough it out' for fear of appearing weak or inferior to their relational partner (Parks 1979). Persons in a complementary relationship covet what the other has while at the same time denying the other's self-definition. The question becomes: What relational control states are associated with *positive* outcomes? There is no clear answer available in the research. Perhaps neutralized and submissive symmetry and the two transitory states produce relatively positive outcomes. More likely, flexibility in patterns of control – movement through the nine relational states as situations change – may conduce to relational health and happiness (Courtright, Millar and Rogers Millar 1979). Finally, we should mention that we have focused upon a particular kind of research in the area of communication and control, research undertaken from a 'Batesonian' perspective (Bateson 1958). A more complete picture would have included research from other perspectives as well (e.g. Good 1979; Zimmerman and West 1975).

Beyond relational definition and control

We will broaden the discussion now to examine briefly other forms of communication in relationships. Although relational definition and the control aspects of interpersonal interaction are very important, there are other things going on in relationships. It is probably important to note at the outset of this section that in the remainder of this chapter we do *not* want to be construed as saying that communication patterns which increase the cohesiveness or equilibrium of relationships are in any sense 'good'. We intend rather more neutrally to describe some connections between communication and relational survival or relational death. Communication is one influence upon the cohesiveness of relational partners. In other words we will not discuss the *effectiveness* of relationships which is another matter altogether, probably best defined by the persons in the relationship, although third parties seem to comment upon such matters quite often (Emler & Fisher 1981). Also, here and elsewhere we do not want to imply that reductions or increases in uncertainty about one's partner or about one's relationship are necessarily associated with feelings of pleasure or pain in any simple, linear fashion. The interpersonal world is more complex than this.

Krueger (in press) provides a good starting point with her close analysis of the talk of a successful and satisfied marital dyad. (This dyad contrasts nicely with the abusive or disconfirming dyads depicted by Parks's axioms.) 'Cal' and 'Rose' were discussing a dual-career decision when they were audiotaped. Their talk pertained to institutional constraints on their decisions (What will our families think? How can we best achieve success as defined by the culture?) and to their decision-making processes. Several patterns were revealed in this talk: (1) discussions of the serious career decision occurred in cycles around more mundane talk; (2) their talk was multi-functional, used for information gathering, identifying obstacles, and generating solutions; (3) topics and sub-topics shifted continuously; (4) interruptions occurred frequently as did (5) mutual affirmation; (6) a topic-extension form occurred frequently where Cal raised a topic and Rose extended it or vice versa; (7) topic shifts were smooth and mutually acknowledged; and (8) overt disagreements were rare. Generally, their decision-making conversation exhibited high mutual awareness of the other's needs and of the other's typical behaviours. Whether Cal's or Rose's conversational style is typical or atypical of the style of effective marital dyads remains to be seen.

The kind of cohesiveness exhibited by Cal and Rose is facilitated by the use of personal idioms. Persons in long-term relationships may develop special terms to refer to each other and to their activities. Such terms were studied recently by Hopper, Knapp and Scott (1981). Eight categories exhausted the varieties of personal idioms described by respondents in their study: teasing insults ('Futtbutt'), confrontations ('jelly beans' – a phrase indicating 'You're talking over my head'), expressions of affection ('hunch nickle' – a phrase meaning 'I love you'), sexual invitations ('Too-hoot'), sexual references and euphemisms ('boogie-woogie'), requests/routines ('Week Thursday' – a phrase indicating 'I'll attend to that at my convenience'), partner nicknames ('Kitten-Snuffy'), and names for others ('motz' indicating a slow, disorganized person). The researchers note that teasing insults and expressions of affection were mentioned most frequently by their 224 respondents. Seventy-five per cent of the idioms received a positive evaluation from both participants and only 5 per cent received a clearly negative evaluation. About 55 per cent of the personal idioms were used exclusively in private contexts with sexual invitations being proportionately the most private, not surprisingly. There was some evidence that personal idioms are more characteristic of the early phase of a relationship than of the mature phase. Speculating upon the functions of these idioms, the researchers say:

> Romantic pairs may use personal idioms as expressions of mutual commitment in the task of working out the integration of their behavioural styles. Personal idioms may assist the couple in coping for the first time with each other's idiosyncracies; sexual euphemisms reduce embarrassment as couples experiment with sexuality. Making a partner's idiosyncracy the subject of everyday teasing comments or gestures may be a way to tell the partner the behaviour is bothersome without threatening the equilibrium of the relationship (p. 32).

Although all of these examples pertain to romantic relationships, partners in other long-term relationships may develop personal idioms also, e.g. to refer to work routines or work areas. Workers in the famous 'Hawthorne studies' of Elton Mayo coined the term 'binging' for a kind of friendly punch delivered to the upper arm of a fellow worker who was frequently exceeding his work quota (Homans 1950).

On the face of it, it would seem that disagreements or arguments are functionally the opposite of personal idioms in that they threaten cohesiveness and equilibrium. But this is simplistic. More accurate is the suggestion that some forms of argument or disagreement threaten equilibrium, whereas other forms have as a primary function the *maintenance* of equilibrium (Jacobs and Jackson 1981). There are several types or species of 'argument', and these seem likely to differ in their relational consequences, although unfortunately there is no experimental research on this matter, so we will have to speculate upon the causal connection between argument type and effect. First, there is the 'fight', a state of affairs where one person attempts to destroy or eliminate the other (Rapoport 1960). The attempt here is not to persuade one's partner or to justify a course of action, but rather simply to eliminate an obstacle to getting one's way. Probably most relationships will not survive many fights of this type. Next, there is the 'primitive argument' (Piaget 1932; Jacobs and Jackson 1981). This is simply an 'unmotivated clash of assertions' (Piaget 1932):

> *John*: You *lied* to me about your mother!
> *Mary*: I did not!
> *John*: You did. You said she was British!
> *Mary*: I did not. I said she was Scottish!
> *John*: British!
> *Mary*: Scottish!

This symmetrical form is literally childish. Primitive argument would seem to be divisive because the form allows no possibility of resolution or compromise. It is not all that far removed from the fight.

Now we move into the realm of 'genuine argument' (Piaget 1932). Generally, these may be conceived as expansions of assertions – the arguer offers a reason for his or her position. But in the context of everyday arguments occurring in conversations of relational partners, an argument may be more clearly conceptualized as an expansion of speech act in a disagreement-relevant situation (Jacobs and Jackson 1981):

> *John*: Would you bring me a piece of cake?
> *Mary*: Why don't you get it yourself?
> *John*: My foot is asleep and I will fall if I try to walk.

Here a request is made, and it is questioned. Mary *may* refuse John's request if he does not provide a convincing reason. He explains his request because Mary questions its legitimacy. Another version of this is not an argument in any sense:

> *John*: Would you bring me a piece of cake?
> *Mary*: OK.
> *John*: Thanks.

Nor is:

> *John*: Would you bring me a piece of cake?
> *Mary*: OK.
> *John*: It's just that my foot is asleep and I will fall if I try to walk.

With interpersonal arguments, it takes two to tango, and the tango occurs in the context of disagreement, potential or actual. Other sorts of argumentation, e.g. philosophical discourses, demand only assertions and reasons; disagreements are not necessarily entailed in these (O'Keefe 1977; Jacobs and Jackson 1981).

In terms of their impact upon relationships, there are few obvious things we can say about genuine arguments. Much depends upon the persons involved and the topics of disagreement. Everything being equal, genuine arguments seem likely to be less damaging to relationships than fights or primitive arguments. More positively, genuine arguments potentially allow disagreements to be aired and dealt with. From the standpoint of relational survival, this objectification of an experienced problem is probably preferable to the situation where a problem smoulders in the subconscious depths, only to break out in the form of ambiguous hostilities. Of course, even genuine arguents can be damaging:

John: You are fundamentally evil.
Mary: I am not.
John: I will prove it to you. First, it is clear to me that you consciously seek the destruction of living things. Both I and you have elsewhere defined this as evil.
Mary: I do not seek to destroy.
John: Item: you step on ants. Item: you eat chicken embryos.
Mary: You are crazy.
John: Perhaps. The important thing is for you to believe that I believe that you are evil. I can prove this to your satisfaction. First, I am asserting that I believe that you are evil. In the absence of contradictory information, you should accept my sincerity, etc.

This rather far-fetched (we hope) scenario illustrates a general point: genuine arguments designed to prove the inferiority, stupidity, badness etc. of the other person's *essence* are almost certainly damaging to the other and to the relationship. The suggestion has been made that relational partners should address the particular *behaviours* which are problematic in terms of *perceptions* and *feelings*: 'You are bad' becomes 'I feel angry when it appears that you do not respond to my questions.' The person addressed, in turn, should acknowledge the validity of the speaker's feeling, although he or she should be free to justify the behaviour: 'I believe you feel angry, but you see often I do not hear you because the kids make so much noise.' But apparently in reality it is difficult to focus upon particular acts, given a pervasive attributional warp in the direction of general dispositional inferences, in this case negative ones (Kelley 1979; Nisbett and Ross 1980).

When we talk of 'genuine arguments' we must again invoke the construct of a 'digital system'. Genuine arguments, which entail propositions and reasons, can be rendered exclusively in a symbolic system such as language. There is no such thing as an analogic argument. Fights, on the other hand, are prototypically analogical.

More generally, Altman and Taylor (1973) hypothesize that eight features of communication typically distinguish newly formed from long-term relationships:

1. *Depth of communication*. Long-term partners reveal more intimate information than do newly related partners.

2. *Breadth of Communication*. Long-term partners talk about a greater variety of topics.
3. *Communication Difficulty*. Communication is more efficient when persons have many experiences in common.
4. *Flexibility*. Developed relationships permit many options for emotional expression, whereas initial interactions are severely constrained by cultural rules for affect display.
5. *Spontaneity*. Intimates are less cautious, less inclined to plan their comunications than are non-intimates. Intimates exhibit a higher degree of mindlessness when they interact.
6. *Smoothness*. The interactions of long-term partners are more highly synchronized than are the interactions of those newly acquainted.
7. *Evaluation*. Intimates are more likely to exchange positive and negative remarks than are non-intimates.
8. *Uniqueness*. The communication of intimates is more personalized than is the communication of non-intimates.

Although folk wisdom has it that intimates talk more to each other than do non-intimates, these theorists do not offer amount of communication as a distinguishing feature, perhaps because its connection to relationship intimacy is a complex one. If anything, there may be a tendency for intimates to exhibit *lower* amounts of communication, if amount refers to number of words uttered per unit of time. See our discussion of abbreviation below.

Knapp, Ellis and Williams (1980) analysed the extent to which Altman and Taylor's eight dimensions of communicative behaviour were salient to persons when they thought about various relational partners who varied in intimacy. For example, with regard to 'lover' and 'acquaintance', respondents were asked to agree or disagree with the following statements, among others: 'We talk to each other in much the same way we talk to a lot of other people'; 'We share secrets with each other'; 'We discuss a wide variety of topics'; 'We have trouble understanding each other'; and 'We choose our words carefully to avoid misunderstandings'. A factor analysis of responess revealed three factors or underlying dimensions of communicative behaviour: *Personalized*, *Synchronized* and *Difficult*. The first factor essentially collapses Altman and Taylor's (1973) uniqueness, depth, flexibility and evaluation dimensions. The second factor collapses difficulty, smoothness and spontaneity. And the third factor collapses difficulty, smoothness and spontaneity also, although different items (statements) are implicated. Probably the second and third factors are correlated although we cannot tell from the research report. At any rate, the first two factors were clearly related to degree of intimacy: Respondents perceived their communication with intimates as being more personal and more highly synchronized. This outcome does not surprise us greatly. Other outcomes were more surprising and potentially more interesting: Males reported being less personal and less synchronized than did females; young respondents (age 22 and below) perceived intimate relationships as being more personal and synchronized than did older respondents (41 and above). Perhaps, for whatever reasons, older males especially are more realistic (or more cynical) than are younger females. Or perhaps the relationships of younger females actually *are* more personal and synchronized from their experiential standpoint.

Finally, we suggest that the communication of partners in fully developed relationships exhibits a high degree of TFG, to use Hopper's abbreviation (1981). This refers to the taken-for-granted or *das Fraglosgegeben* (Schutz 1967). Hopper (1981) says about TFG:

> the concern is with messages not actualized in physical speech, but nevertheless ordinarily understood in common (or at least thought to be so understood) by senders and receivers of the talk . . . . Uncoded, 'between-the-lines' information is referred to . . . . as taken for granted. (p. 196)

As persons become increasingly certain about the way their partners think and increasingly certain about their partner's certainty about the way they think, they will become increasingly likely to abbreviate their messages. This is a particular manifestation of lack of communication difficulty (Knapp, Ellis and Williams 1980; Altman and Taylor, 1973). An abbreviated message entails less expenditure of interpersonal energy than does a completely elaborated one (Miller and Steinberg 1975; Zipf 1935), so if persons are certain that their partners will grasp the meaning of the abbreviated form it is rational to abbreviate. The following example of abbreviation concludes this section; it illustrates, by the way, how partners in long-term relationships may develop conversational rules which are culturally deviant:

John: Hi.
Mary: Of course she did. You know that she did and you should reciprocate.
John: Right.
Mary: Now don't invent excuses, a simple note of congratulations will suffice.
John: Yes.
Mary: Good idea, a telephone call would be better.
John: Right.
Mary: An even better idea! Good for you! She would love you to visit and to bring those funny little candies that she likes so much.

Fractural communication

The heading of this section implies that relationships 'break up', and indeed this term is used by persons in everyday talk to describe the termination of relationships. We could have entitled this section with equal justification *Dissolving Communication* or *Decaying Communication*. Some relationships wane organically, while others end volcanically. In any case, we will briefly discuss communication patterns in relationships which are 'on the rocks' or 'melting down'. We say briefly because until recently there has not been concerted research on this topic. Perhaps in the past, communication researchers found the topic too depressing to pursue. Now we are in more cynical times. Sociologists, on the other hand, have always been interested in divorce and related topics. (Perhaps sociologists have always been cynical.) But they have seldom examined communication behaviours associated with relational death.

The specific causes of relational termination are of course various. But generally, mutual judgements of low rewards and high costs are probably typically involved. Two kinds of rewards and costs seem important, and these can be labelled 'intrinsic' and 'extrinsic' (Thibaut and Kelley 1959). Intrinsic rewards (or costs) are a product of the relationship itself (companionship) and extrinsic rewards (or costs) are a *by*-product of the relationship (economic security). Further, mutual judgements of the availability of better relational options are also an important factor (Thibaut and Kelley 1959). Given our focus, the precipitators of relational death are interesting only to the extent that they entail communication. That is, to oversimplify a bit, economic correlates of relational breakdown are not interesting, symbolic ones are.

Initially we can invoke again Altman and Taylor's social penetration model (1973). They argue that as relationships decline, partners engage in 'depenetration'. These partners move from intimate mutual self-revelations to superficial chatter. Specifically, communication becomes inflexable, cautious, difficult, dissynchronized, non-evaluative, superficial, narrow and de-personalized. We have seen deviations from this pattern, however. Where both partners have nothing left to lose – the relationship *is* over – caution may be low, evaluation (negative) and personalization may be high as in: 'You never were good for anything, Weak John, you #&*!!@$%!.' In this case words may be used as weapons. Persons may grimly and wilfully exploit their deep knowledge of the other to inflict painful psychic wounds.

But where the Altman and Taylor pattern is followed, we can suggest that the behaviour of partners whose relationship is dying resembles that of new acquaintances. This raises the question: Given a relationship that is nearing termination, is the mutual uncertainty of partners high or low? This is a complex question. Some relationships appear to move toward termination when one of the partners changes suddenly, as in mid-life crisis. Thompson (1981) provides evidence that in the case of a serious physical trauma, e.g. a debilitating injury experienced by one of the partners, intimate relational communication decreases. These sorts of abrupt changes in one partner should increase the other partner's uncertainty (cf. Kleck, Ono and Hastorf 1966). This is the 'It's-as-if-I-don't-even-know him (her)' syndrome, alternatively labelled the 'He's (She's)-become-a-total-stranger-over-night' syndrome. (These syndromes were skillfully dramatized in both film versions of *The Body Snatchers*, where overnight persons became literally alienated from their partners.)

In the case of dissolving relationships, where neither partner changes abruptly, the answer to the uncertainty question is less clear. Where an affair occurs, and this is a common indicant or cause of relational decay (Bradford 1980), the 'injured' party may experience uncertainty about the partner's behaviour and feelings in this one area while remaining certain about other behaviours and feelings. In most, perhaps all, instances of relational decline, at some point one or both partners will experience uncertainty about the relationship. This should precipitate much information seeking (Berger and Calabrese 1975). Specifically, the uncertain partner will seek information from the other about his or her perceptions of the relationship and will seek information from friends about their relationships for the purpose of social comparison (Festinger 1954). The result of this information seeking will be reduced uncertainty. The information seeker may realize that the relationship is basically sound, that it is like the relationships of others, and that alternative relationships are not more attractive (Thibaut and Kelley 1959). This may throw the relationship, at least temporarily, back to an earlier pre-crisis stage. Contrarily, the information seeker may discover that the relationship is fatally flawed and that he or she must anticipate increasingly dwindling rewards. In either case a decision will be made, and following this self-justifications will be invented (Aronson 1980). For a while, uncertainty will be low.

In addition to much information seeking about the relationship, there may be other communicative manifestations of uncertainty. There may be long periods of silence, the clearest case of this being physical separation which precludes talk. These silences will be difficult and partners will be highly aware of them. Some silences will be strategic as when one partner gives the other the 'silent treatment'. Other silences will be the product of spontaneous ruminations about the relationship. At some point one or both partners may engage in verbal projections of relational death: 'What will become of us when it ends?' They will construct scenarios of what each will do following termination of the relationship. These projections may facilitate decision making and, if they are realistic, they may usefully guide behaviour following the break-up. And, of course, at some point partners will talk about the details of ending the contract, what will be done prior to termination – consulting lawyers, publicizing the dissolution, dividing properties, etc.

Both partners, individually or jointly, will search for explanations of the fracture. From the standpoint of each partner there are four major causal possibilities: Mary sees John as the cause; Mary sees herself as the cause; Mary sees the relationship as precipitating its own destruction ('We were doomed from the start because of our attitudinal differences'); and Mary sees one or more situational factors as the cause ('The lack of money caused us to fight a lot'). The first two explanations are internal and the second two are external. The notion of a 'fundamental attribution error' suggests that each partner as an observer of the other person will be strongly inclined to view the other's behaviour as internally motivated instead of situationally coerced (Sillars 1980a; Nisbett and Ross 1980). This may result in mutual, intensifying character assassination. Indeed there is evidence that persons experiencing marital difficulties are especially likely to see their partner as the causal agent (Harvey, Wells and Alvarez 1978; Orvis, Kelley and Butler 1976). Harvey, Wells and Alvarez (1978) suggest that data from two studies indicate that efforts at explaining relational difficulties are likely to be especially strong following physical separation:

> Our interview and written record data suggest that, if anything, individuals are overly 'mindful' during separation. . . . Our data suggest that these vigilant, restless periods may be filled often with incessant causal analyses. . . . The results of these studies may be interpreted to suggest that there is a complex interplay between behaviour and attribution in the development of conflict and separation in close relationships. . . . (p. 256)

Probably immediately after separation persons will offer explanations to close friends in an attempt to gain support for their interpretation of events. Friends' agreements and elaborations of the interpretation should facilitate uncertainty reduction. It is worth noting that causal explanations to friends or to self demand a digital mode of communication. There is no such thing as an analogic description of a causal pattern. The analogic aspect of language may, however, signal to friends the intensity of one's feelings about the causal relationship.

At this point a reasonable question is: What sorts of causal interpretations are associated with relational termination or with conflict resolution? A recent study by Sillars (1980a) begins to point to an answer. This researcher investigated the attributions made by roommates experiencing conflict. He related these to communication patterns and to roommates' perceptions of degree of conflict resolution and degree of satisfaction with the partner. Subjects' accounts of conflicts with their roommates were coded in terms of three basic categories: 'passive – indirect' conflict resolution strategies, 'distributive' strategies and 'integrative' strategies. The first category included, for example, disregarding the issue, avoiding the person, hinting, and yielding. The second category included demanding, persuading and threatening. The third category included self-disclosure and problem solving. The following pattern is suggested by Sillars's results:

1. Roommates tended to blame their partners for conflicts more than themselves.
2. Attribution of blame to the other was associated with 'passive-indirect' and 'distributive' strategies, whereas attribution of blame to self was associated with 'integrative' strategies.
3. 'Integrative' strategies were associated with a greater likelihood of perceived conflict resolution and greater satisfaction with one's partner than were 'passive-indirect' and 'distributive' strategies.

The implication is that mutual recriminations are associated with communication strategies which inhibit conflict resolution and diminish relational cohesiveness. This pattern is consistent with one obtained by Baxter (1979) in a study of relationship disengagement. Respondents' intentions to disengage from a relationship, which we assume reflected low satisfaction, were associated with the reported use of indirect strategies and with low amounts of self-disclosure.

Finally, two points should be made. First there is a need for much more research on the communicative behaviours occurring in various types of partnerships which are in relational crisis. Because of the paucity of research in this area, many of our suggestions should be taken as highly tentative. Second, to emphasize a point we made previously, our use of terms like 'relational death', 'relational decay', and 'relational decline' should not lead the reader to infer that we are 'pro-relationship', that we view relational dissolution or fracture as a negative outcome. We fully realize that in many cases one or both partners are better off alone than together. Some persons are generally obnoxious and their obnoxiousness is intensified by the presence of others.

Summary

Relational communication was the subject of this chapter. We explored the difficulties of defining relationships and the ways in which persons attempt to do so. Here we considered explicit modes of communication. Controlling messages, on the other hand, were viewed as a kind of implicit communication about relationships. We subsequently examined interpersonal arguments along with verbal indicants and determinants of cohesiveness. We also scrutinized Altman and Taylor's (1973) suggestions regarding forms of communication as a function of relational intimacy. The point was made that long-term partners are free to abbreviate their messages. A high degree of shared knowledge allows these persons to take much for granted. Finally, we touched upon 'fractural' communication. Of special interest was the research on attributions made by partners in a declining, conflict-ridden relationship.

This chapter shows that 'naive scientists' attempt to reduce uncertainty about others throughout the lifespan of a relationship. Uncertainty shifts back and forth from one's uncertainty about the other to one's uncertainty about the relationship. While generally uncertainty decreases as relationships develop, this decrease is not linear. Particular events will cause highly predictable relationships to become suddenly unpredictable. These relational crises are resolved one way or another, and when they are the uncertainty of both partners becomes low once more.

The next chapter concludes this volume. We summarize our overall argument and address some issues which have been lurking in the shadows. We also assume a prophetic stance as we talk about the future of language and social knowledge.

6

Language and social knowledge: conclusion and prospect

Silence is the perfectest herald of joy: I were but little happy, if I could say how much.

Shakespeare

Speech is civilization itself. The word, even the most contradictory word, preserves contact – it is silence which isolates.

Thomas Mann

We can now stand back from the many particular facts and examples we have discussed and highlight certain patterns in the data. We will begin by summarizing the argument made in the preceding five chapters. We will next develop some axioms or basic assumptions which undergird the argument and we will briefly discuss these. This will be followed by a discussion of some issues suggested by the argument and the many studies cited in support of it. Some of the issues have been hinted at or briefly discussed in the previous chapters but here we state them explicitly. Finally, we will talk about the future of research in this area and we will speculate about the future of the phenomena examined in research, i.e. the future of language and interpersonal communication.

The argument recapitulated

We view interpersonal communication as the exchange of analogic and digital messages. These both *cause* relational development (or preclude this development) and at some point *constitute* the relationship fundamentally. Messages exchanged in interpersonal contexts have as their primary function the reduction of mutual uncertainty. Interactants become increasingly capable of explaining or accounting for the behaviour of the other and increasingly capable of accurately predicting the rewards and costs of future interaction. In other words, interactants make 'retroactive' and 'proactive' attributions (Berger 1975) as relationships develop. Thus, interpersonal communicators are 'naive scientists' who make causal attributions about behaviour (Heider 1958).

In a sense these 'naive scientists' conduct both descriptive and experimental research. That is, they assess the behaviour of others unobtrusively, without interference with that behaviour and they manipulate situations for the purpose of observing behavioural consequences. The descriptive technique of knowledge acquisition was previously labelled 'passive', while the experimental approach was designated 'active' and 'interactive'. The primary goal of this

112

interpersonal research is the formulation of hypotheses about internal and external behavioural causes. Of course, the researches of 'naive scientists' are typically highly flawed, biased and non-objective (Nisbett and Ross 1980), and their hypotheses are accordingly frequently erroneous from a scientific standpoint. But these objectively erroneous hypotheses crucially affect the hypothesizer's behaviour toward the object of hypothesis formation.

There are several determinants of internal and external attributions. For example, socially undesirable actions tend to have few alternative explanations and are usually seen as dispositional (Jones and Davis 1965). Or a response which is low in distinctiveness (John says nice things to everybody), low in consensus (nobody else says nice things to John's particular interlocutor, Mary), and high in consistency (John consistently says nice things to Mary) will be seen as indicating something about John's personality rather than about the external stimuli provided by Mary (Kelley 1967). Both internal and external attributions serve to reduce (or in some cases to increase) uncertainty. Thus, if we attribute a particular quality to John (he is a friendly person) and if we have a particular script for dealing with persons exhibiting this quality (Schank and Abelson 1977), our uncertainty should be reduced. Contrarily, if we see John's behaviour as caused by a particular stimulus, say, Mary, and if we know nothing about this stimulus (Mary is a stranger to us and she has no especially distinguishing attribute), our uncertainty about John will *not* be reduced – it may even be increased.

But persons do not ceaselessly search for internal and external causes of others' behaviours. In many situations behaviours are not consciously thought about by 'naive scientists'. This occurs when the behaviours are highly familiar or expected. Such behaviours produce a state of mindlessness (Langer 1978). On the other hand, unexpected and surprising behaviours engage the 'naive scientist's' explanatory apparatus; they produce a state of high vigilance or mindfulness (Pysczynski and Greenberg 1981). The object of a mindful state is typically the behaviour of another person or a situational artefact (a spilled platter of food). But in some cases persons become mindful of themselves, a state which has been labelled 'objective self-awareness' (Duval and Wicklund 1972).

The fact that persons' conscious attention may or may not be focused upon the interactions of which they are a part suggests that one might distinguish between *thoughtful* and *thoughtless* speech (Berger and Roloff 1980). At times, and for various reasons, persons may pay very close attention to what they and their interaction partner are saying and doing in the social situation. At other times, persons may pay minimal attention to their own as well as others' actions in given social situations. Although it is tempting to argue that thoughtful speech is preferable to thoughtless speech, we would contend that many everyday, highly repetitive interaction sequences do not deserve a great deal of our attention. A.N. Whitehead (as cited by Langer 1978, p. 40) has noted,

> It is a profoundly erroneous truism, repeated by all copy-books and by eminent people making speeches, that we should cultivate the habit of thinking of what we are doing. The precise opposite is the case. Civilization advances by extending the number of operations which we can perform without thinking about them. Operations of thought are like cavalry charges in a battle – they are strictly limited in number, they require fresh horses, and must only be made at decisive moments.

The time and energy required for thinking is a relatively scarce resource which should be reserved for important interactions.

Another justification for thoughtless speech concerns the consequences which occur when it is interrupted by thought. In a recent study, Langer and Weinman (1981) asked persons to discuss either a novel or a familiar issue. Some subjects were given time to think about the issue before discussing it while other subjects were not. In addition, a third group of subjects were explicitly told to think about the issue before saying anything. Subjects then recorded their opinions on the issue. Analyses of the tapes revealed that persons who had time to think about the familiar issue or persons who were explicitly encouraged to think about the familiar issue manifested more filled pauses in their speech than did persons who were not given thinking time. By contrast, persons who were given time to think about the novel issue and persons who were explicitly directed to think about the novel issues showed significantly fewer filled pauses in their speech than did persons who were given no such time for thought. Given that filled-pause rates might be one indicator of uncertainty, these findings suggest that when persons have well developed scripts and they are asked to think about their performance of these scripts, they will become uncertain and their performance will be debilitated. The opposite is the case with persons who do not have well developed scripts; thinking will facilitate performance. It is interesting to note that the sports pages of newspapers provide supporting testimony for the potential debilitating effects of thinking about what one is doing. Sports stars who experience slumps in performance frequently attribute their poor showing to the fact that they are thinking too much about what they are doing and not letting their performance 'come naturally'. We would argue that some of the most competent social interactors are those who have to think very little about what they are doing in a given social situation. The performances of such persons are likely to be both fluent and effective when compared with the performances of those who have to monitor closely what they are saying and doing in the situation.

The behavioural object of mindful persons' attention which is of special interest to us is performed language or speech. Speech has an expressive function. It yields information about speakers which 'naive scientists' use in their attempts to reduce uncertainty. Both the analogic and the digital aspects of speech are potentially expressive. Virtually every phonological, semantic, syntactic and pragmatic language variable is capable of conveying information about speakers (Bradac, Bowers and Courtright 1979, 1980). Specifically, research and theory have implicated the following aspects of language in the attribution process: lexical familiarity and goodness, immediacy and intensity, elaboration/restriction and fluency, grammar, powerful/powerless speech, talk and silence patterns, pitch and intonation, phonetic variation, volume and rate, and pragmatic deviation and normalcy. These language variables can cause interactants to search for internal and external explanations of the other's behaviour. For example, low lexical diversity may produce an attribution of low ability and high effort (Bradac, Konsky and Davies 1976). High loudness may produce an attribution of high extroversion (Scherer 1979a). On the other hand, external attributions are produced by particular phonological, lexical and syntactic patterns. 'Dialects' signal membership in various social groups differing in prestige (Giles and Powesland 1975). They may also produce hypotheses about birthplace, family background, and other external determinants of a speaker's behaviour.

In addition to its expressive function, spoken language has referential and persuasive functions. Language is an instrument. People do things with words (Austin 1962). From our standpoint an important fact is that language is crucial to relationship definition. Persons talk about their relationship, often using explicit labels such as 'friend' or 'lover'. Such labels specify rights and obligations of relational partners. Persons also convey their attitudes toward their relationships implicitly through 'controlling' messages (Watzlawick, Beavin and Jackson 1967). Language is also used as an instrument for finding things out about others and for revealing information about self. The prototype of interrogation is the illocutionary act of requesting and this is done politely to avoid violating a regulative rule. When interrogated, persons refer to aspects of their minds and bodies using the lexicon of *psyche* and *soma*. Like interrogations these self-disclosures are subject to regulative rules which specify certain forms and prohibit others. So, for both requesters and revealers the possibilities of reducing uncertainty are limited by culturally mandated constraints. Perlocutionary acts, e.g. persuasion, are important throughout the lifespan of relationships – persons persuade others to reveal information about themselves and they persuade others that a divorce is necessary.

When relationships are formed, communication has as a primary function the maintenance of equilibrium. On the one hand, personal idioms serve to increase unity or cohesiveness (Hopper, Knapp and Scott 1981), as do linguistic forms associated with smooth interaction (Knapp, Ellis and Williams 1980; Krueger, in press; Altman & Taylor 1973). On the other hand, arguments allow individuals to assert their separateness in the context of disagreements; 'genuine arguments' may allow relational partners to disagree without fatal rupture (Piaget 1932; Jacobs and Jackson 1981). Communication is an instrument for maintaining the precarious and necessary tension between the 'I' and the 'we'.

But it is an imperfect instrument in this respect. It often fails, as witnessed by current divorce statistics. When it does fail, speech may become a weapon for inflicting damage upon one's partner. In this case it becomes an instrument for strongly or even viciously asserting the rights of the self over the 'us'. More neutrally, words may become the means for extracting oneself from a relationship which has failed or, less drastically, for altering the relationship before it is irreparably damaged. During relational crises, language spoken to others or to self serves to reduce uncertainty about the relationship. Partners explain the reasons for the problem and they justify courses of action. Following relational termination, uncertainty about the relationship will be low (often approaching zero), but uncertainty about relationships in general or about one's former partner may be high. Again, we must affirm that relational failure may be a highly desirable outcome from the standpoint of one or both partners or from the standpoint of interested third parties.

Thus, our uncertain knowledge of self and other waxes and wanes during the life of a relationship, and spoken language is crucially implicated in the relational ebb and flow. Aspects of our knowledge remain uncertain even after relational death. This necessary incompleteness of interpersonal knowledge is a blessing or a curse, depending upon one's preferences for finality or possibility, for stasis or fluxion.

Although language serves the functions outlined above, it is important to keep in mind that verbal language is but *one source* of information that we have about others. Because educational institutions in many cultures stress the importance of spoken and written language, we tend to become 'word centered' or logocentric. This kind of bias extends to persons who do research concerned with human interaction. For example, research done in the area of impression formation has frequently asked persons to indicate whether or not they like a given 'person' who is represented by a list of adjectives printed on a sheet of paper. This particular manifestation of the 'logocentric fallacy', as the first author has called it, suggests that we may make the mistake of over-attributing the impact that words themselves have upon impression formation. In any social interaction, persons who are sighted have access to large amounts of *visual information* which may have considerable impact upon the kinds of impressions they form about others. In fact, this information can be obtained *without* any verbal interaction whatsoever. Thus, in everyday life, persons may form impressions of others without any direct interaction or verbal exchange with them.

Another manifestation of the logocentric fallacy is the belief that words can fully represent one's experience. We would contend that when persons attempt to talk about their visual worlds, words may not be useful for describing their visual experiences for a variety of reasons. First, the visual experiences themselves may be too complex to describe fully. Second, the language system may not have an adequate lexicon for describing the experience. Third, persons may not be able to translate their visual experiences into a linguistic form; that is, they can 'picture it' but not talk about it. Thus, as we have pointed out, verbal communication has limitations as both a source of information about a person and as a tool of expression. Some domains of social experience are indeed beyond words.

Axioms

In this section we offer and discuss six axioms of language and social knowledge. Here we are using the term 'axiom' to refer to a basic assumption, not to a demonstrated causal relationship between variables (Berger and Calabrese 1975; Blalock 1969). It seems to us that these six axioms must be accepted if one is to accept our overall argument.

Axiom 1: Persons are sometimes aware and sometimes unaware of self, others, and the behaviours of self and others in social interaction.

This is an especially safe axiom, one which is almost undebatable, it seems to us. The only alternative is the claim that persons are *always* aware or *never* aware of self, others and the behaviours of self and others. Awareness fluctuates with various environmental contingencies, e.g. the presence of mirrors (Duval and Wicklund 1972) and unexpected performances (Pysczynski and Greenberg 1981). It also fluctuates with personality. To use extreme examples, paranoids are hyper-aware of particular aspects of their environment, whereas autistic persons seem uniquely unaware of their surroundings. More mundanely, some persons are more vigilant or more introspective than others, as in the cases of Captain Ahab and Hamlet, respectively.

Axiom 2: Fluctuations in awareness of self and others influences both communicative competence and performance in social interaction situations.

As we have pointed out in several places in this volume, levels of self-monitoring and thinking have an impact upon communicative performance. Moreover, these variables help to determine how persons process information about others in their environments, especially persons with whom they will interact. It is important to note with reference to this axiom that increased awareness is not always associated with increased communicative competence. While introductory textbooks in the area of speech communication frequently assert that greater awareness of self and others is likely to give rise to higher quality communication, we contend that the evidence suggests many limitations to this proposition. As we have tried to point out, thinking about self and others may actually interfere with communicative performance when the interaction is routine. By contrast, thinking may improve interactions in novel situations. In short, there is no simple relationship between such variables as awareness or thought and communicative performance.

Axiom 3: Persons see the social world as a product of internal and external forces.

The internal/external distinction is basic to naive thinking and it runs throughout this book (Heider 1958). Internal causes are volitional and appetitive; external causes are coercive. The major alternative to this axiom would argue that society and social behaviour are not subject to forces, that they are not caused. Claimants to this position would argue, furthermore, that the social world arises spontaneously and changes in it occur randomly. Both 'naive' and 'sophisticated' social scientists reject this position, opting instead for some form of causation. But an alternative to causation on the one hand and to randomness on the other is a 'systems' perspective, where characterization of the components of a system and the interrelationships among these components yields a structural explanation which is deemed sufficient (Monge 1973). This perspective seems not to have caught on with 'naive scientists, nor indeed has it caught on with most 'sophisticated' social scientists who are locked into a pre-twentieth-century model of physics with its emphasis on mechanical causation.

Axiom 4: Uncertainty reduction is a powerful drive in the human organism.

We could probably extend this axiom to most non-human organisms as well, if uncertainty is defined as the inability to structure the environment so as to render it predictable. Anticipating environmental changes for the purpose of gaining rewards (eating) and avoiding costs (being eaten) has survival value for individual species and organisms. At any rate, humans desire to know; we seek meaningful patterns even in the face of chaos (Watzlawick 1977). But there may be an optimal level of certainty; complete certainty is stifling (Berlyne 1971; Fiske and Maddi 1961). There is a competing drive for novelty, for exposure to a diverse range of stimuli.

Also, there are differences among persons in the strength of the uncertainty reduction drive. Again to use extreme examples, persons with obsessive–compulsive neuroses are driven to achieve high levels of certainty (Salzman 1968), whereas manic personalities seem driven to bounce impulsively from one novelty to another. More familiarly, clinically 'normal' persons may be driven to seek high certainty in times of stress and to seek high novelty in times of relaxation.

Axiom 5: Spoken language is important to persons in their attempts to reduce interpersonal uncertainty.

Language allows persons to ask questions of others and it allows the others to give information when asked. Language also yields information about others quite apart from their intentions. One can imagine a world in which this axiom does not hold true, but a very bizarre world it would be – a science-fiction world, one which is not *humanly* possible. The inhabitants of this world – we will call it Antilogos – gain information about others exclusively through observing their actions. Accordingly, Antilogians have developed a powerful visual technology for spying upon others at work and play and many counter-devices for blinding spies. Language exists on Antilogia but laws forbid its use in interpersonal contexts. The difficulty of specifying the meaning of 'interpersonal' has led Antilogians to avoid the use of language in all situations in which others are present. However, some Antilogians behave illegally when they feel certain they are not being spied upon: they talk to others, soliciting and revealing information. But talk is not believed. Nonverbal action alone is trusted. In fact, Antilogians assume that utterances bear no correspondence to the utterer's intention. Utterances and intentions are either (1) randomly paired or (2) exactly antithetical so that utterers mean the opposite of what they say. The uncertainty about the true state of affairs regarding intentions and utterances renders talk useless.

Less exotically, there is evidence supporting the axiom, evidence that speech is a potent determinant of inferences about speakers (Triandis, Loh and Levin 1966), although particular situations may predispose interactants to rely more heavily upon other modalities (Scherer, Scherer, Hall and Rosenthal 1977). Also, some interpersonal intentions, e.g. promising, *demand* language for their fulfilment (Searle 1969). Indeed one could not even *have* the intention of promising were it not for language. So, broken promises and promises kept and the reduction or increase of uncertainty which these may produce would not be possible without language.

Axiom 6: Language is a powerful instrument in the creation of social reality.

Language constitutes an aspect of most interpersonal relationships, as in the sexist 'I pronounce you man and wife'. (An ideologically better version is 'I pronounce you persons-related-voluntarily'). Contractual relationships of any kind demand language for their creation. In the social world, saying it makes it so. When we say: 'Let's have a party', 'Let's play cricket', or 'Let's get a divorce', we exploit our knowledge of language and we assume identical linguistic knowledge in our hearer. Parties, games and divorces are invented institutional entities which are defined culturally and symbolically (Searle 1969). A symbolic system is *necessary* to formulate rules such as: A party includes a host (or hosts) and guests; when one is a host, one should assume responsibility for entertainment, food, drink, etc.

This axiom is *not* a version of the Sapir–Whorf hypothesis which asserts, in its strong form, that language determines our perceptions of physical reality (Fishman 1960). *Physical* reality is perceivable without language, as any pet-owner knows. Language facilitates communication about physical distinctions perceived by members of cultural groups. And language may *influence* (as opposed to determine) our perceptions of physical reality; i.e. our knowledge of particular words or concepts may predispose us to attend to certain physical features. We could accept a version of the Sapir–Whorf hypothesis which reads something like: Language influences and sometimes determines our perception of *social* reality. Language may determine our perception of an act which has meaning in a particular institutional context, e.g. when we *see* a *goal* scored in a soccer match instead of a man having merely kicked a ball. Language may influence our perception of other actions, e.g. when we define one person's hitting another in the face as a 'slap' instead of a 'punch'.

Taken together, the axioms picture an organism which is sometimes aware of social phenomena and their causes. This awareness is influenced by language. Awareness is incomplete and accordingly the organism experiences uncertainty which is reduced by using and observing speech and other aspects of the social context.

Issues

For us there are several important, interrelated issues which revolve around the concept of the *validity* or *accuracy* of our knowledge of language and social interaction. In Chapter 3, we suggested that the linguistic stereotypes of 'naive scientists' may be objectively inaccurate and only hazardously applied to the single case. Yet, these stereotypes importantly affect 'naive scientists' judgements of personality and background and importantly affect their behaviours toward those who are stereotyped. So, from the standpoint of 'sophisticated' science, *valid* statements about the consequences of these potentially *invalid* stereotypes can be made. This sort of paradox is at the heart of the study of 'folk psychology' (Heider 1958).

In Chapter 4, we suggested a difficulty in self-presentation which raises another validity issue: if self-reports do not correspond highly to persons' cross-situational behaviours and if these cross-situational behaviours are themselves only weakly associated, what is the truth value of a statement like: 'I am an aggressive person'? Several studies suggest that the validity of self-reports can be influenced by factors related to self-awareness. Pryor, Gibbons, Wicklund, Fazio and Hood (1977) found that persons who were made objectively self-aware gave more accurate self-reports than persons who were not made objectively self-aware. Scheier, Buss and Buss (1978) also found that persons with high levels of private self-consciousness provided more accurate reports of their aggressiveness levels than persons with low levels of private self-consciousness. These findings suggest that persons who are more self-aware are better able to give accurate assessments of their own behaviour. However, even if the statement 'I am aggressive' is objectively inaccurate to some extent, if the revealer *believes* this statement his or her behaviour may be importantly affected. Once again the effect of this sort of erroneous belief can be studied by 'sophisticated scientists'.

The difficulty of self-reports, their possible invalidity, brings us to the problem of validity in 'sophisticated' claims about language and social interaction. Cognitive approaches to social science necessarily exploit the self-report as an essential research tool. Our only access to the 'black box' of social cognition is through the cognizer's reports. To the extent that we are interested in meanings, attitudes, judgements and 'folk' explanations, we have to *ask* respondents about social phenomena. But there are some things we can do to improve the likelihood of high validity.

First, we should recognize that for some kinds of research problems, those where the essential concern is with social cognition *per se*, the problem of validity does not exist as long as our respondents are (1) reliable, i.e. consistent in their statements, and (2) honest. If an honest person consistently claims that X and Y are causally associated, this is a valid statement about his belief, and the structure of this sort of belief may be just what we are interested in.

If, on the other hand, we are interested in the relationship between social cognition and overt behaviour, the validity problem becomes thornier. To the extent that we obtain a high correspondence between cognitions and behaviours – if this is what we are predicting – there is no problem, but: which behaviours should we observe? How many? In which situations? Who should observe? Will the observer alter the situation–behaviour relationship by virtue of his or her mere presence (Zajonc 1965)? There are no easy answers to these questions. Probably usually we should try to make as many theoretically motivated reliable observations as we can in a search for cognitive–behavioral correspondence. We should not *expect* correspondence between those classes of behaviour or classes of situations which our theory claims are *distinct*.

Also, some of the difficulties with self-reports may be minimized if we make as few demands as possible upon our respondents' encoding abilities. Persons may be very poor verbalizers when it somes to distinctions which they consistently make but are typically not aware of. For example, most untutored speakers of English will recognize some kind of difference and some kind of similarity between active and passive sentence forms ('John hit the ball' versus 'The ball was hit by John'), but they will be hard pressed to give a detailed verbal account of just *how* the sentences are both similar and dissimilar. A linguist is in a better position to do this as a result of the explicit lexicon and logic of linguistic theory. Yet it is important to the linguist to obtain information about normal speakers' judgement of similarity and dissimilarity. This can be done simply by having the respondent nod 'yes' or 'no' after listening to sentences. These minimal responses indicating perceived similarity or dissimilarity can then be elaborately interpreted, characterized and explained by the linguist. The same sort of minimal response procedure can be used with non-linguistic stimuli as well, e.g. 'How similar or dissimilar are the following pairs of situations? Hold up one finger if they are very similar and five fingers if they are very dissimilar. Hold up three fingers if they are neither similar nor dissimilar.' The situations are: a party and a funeral (five fingers), a party and a wedding (two fingers), attending a movie and attending a stage play (one finger), etc.

Another issue in the validity of 'sophisticated' research on language and social interaction might be labelled the 'sampling problem'. This is rather different from the 'measurement problem' just discussed. A paradigm case of the 'sampling problem' involves experiments on the effects of language, some of which were cited in the previous chapters. A study might, for example, have subjects rate sentences for language intensity (Greenberg 1976) or for grammaticality (Greenbaum and Quirk 1970). Let us say that the sentence 'The man hit the elephant very hard' is rated both highly intense and grammatical. We infer, perhaps on the bases of our theory, that declarative sentences with subject–verb–object order are grammatical and that sentences with the adjective 'very' preceding other adjectives or adverbs will tend to be judged high in intensity. These are hazardous inferences in this case, because the judgements of grammaticality or intensity may be related to sentence attributes other than the sentence's declarative status and the presence of 'very'. Our one sentence contains other lexical items and exhibits other lexical patterns. Maybe any sentence beginning with the word 'the' will be judged grammatical. Maybe any sentence with the word 'elephant' will be rated as highly intense. Our sentence is a biased sample of the declarative sentences of English and of the English sentences containing 'very'. We simply cannot assert in this case that 'very' and declarative status are causes of judgements of intensity and grammaticality, respectively. In a somewhat different form, this problem has been labelled the 'language-as-fixed-effect' fallacy (Clark 1973; Jackson and Jacobs, in press).

The problem of potentially biased sampling is especially severe in language-effects studies because of the millions of common lexical and syntactic combinations which are possible. But other sorts of non-linguistic stimuli which are judged by research respondents are subject to the same problem, although the magnitude of the problem is perhaps reduced. For example, in studies of judgements of human faces, the inference may be made that beards connote aggression when in fact the researcher has used only a small and biased sample of types of bearded faces. The practical solution is to have respondents judge many objects which exhibit the hypothesized attribute of importance, while exhibiting also as many theoretically irrelevant attributes as possible. If in spite of the confounded irrelevancies, the hypothesized attribute continues to function as predicted, one's confidence in the correctness of the hypothesis increases (Campbell and Stanley 1966).

Related to the problem of sampling, at least indirectly, is that of the nature of the situation in which researchers collect data. At one extreme, we have respondents exposed to taperecorded linguistic stimuli making judgements of communicators along attitude scales (Bradac, Konsky and Davies 1976). At the other extreme, we have researchers observing persons' language behaviour in situations where the speakers are behaving 'naturally', unaware of the observer's presence or research purpose. The former sort of experimental study has the advantages of control over stimuli and precision of measurement and the disadvantage of the special context which is unlike most contexts in which persons respond to language. The latter sort of study has the advantage of contextual typicality and the disadvantages of low control and imprecision. Experiments constitute a biased sample of the research techniques available, as do 'naturalistic' descriptive studies. The best advice here is to increase generalizability of findings by exploiting as many research procedures as possible, using designs which vary in degree of respondent awareness of the research purpose and researcher control (Bowers and Bradac, forthcoming; Campbell and Stanley 1966; Robinson, Giles and Smith, 1980).

While the sampling problem discussed above is one with which 'sophisticated' observers of the social scene must deal, it is also a problem which naive observers must face. In making judgements concerning the 'personality' of another person, observers must establish some kind of informal criteria by which they are willing to evaluate the adequacy of the sample of observations they make in order to form their impressions. For example, if John always talks to Mary about chemistry problems in the dormitory lounge, to what extent does this kind of sample of Mary's behaviour provide John with adequate information upon which to base an impression of Mary? Assume that instead of always talking to Mary in the dormitory lounge about chemistry, John also talks with Mary in a wide variety of different social contexts, e.g. in a pub, at the beach, in church, etc. In all likelihood we would be confident that John's impression of Mary would be more accurate if his impression of her were the product of sampling over a wide variety of situations rather than just one situation.

As we pointed out earlier, many theorists have argued that we all can display a number of different selves; depending upon the particular situation in which we are involved. Thus, in terms of knowledge gaining, it would seem most desirable to sample a person's behaviour across a number of heterogeneous situations *before* forming some kind of impression. Alas, however, the evidence suggests that persons are frequently and inordinately influenced by their *first impressions* of others and that subsequent information which contradicts first impressions is often ignored or discounted (Jones and Goethals 1971). This state of affairs suggests that persons are not very good samplers of others' behaviours and that persons do not generally withhold judgements about others for very long periods of time. It would seem that one crucial educational task would be to develop ways to encourage persons to employ large and diverse samples of others' actions before forming confident impressions of them and to encourage persons to be willing to accept the possibility that the same person can exhibit actions which are contradictory both across different situations and in the same situation at different times. Of course, it is one thing to discuss these problems and potential solutions, but it is quite another to develop educational strategies for producing the necessary changes in persons' knowledge gaining strategies.

A final issue we will raise is of a different sort. Rather obviously, we believe that an important goal is the creation of a valid theory of language and social phenomena. Our book is a step in that direction, we hope, as is the entire series of which this book is a part. But in the past and even currently, the creation of such a theory has been hampered by the unfortunate independence of theorists of language and theorists of society. Important exceptions to this rule exist or have existed, e.g. Cicourel (1973), McGee (1980), Habermas (1979), and George Herbert Mead (1934), but typically social scientists interested in social interaction have paid very little attention to the details of language and, conversely, linguists have paid very little attention to language's essentially social character (cf. Giles 1979b; Hudson 1980). Why this has been and continues to be so need not concern us. The important thing is for students of language and social interaction to become expert in both social theory and linguistics with the purpose of transcending this disciplinary dichotomy. There are several encouraging signs in this respect, e.g. the journal *Language and Social Psychology* was recently established, and some of the best current research on language acquisition and language pragmatics assumes the social basis of language (Olson 1980).

It seems to us that both linguists and social theorists will benefit by a merger. Linguists have various refined theoretical apparatus for uncovering the structure of language. This structure is crucially related to human cognitive processes or 'mind', although the details of this connection are a subject of continuing debate (Elliott 1978). Theorists concerned with social cognitions must understand the linguistic structures which such cognitions exploit. Conversely, the structure of language may be to some extent a product of social interaction (Bruner 1975). Also, linguists' arguments regarding the well-formedness of language structures, which are crucial to linguistic theorizing, are influenced by many social factors including membership in particular theoretical camps and the situation or context in which linguistic structures are scrutinized (Bradac, Martin, Elliot and Tardy 1980; Carroll, Bever and Pollack 1981).

The future of the enterprise

In this concluding section we offer prophecies about research on language and interpersonal communication and about the future of the very phenomena which this research investigates. This final section is the safest for us to write because 'the future' can be taken to be, let us say, 50 years from now when the authors will probably be retired or dead or both, certainly no longer accountable.

First, we will sketch the future of research. Our assumption here is that incipient current trends will continue. Linguists, communication researchers and social psychologists will focus increasingly on messages in context. The long-range goal of this pursuit will be a unified theory of messages. Some researchers will become increasingly phenomenological in their studies, examining the unique constructs which various types of persons impose upon speech in social contexts. The goal here will not be the creation of a catalogue of idosyncracies, but rather a coherent theory of language and social interaction which incorporates the full range of meanings which speech can have. Other researchers will pursue 'hard' behavioural data, examining the ways in which persons respond to language quite apart from how they say they will respond. Behavioural data will be obtained increasingly in 'naturalistic experiments', where respondents are initially unaware of their status as experimental subjects (Cantor 1979; Bourhis, Giles, Leyens and Tajfel 1978; Cialdini and Schroeder 1976). Language-attitude research should benefit greatly from the data which this sort of study will yield. A third group of researchers, who might be labelled 'rules scholars', will explore the details of pragmatic knowledge – the kinds of things which humans have to know in order to construct coherent messages and to coordinate messages in social interaction. A fourth approach has been labelled 'transactional'. Researchers taking this approach will increasingly investigate patterns of message sending in relationships (Courtright, Millar and Rogers-Millar 1979). The transactional perspective will 'look directly at the combinatorial rules characterizing the . . . message-exchange process and not at individual characteristics brought to the situation by . . . individual participants' (Millar and Rogers 1976, p. 90). It will require 'social scientists to look for multiple causes and multiplicative effects, rather than unidimensional and additive cause-effect sequences. [It will necessitate] the development of reciprocal or nonrecursive, as well as recursive models of behaviour' (Millar and Rogers 1976, p. 90).

A fifth approach which is closely related to the 'transactional' approach outlined above concerns the role that interpersonal communication plays in the growth and decline of interpersonal relationships. The beginnings of this approach are represented by the material we have presented in this book. Increasingly, researchers in the areas of social psychology and sociology are becoming interested in the general issue of relationship formation and dissolution from a variety of different theoretical perspectives (Altman and Taylor 1973; Duck 1977; Gilmour and Duck 1980; Levinger and Raush 1977; Burgess and Huston 1979). In contrast to the approach taken in this book, several of these researchers have elected to explain relationship growth and development on the basis of rewards and costs exchanged in the relationship. Simply put, relationships grow to the extent that rewards outweigh costs and deteriorate when costs exceed rewards. We believe that while these social-exchange approaches may explain some aspects of relationship growth and decay, much more could be learned about relational development from the study of communication in developing relationships. As we have pointed out, communication can serve as an *indicator* of relational closeness to the outside observer and may be viewed as an integral part of what it means to have a relationship with another person. We expect that in the future those who are interested in relationship development will turn more of their attention to the issue of the critical role that communication plays in the growth, maintenance and decline of various types of interpersonal relationships.

These approaches are and will be complementary. We believe that it is a mistake and probably will be a mistake in the future to view one or another of the approaches as *the* correct one which must compete with the others for the purpose of annihilating them (cf. McGuire 1980). We hope that both within approaches and across approaches researchers will engage increasingly in programmatic efforts with the goal of constructing higher-order theories with greater and greater scope. Until very recently, research on language and social interaction was plagued by atheoretical, 'bits-and-pieces' studies. This rather sterile activity began to change somewhere around the mid-1970s, happily.

Finally, apart from the pursuit of these different research strategies, new variables will be explored. We cannot get very specific here, but a few possibilities occur to us. The idea of 'metaphor' will be reconceptualized, taken from the Renaissance handbooks of rhetoric and transplanted into an interpersonal context. Researchers will talk of the metaphors which persons live by in the conduct of relationships (Bochner 1978). Lakoff and Johnson (1980) clearly have something like this in mind when they write:

> Metaphor is for most people a device of the poetic imagination and the rhetorical flourish – a matter of extraordinary rather than ordinary language. Moreover, metaphor is typically viewed as characteristic of language alone; a matter of words rather than thought or action. . . . We have found, on the contrary, that metaphor is pervasive in everyday life, not just in language but in thought and action. Our ordinary conceptual system, in terms of which we both think and act, is fundamentally metaphorical in nature. (p. 3)

Another variable which will be examined increasingly is awareness. As we suggested in Chapter 4, this variable is potentially very complex – awareness of awareness of awareness, etc. But it should be extremely useful to examine when and how persons plan communication strategies on the one hand and when and how communicators function 'on automatic pilot' on the other (Berger 1980; Berger and Roloff 1980). The role of awareness in the construction of interpersonal messages has been researched hardly at all, so there is much room for research activity. Quite opposite to this pursuit is the search for factors which affect interpersonal behaviour totally outside of interactants' awareness. Several variables may prove to be important here, e.g. hormonal levels, tidal forces, humidity (Lester 1977), and pheremones or subliminal olfactory stimuli (Hopson 1979).

Moving away from the future research front, what will the phenomena researchers investigate look like 50 years from now? Were we to get specific here, the reader would rightly accuse us of quackery. Language and social forms will change in unspecifiable ways as a result of technological changes which we cannot predict. New words will come into the language to reflect these changes, phonological shifts will occur, etc. But this is obvious and uninteresting. This has always happened. At a more general and more interesting level, we can suggest a few alternative futures which hinge on a set of contingencies. Accordingly, these future worlds will be offered in 'if–then' form:

1. If the future yields more efficient transportation and communication, if this results in increased interchanges among speakers of diverse languages and cultures, and if these interchanges are frequent and widespread, then 'naive scientists' ' cognitive construals of language and social interaction will become increasingly complex and elaborate. The assumption here is that diversity increases complexity. Relatively complex cognitions of language and social interaction will in turn increase the range of communication behaviours in 'naive scientists' ' repertoires (Delia 1977).

2. If the future yields increasingly fewer interchanges among members of diverse cultures (as a result of the increasing expense of various forms of energy, for example) or if one culture and its language achieves virtual hegemony over others, then 'naive scientists' ' construals of language and social interaction will become increasingly simple and their communicative repertoires increasingly restricted. In such a case 'naive scientists' may communicate very efficiently among members of their own group but they will be ill equipped for communication with persons from other cultures.

3. If the knowledge produced by 'sophisticated' research on language and social interaction is increasingly assimilated by 'naive scientists', then 'naive scientists' will become increasingly mindful of their speech and the speech of others. This assumes that explicit knowledge increases awareness of the subject of that knowledge.

4. If 'naive scientists' consciously alter their speech as a result of 'sophisticated' knowledge, then that knowledge will become to some extent invalid. For example, if it is established by 'sophisticated' research that experienced and perceived communication anxiety is directly associated with speech rate, if rate is controllable by anxious speakers, if anxious speakers wish to appear non-anxious, and if they for this reason slow their rate, then the claim of a direct relationship between experienced anxiety and speech rate would become incorrect. But this paradox of knowledge could be transcended in subsequent research with 'sophisticated' researchers seeking distinctions between controlled and uncontrolled speech rates, for example, with the purpose of once again establishing a valid link between speech and experienced anxiety: control

+ slow speech = high anxiety (under conditions X and Y) etc. (cf. Gergen 1973).

5. If doctors, counsellors, teachers, and others in the 'helping' professions become increasingly aware of 'sophisticated' research findings, then the nature of their communication with patients or students will be altered. There are four alternative possibilities here:

(i)   The helper acquires invalid knowledge and has a good purpose, e.g. fostering client autonomy and intelligence. The outcome will be comic or tragic depending upon the details of the scenario. This resembles early 1960s attempts to teach American Black children 'school-talk' English based upon the premise that such children had *no language at all* (!) upon entering school. One could argue that the purpose of teaching Black children 'school-talk' is bad, in which case the example belongs to the next possibility.

(ii)   The 'helper' acquires invalid knowledge and has a bad purpose. The best that can be said about this case is that the 'helper' will probably fail.

(iii) The 'helper' acquires valid knowledge and has a bad purpose. This is the gloomiest possibility. Such a world would see 'helpers' fostering dependency in clients for the 'helpers' ' exclusive benefit using effective manipulative strategies. This sounds a bit like the worst aspects of the 'Madison Avenue' culture of the USA and much of the Western world for that matter.

(iv)   The 'helper' acquires valid knowledge and has a good purpose. The 'helper' succeeds in facilitating client autonomy and intelligence.

The last alternative world is the one which the authors desire, which is not surprising we hope. We want our 'sophisticated' knowledge to be used *by* 'naive scientists' in their everyday lives and *for* 'naive scientists' by 'sophisticated' helpers. We hope that the naive–sophisticated and helper–client distinctions will eventually disappear or at least will *not* indicate different persons but will instead refer to the same person in different situations – sometimes we are helpers, sometimes we are sophisticated, sometimes clients, sometimes naive. The goal of our efforts should be the creation of a climate in which *communicatively competent* individuals will *flourish* (Wiemann 1977; Wiemann and Kelly 1981). Knowledgeable, empathic, creative and autonomous and fostering knowledge, empathy, creativity and autonomy, such individuals will hedge against the gloomy spectre of a society *of* and *for* evil technocrats who largely get their way.

References

AAMOT, S. 1978: Reactions to facial deformities: Autonomic and social psychological. *European Journal of Social Psychology* **8**, 315–33.

ABELSON, R.P. 1976: Script processing in attitude formation and decision making. In Carroll, J.S. and Payne, J.W., editors, *Cognition and social behavior* (Hillsdale, NJ: Lawrence Erlbaum Associates) 33–45.

ADAMS, J.S. 1965: Inequity in social exchange. In Berkowitz, L., editor, *Advances in experimental social psychology* (New York: Academic Press) 267–300.

ALLPORT, G.W. and CANTRIL, H. 1934: Judging personality from voice. *Journal of Social Psychology* **5**, 37–54.

ALTMAN, I. and TAYLOR, D.A. 1973: *Social penetration: The development of interpersonal relationships.* New York: Holt, Rinehart & Winston.

ARISTOTLE. 1932: *The rhetoric.* Cooper, L., translator. New York: Appleton & Co.

ARONSON, E. 1980: Persuasion via self-justification: Large commitments for small rewards. In Festinger, L., editor, *Retrospections on social psychology* (New York: Oxford University Press) 3–21.

AUSTIN, J.L. 1962: *How to do things with words.* Cambridge, Mass.: Harvard University Press.

BADZINSKI, D.M. 1982: *An analytic expansion of talk-silence states.* Unpublished manuscript, University of California, Santa Barbara.

BARNES, B. 1980: *Surfing terminology.* Unpublished manuscript, University of California, Santa Barbara.

BATESON, G. 1958: *Naven*, 2nd edn. Stanford: Stanford University Press.

—1979: *Mind and nature: A necessary unity.* New York: Dutton.

BAUCHNER, J.E., KAPLAN, E.A. and MILLER, G.R. 1980: Detecting deception: The available information to judgmental accuracy in initial encounters. *Human Communication Research* **6**, 253–64.

BAXTER, L.A. 1979: Self-disclosure as a relationship disengagement strategy: An exploratory investigation. *Human Communication Research* **5**, 257–69.

BERGER, C.R. 1973a: Attributional communication, situational involvement, self-esteem and interpersonal attraction. *Journal of Communication* **23**, 284–305.

—1973b: The acquaintance process revisited: Explorations in initial interaction. Paper presented at the annual convention of the Speech Communication Association, New York, November.

—1975: Proactive and retroactive attribution processes in interpersonal communications. *Human Communication Research* **2**, 33–50.

—1980: Self-consciousness and the study of interpersonal interaction: Approaches and issues. In Giles, H., Robinson, W.P. and Smith, P., editors, *Language: Social psychological perspectives* (Oxford: Pergamon Press) 49–53.

BERGER, C.R. and CALABRESE, R.J. 1975: Some explorations in initial interaction and beyond: Toward a developmental theory of interpersonal communication. *Human Communication Research* **1**, 99–112.

BERGER, C.R. and DOUGLAS, W. 1981: Studies in interpersonal epistemology III: Anticipated interaction, self-monitoring, and observational context selection. *Communication Monographs* **48**, 183–96.

BERGER, C.R., GARDNER, R.R., CLATTERBUCK, G.W. and SCHULMAN, L.S. 1976: Perceptions of information sequencing in relationship development. *Human Communication Research* **3**, 29–46.

BERGER, C.R., GARDNER, R.R., PARKS, M.R., SCHULMAN, L. and MILLER, G.R. 1976: Interpersonal epistemology and interpersonal communication. In Miller, G.R., editor, *Explorations in interpersonal communication* (Beverly Hills: Sage Publications) 149–71.

BERGER, C.R. and PERKINS, J.W. 1978: Studies in interpersonal epistemology I: Situational attributes in observational context selection. In Ruben, B.D., editor, *Communication yearbook II* (New Brunswick, NJ: Transaction Press) 171–84.

—1979: Studies in interpersonal epistemology II: Self-monitoring, involvement, facial affect, similarity and observational context selection. Paper presented at the annual convention of the Speech Communication Association, San Antonio, Texas, November.

BERGER, C.R. and ROLOFF, M.E. 1980: Social cognition, self-awareness in interpersonal communication. In Dervin, B. and Voigt, M., editors, *Progress in communication sciences: Volume 2* (Norwood, NJ: ABLEX Publishing Corporation) 1–49.

BERGER, C.R., WEBER, M.D., MUNLEY, M.E. and DIXON, J.T. 1977: Interpersonal relationship levels and interpersonal attraction. In Ruben, B.D., editor, *Communication yearbook I* (New Brunswick, NJ: Transaction Press) 245–361.

—1980: Interpersonal relationship levels and interpersonal attraction. In Morse, B.W. and Phelps, L.A., editors, *Interpersonal communication: A relational perspective* (Minneapolis, Minn.: Burgess Publishing Company) 132–50.

BERLYNE, D. 1971: *Psychobiology and aesthetics.* New York: Appleton-Century Crofts.

BERNSTEIN, B. 1971: *Class, codes, and control.* Vols. 1, 2. London: Routledge & Kegan Paul.

BERSCHEID, E., DION, K.K., WALSTER, E. and WALSTER, G.W. 1971: Physical attractiveness and dating choice: A test of the matching hypothesis. *Journal of Experimental Social Psychology* **7**, 173–89.

BERSCHEID, E., GRAZIANO, W., MONSON, T. and DERMER, M. 1976: Outcome dependency: Attention, attribution, and attraction. *Journal of Personality and Social Psychology* **34**, 978–89.

BERSCHEID, E. and WALSTER, E.E. 1974: Physical attractiveness. In Berkowitz, L., editor, *Advances in experimental social psychology* (New York Academic Press).

BISHOP, G.D. 1979: Perceived similarity in interracial attitudes: The effects of belief and dialect style. *Journal of Applied Social Psychology* **9**, 446-65.

BLAKAR, R.M. in press: Towards a theory of communication in terms of preconditions: A conceptual framework and some empirical explorations. In Giles, H. and St Claire, R., editors, *Language and the paradigms of social psychology* (Hillsdale, NJ: Lawrence Erlbaum Associates).

BLALOCK, H.M. 1969: *Theory construction: From verbal to mathematical formulations*. Englewood Cliffs, NJ: Prentice-Hall.

BLAU, P. 1964: *Exchange and power in social life*. New York: Wiley.

BOCHNER, A. 1978: On taking ourselves seriously: An analysis of some persistent problems and promising directions in interpersonal research. *Human Communication Research* **4**, 179-91.

BOURHIS, R.Y. and GILES, H. 1977: The language of intergroup distinctiveness. In Giles, H., editor, *Language, ethnicity, and intergroup relations* (London: Academic Press).

BOURHIS, R.Y., GILES, H., LEYENS, J.P. and TAJFEL, H. 1978: Psycholinguistic distinctiveness: Language divergence in Belgium. In Giles, H. and St Clair, R.N., editors, *Language and social psychology* (Baltimore: University Park Press) 158-85.

BOURHIS, R.Y., GILES, H. and TAJFEL, H. 1973: Language as a determinant of Welsh identity. *European Journal of Social Psychology* **3**, 447-60.

BOWER, G.H., BLACK, J.B. and TURNER, T.J. 1979: Scripts in memory for text. *Cognitive Psychology* **11**, 177-220.

BOWERS, J.W. 1963: Language intensity, social introversion, and attitude change. *Speech Monographs* 30, 345-52.

—1974: Editor's introductions: Beyond threats and promises. *Speech Monographs* **41**, ix-xi.

BOWERS, J.W. and BRADAC, J.J. forthcoming: Contemporary problems in human communication theory. In Arnold, C.C. and Bowers, J.W., editors, *Handbook of rhetorical and communication theory* (Boston: Allyn & Bacon).

BOWERS, K.S. 1973: Situationism in psychology: An analysis and critique. *Psychological Review* **80**, 307-36.

BRADAC, J.J. in press: A rose by another name: Attitudinal consequences of lexical variation. In Ryan, E.B. and Giles, H., editors, *Language attitudes: Social and applied contexts* (London: Edward Arnold).

BRADAC, J.J., BOWERS, J.W. and COURTRIGHT, J.A. 1979: Three language variables in communication research: Intensity, immediacy, and diversity. *Human Communication Research* **5**, 257-69.

—1980: Lexical variations in intensity, immediacy, and diversity: An axiomatic theory and causal model. In St Clair, R.N. and Giles, H., editors, *The social and psychological contexts of language* (Hillsdale, NJ: Lawrence Erlbaum Associates) 193-223.

BRADAC, J.J., COURTRIGHT, J.A. and BOWERS, J.W. 1980: Effects of intensity, immediacy, and diversity upon receiver attitudes toward a belief-discrepant message and its source. In Giles, H., Robinson, W.P. and Smith, P., editors, *Language: Social psychological perspectives* (Oxford: Pergamon Press)

217–21.

BRADAC, J.J., COURTRIGHT, J.A., SCHMIDT, G. and DAVIES, R.A. 1976: The effects of perceived status and linguistic diversity upon judgments of speaker attributes and message effectiveness. *Journal of Psychology* **93**, 213–20.

BRADAC, J.J., DAVIES, R.A. and COURTRIGHT, J.A. 1977: The role of prior message context in evaluative judgments of high- and low-diversity messages. *Language and Speech* **20**, 295–307.

BRADAC, J.J., DAVIES, R.A., COURTRIGHT, J.A., DESMOND, R.J. and MURDOCK, J.I. 1977: Richness of vocabulary: An attributional analysis. *Psychological Reports* **41**, 1131-4.

BRADAC, J.J., DESMOND, R.J. and MURDOCK, J.I. 1977: Diversity and density: Lexically determined evaluative and information consequences of linguistic complexity. *Communication Monographs* **44**, 273–83.

BRADAC, J.J., HEMPHILL, M.R. and TARDY, C.H. 1981: Language style on trial: Effects of 'powerful' and 'powerless' speech upon judgements of victims and villains. *Western Journal of Speech Communication* **45**, 327–41.

BRADAC, J.J., HOSMAN, L.A. and TARDY, C.H. 1978: Reciprocal disclosures and language intensity: Attributional consequences. *Communication Monographs* **45**, 1–17.

BRADAC, J.J., KONSKY, C.W. and DAVIES, R.A. 1976: Two studies of the effects of linguistic diversity upon judgements of communicator attributes and message effectiveness. *Communication Monographs* **43**, 70–9.

BRADAC, J.J., MARTIN, L.W., ELLIOTT, N.D. and TARDY, C.H. 1980: On the neglected side of linguistic science: Multivariate studies of sentence judgement. *Linguistics: An International Journal for the Language Sciences* **18**, 967–95.

BRADAC, J.J., SANDELL, K.I. and WENNER, L.A. 1979: The phenomenology of evidence: Information-source utility in decision making. *Communication Quarterly* **27**, 35–46.

BRADAC, J.J., SCHNEIDER, M.J., HEMPHILL, M.R. and TARDY, C.H. 1980: Consequences of language intensity and compliance-gaining strategies in an initial heterosexual encounter. In Giles, H., Robinson, W.P. and Smith, P., editors, *Language: Social psychological perspectives* (Oxford: Pergamon Press) 71–6.

BRADAC, J.J., TARDY, C.H. and HOSMAN, L.A. 1980: Disclosure styles and a hint at their genesis. *Human Communication Research* **6**, 228–38.

BRADFORD, L. 1980: The death of a dyad. In Morse, B.W. and Phelps, L.A., editors, *Interpersonal communication: A relational perspective* (Minneapolis, Minn.: Burgess Publishing Company) 497–508

BRADLEY, P.H. 1981: The folk-linguistics of women's speech: An empirical examination. *Communication Monographs* **48**, 73–90.

BROMLEY, D.B. 1977: *Personality description in ordinary language.* New York: John Wiley.

BROUWER, D., GERRITSEN, M. and DEHAAN, D. 1979: Speech differences between women and men: On the wrong track? *Language in Society* **8**, 33–50.

BROWN, B.L. 1980: Effects of speech rate on personality attributions and competency evaluations. In Giles, H., Robinson, W.P. and Smith, P.M., editors, *Language: Social psychological perspectives* (Oxford: Pergamon Press)   293–300.

BROWN, P. and FRASER, C. 1979: Speech as a marker of situation. In Scherer, K.R. and Giles, H., editors, *Social markers in speech* (Cambridge: Cambridge University Press) 33–62.

BROWN, R. 1978: A new paradigm of reference. In Miller, G.A. and Lenneberg, E., editors, *Psychology and biology of language and thought: Essays in honor of Eric Lenneberg* (New York: Academic Press) 151–66.

BRUNER, J.S. 1975: The ontogenesis of speech acts: *Journal of Child Language* **2**, 1–19.

BURGESS, R.L. and HUSTON, T.L. 1979: *Social exchange in developing relationships*. New York: Academic Press.

BURGOON, M., JONES, S.B. and STEWART, D. 1975: Toward a message-centered theory of persuasion: Three empirical investigations of language intensity. *Human Communication Research* **1**, 240–56.

CAIN, W.S. 1981: Educating your nose. *Psychology Today* **15**, 48–56.

CALABRESE, R.J. 1975: *The effects of privacy and probability of future interaction on initial interaction patterns*. Unpublished doctoral dissertation, Department of Communication Studies, Northwestern University, Evanston, Illinois.

CAMPBELL, D.T. and STANLEY, J.C. 1966: *Experimental and quasi-experimental designs for research*. Chicago: Rand McNally.

CANTOR, J.R. 1979: Grammatical variations in persuasion: Effectiveness of four forms of request in door-to-door solicitations for funds. *Communication Monographs* **46**, 296–305.

CAPPELLA, J.N. 1979: Talk-silence sequences in informal conversations I. *Human Communication Research* **6**, 3–17.

—1980: Talk and silence sequences in informal conversations II. *Human Communication Research* **6**, 130–45.

CARROLL, J.M., BEVER, T.G. and POLLACK, C.R. 1981: The non-uniqueness of linguistic intuitions. *Language* **57**, 368–83.

CARTRIGHT, D. and ZANDER, A. 1968: *Group dynamics*, 3rd edn. New York: Harper & Row.

CHAIKIN, A.L. and DERLEGA, V.J. 1974: Liking for the norm-breaker in self-disclosure. *Journal of Personality* **42**, 117–29.

CHIESI, H.L., SPILICH, G.J. and VOSS, J.F. 1979: Acquisition of domain-related information in relation to high and low domain knowledge. *Journal of Verbal Learning and Verbal Behavior* **18**, 257–73.

CHOMSKY, N. 1965: *Aspects of the theory of syntax*. Cambridge, Mass.: MIT Press.

CIALDINI, R.B. and SCHROEDER, D.A. 1976: Increasing compliance by legitimizing paltry contributions: When even a penny will help. *Journal of Personality and Social Psychology* **34**, 599–604.

CICOUREL, A.W. 1973: *Cognitive sociology*. Harmondsworth: Penguin Education.

CLARK, H.H. 1973: The language-as-fixed-effect fallacy: A critique of language statistics in psychological research. *Journal of Verbal Learning and Verbal Behavior* **12**, 335–59.

CLATTERBUCK, G.W. 1979: Attributional confidence and uncertainty in initial interaction. *Human Communication Research* **5**, 147–57.

CLINE, R. and JOHNSON, B. McD. 1976: The verbal stare: Focus of attention in conversation. *Communication Monographs* **43**, 1–10.

COHEN, M.M. and SAINE, T.J. 1977: The role of profanity and sex variables in interpersonal impression formation. *Journal of Applied Communications Research* **5**, 45–51.

COURTRIGHT, J.A., MILLAR, F.E. and ROGERS-MILLAR, L.E. 1979: Domi neeringness and dominance: Replication and extension. *Communication Monographs* **46**, 179–92.

DANCE, F.E.X. and LARSON, C.E. 1976: *The functions of human communication: A theoretical approach*. New York: Holt, Rinehart & Winston.

DELIA, J.G. 1972: Dialects and the effects of stereotypes on interpersonal attraction and cognition processes in impression formation. *Quarterly Journal of Speech* **58**, 285–97.

—1976: A constructivist analysis of the concept of credibility. *Quarterly Journal of Speech* **62**, 361–75.

—1977: Constructivism and the study of human communication. *Quarterly Journal of Speech* **63**, 66-83.

DE SAUSSURE, F. 1966: *Course in general linguistics*. Baskin, W., translator. New York: McGraw-Hill.

DICKSON-MARKMAN, F. and WHEELESS, V.E. 1980: Toward a delineation of friendship types. Paper presented at the meeting of the Speech Communication Association, New York.

DRAKE, G.F. 1980: The social role of slang. In Giles, H., Robinson, W.P. and Smith, P., editors, *Language: Social psychological perspectives* (Oxford: Pergamon Press) 63–70.

DUCK, S.W. 1973: Personality similarity and friendship choice: Similarity of what, when? *Journal of Personality* **41**, 543–58.

DUCK, S. 1977: *Theory and practice in interpersonal attraction*. London: Academic Press.

DUNCAN, H.D. 1962: *Communication and social order*. New York: The Bedminster Press.

DUNCAN, J.R., SJ 1973: Toward a grammar for dyadic conversation. *Semiotica* **9**, 29–46.

DUVAL, S. and WICKLUND, R.A. 1972: *A theory of objective self-awareness*. New York: Academic Press.

DUVAL, S., WICKLUND, R.A. and FINE, R.L. 1971: Cited in Duval, S. and Wicklund, R.A. 1972: *A theory of objective self-awareness* (New York: Academic Press) 16–21.

EBBESEN, E. 1980: Cognitive processes in understanding ongoing behavior. In Hastie, R., Ostrom, T.M., Ebbesen, E., Wyer, R.S., Hamilton, D.L. and Carlston, D.E., editors, *Person memory: The cognitive basis of social perception* (Hillsdale, NJ: Lawrence Erlbaum Associates).

EHRLICH, H.J. and GRAEVEN, D.B. 1971: Reciprocal self-disclosure in a dyad. *Journal of Experimental Social Psychology* **7**, 389–400.

EISER, J.R. and PANCER, S.M. 1979: Attitudinal effects of the use of evaluatively biased language. *European Journal of Social Psychology* **9**, 39–47.

EKMAN, P. 1975: *Unmasking the face: A guide to recognizing emotions from facial clues*. Englewood Cliffs, NJ: Prentice-Hall.

EKMAN, P. and FRIESEN, W. 1969: Nonverbal leakage and clues to deception. *Psychiatry* **63**, 88–106.

ELLIOTT, G.C. 1979: Some effects of deception and level of self-monitoring on planning and reacting to self-presentation. *Journal of Personality and Social Psychology* **37**, 1282–92.

ELLIOTT, N.D. 1978: *The general relationship between language and cognition in the developing child*. Unpublished doctoral dissertation, University of Iowa.

EMLER, N. and FISHER, S. 1981: Gossip and the nature of the social environment. Paper presented at the meeting of the British Psychological Society's Social Psychological Section. Oxford.

ENZLE, M.E., HARVEY, M.D. and WRIGHT, E.F. 1980: Personalism and distinctiveness. *Journal of Personality and Social Psychology* **39**, 542–52.

ERICKSON, B., LIND, A.E., JOHNSON, B.C. and O'BARR, W.M. 1978: Speech style and impression formation in a court setting: The effects of 'powerful' and 'powerless' speech. *Journal of Experimental Social Psychology* **14**, 266–79.

ERVIN-TRIPP, S. 1980: Speech acts, social meaning and social learning. In Giles, H., Robinson, W.P. and Smith, P.M., editors, *Language: Social Psychological perspectives* (Oxford: Pergamon Press) 389–96.

FALBO, T. 1977: Multidimensional scaling of power strategies. *Journal of Personality and Social Psychology* **35**, 537–47.

FEATHER, N.T. 1969: Attribution of responsibility and valence of success and failure in relation to initial confidence and task performance. *Journal of Personality and Social Psychology* **13**, 129–44.

FEATHER, N.T. and SIMON, J.G. 1971: Attribution of responsibility and valence of outcome in relation to confidence and success and failure of self and other. *Journal of Personality and Social Psychology* **18**, 173–88.

FENIGSTEIN, A. 1979: Self-consciousness, self-attention, and social interaction. *Journal of Personality and Social Psychology* **37**, 75–86.

FENIGSTEIN, A., SCHEIER, M.F., and BUSS, A.H. 1975: Public and private self-consciousness: Assessment and theory. *Journal of Consulting and Clinical Psychology* **43**, 522–7.

FESTINGER, L. 1954: A theory of social comparison processes. *Human Relations* **7**, 117–40.

—1957: *A theory of cognitive dissonance*. Evanston, Ill.: Row, Peterson.

FISHMAN, J.A. 1960: A systematization of the Whorfian hypothesis. *Behavioral Science* **5**, 323–9.

FISHMAN, P.M. 1980: Conversational insecurity. In Giles, H., Robinson, W.P. and Smith, P.M., editors, *Language: Social psychological perspectives* (Oxford: Pergamon Press) 127–32.

FISKE, D.W. and MADDI, S.R. 1961: *Functions of varied experience*. Homewood, Ill.: Dorsey Press.

FITZPATRICK, M.A. and BEST, P. 1979: Dyadic adjustment in relational types: Consensus, cohesion, affectional expression, and satisfaction in enduring relationships. *Communication Monographs* **46**, 167–78.

FORGAS, J. 1975: The perception of social episodes: Categorical and dimensional representations in two different social milieus. *Journal of Personality and Social Psychology* **34**, 199–209.

—1978a: Social episodes and social structure in an academic setting: The social environment of an intact group. *Journal of Experimental Social Psychology* **14**, 434–48.

—1978b: The effects of behavioural and cultural expectation cues on the perception of social episodes. *European Journal of Social Psychology* **8**, 203–13.

GEIZER, R.S., RARICK, D.L. and SOLDOW, G.F. 1977: Deception and judgement accuracy: A study in person perception. *Personality and Social Psychology Bulletin* **3**, 446–9.

GERGEN, K.J. 1973: Social psychology as history. *Journal of Personality and Social Psychology* **26**, 309–20.

GILBERT, S.J. and HORENSTEIN, D. 1975: The dyadic effects of self-disclosure: Level versus valence. *Human Communication Research* **1**, 316–22.

GILES, H. 1977: The social context of speech: A social psychological perspective. *ITL: A Review of Applied Linguistics* **35**, 27–42.

—1979a: Ethnicity markers in speech. In Scherer, K.R. and Giles, H., editors, *Social markers in speech* (Cambridge: Cambridge University Press) 251–89.

—1979b: Sociolinguistics and social psychology: An introductory essay. In Giles, H. and St Clair, R.N., editors, *Language and social psychology* (Baltimore: University Park Press) 1–20.

GILES, H., HEWSTONE, M. and ST CLAIR, R.N. in press: Cognitive structures and a social psychology of communication, new integrative models and an introductory overview. In Giles, H. and St Clair, R.N., editors, *The social psychological significance of communication* (Hillsdale, NJ: Lawrence Erlbaum Associates).

GILES, H. and POWESLAND, P.F. 1975: *Speech style and social evaluation*. New York: Academic Press.

GILES, H., SCHERER, K.R. and TAYLOR, D.M. 1979: Speech markers in social interaction. In Giles, H. and Scherer, K.R., editors, *Social markers in speech* (Cambridge: Cambridge University Press) 343–81.

GILES, H. and SMITH, P.M. 1979: Accommodation theory: Optimal levels of convergence. In Giles, H. and St Clair, R.N., editors, *Language and social psychology* (Baltimore: University Park Press) 45–65.

GILES, H., WILSON, P. and CONWAY, T. 1981: Accent and lexical diversity as determinants of impression formation and employment selection. *Language Sciences* **3**, 91–103.

GILMOUR, R. and DUCK, S., editors, 1980: *The development of social psychology*. London: Academic Press.

GOFFMAN, E. 1959: *The presentation of self in everyday life*. Garden City, NY: Doubleday, Inc.

GOOD, C. 1979: Language as social activity: Negotiating conversation. *Journal of Pragmatics* **3**, 151–67.

GOULDNER, A.W. 1960: The norm of reciprocity: A preliminary statement. *American Sociological Review* **25**, 161–78.

GRAESSER, A.C., GORDON, S.E. and SAWYER, J.D. 1979: Recognition memory for typical and atypical actions in scripted activities: Tests of the script pointer + tag hypothesis. *Journal of Verbal Learning and Verbal Behavior* **18**, 319–32.

GREENBAUM, S. and QUIRK, R. 1970: *Elicitation experiments in English: Linguistic studies in use and attitude*. Coral Gables, FL: University of Miami Press.

GREENBERG, B.S. 1976: The effects of language intensity modification on perceived verbal aggressiveness. *Communication Monographs* **43**, 130–9.

HABERMAS, J. 1979: *Communication and the evolution of society*. Translated and introduced by McCarthy, T. Boston: Beacon Press.

HALL, E.T. 1959: *The silent language*. Garden City, NY: Doubleday.

—1966: *The hidden dimension*. Garden City, NY: Doubleday.

HARVEY, J.H., WELLS, G.L. and ALVAREZ, M.D. 1978: Attribution in the context of conflict and separation in close relationships. In Harvey, J.H., Ickes, W. and Kidd, R.F., editors, *New directions in attribution research: Volume 2* (Hillsdale, NJ: Lawrence Erlbaum Associates) 235–60.

HARVEY, J.H., YARKIN, K.L., LIGHTNER, J.M. and TOWN, J.P. 1980: Unsolicited interpretation and recall of interpersonal events. *Journal of Personality and Social Psychology* **38**, 551–68.

HEIDER, F. 1958: *The psychology of interpersonal relations*. New York: John Wiley.

HELFRICH, H. 1979: Age markers in speech. In Scherer, K.R. and Giles, H., editors, *Social markers in speech* (Cambridge: Cambridge University Press) 63–107.

HESS, A.K. and GOSSETT, D. 1974: Nixon and the media: A study of non-immediacy in newspaper editorials as reflective of geographical attitude differences. *Psychological Reports* **34**, 1055–8.

HEWES, D.E. and HAIGHT, L. 1979: The cross-situational consistency of communicative behaviors: A preliminary investigation. *Communication Research* **6**, 243–70.

HEWSTONE, M. and JASPARS, J. in press: Social dimensions of attribution: A European perspective. In Tajfel, H., editor, *The social dimension: European developments in social psychology* (Cambridge/Paris: Cambridge University Press/Maison des Sciences de l'Homme)

HOCKETT, C. 1960: The origin of speech. *Scientific American* **203**, 88–96.

HOMANS, G. 1950: *The human group*. New York: Harcourt, Brace.

HOMANS, G.C. 1961: *Social behavior: Its elementary forms*. New York: Harcourt Brace Jovanovich.

HOPPER, R. 1981: The taken-for-granted. *Human Communication Research* **7**, 195–211.

HOPPER, R., KNAPP, M.L. and SCOTT, L. 1981: Couples' personal idioms: Exploring intimate talk. *Journal of Communication* **31**, 23–33.

HOPSON, J.L. 1979: Scent and human behavior: Olfaction or fiction? *Science News* **115**, 282–3.

HOSMAN, L.A. 1978: *Communication competence: Adults' understanding of direct and indirect speech acts*. Unpublished doctoral dissertation, University of Iowa.

HOVLAND, C.I., JANIS, I.L. and KELLEY, H.H. 1953: *Communication and persuasion*. New Haven, Conn.: Yale University Press.

HUDSON, R.A. 1980: *Sociolinguistics*. Cambridge: Cambridge University Press.

ICKES, W. and WICKLUND, R.A. 1971: Cited in Duval, S. and Wicklund, R.A. 1972: *A theory of objective self-awareness* (New York: Academic Press) 24–7.

JACKSON, S. and JACOBS, S. in press: Generalizing about messages: Suggestions for design and analysis of experiments. *Human Communication Research*.

JACOBS, S. and JACKSON, S. 1981: Argument as a natural category: The routine grounds for arguing in conversation. *The Western Journal of Speech Communication* **45**, 118–32.

JAKOBSON, R. 1972: Verbal communication. *Scientific American* **227**, 72–80.

JAMES, W. 1892: *Psychology: The briefer course*. New York: Henry Holt.

JOHNSON, T.J., FEIGENBAUM, R. and WEIBEY, M. 1964: Some determinants and consequences of the teacher's perception of causality. *Journal of Educational Psychology* **55**, 237–46.

JONES, E.E. 1964: *Ingratiation: A social psychological analysis*. New York: Appleton-Century-Crofts.

JONES, E.E. and DAVIS, K.E. 1965: From acts to dispositions: The attribution process in person perception. In Berkowitz, L., editor, *Advances in experimental social psychology* (New York: Academic Press) 219–66.

JONES, E.E. and GOETHALS, G.R. 1972: Order effects in impression formation: Attribution context and the nature of the entity. In Jones, E.E., Kanouse, D.E., Kelley, H.H., Nisbett, R.E., Valins, S. and Weiner, B., editors, *Attribution: Perceiving the causes of behavior* (Morristown, NJ: General Learning Press) 27–46.

JONES, E.E. and NISBETT, R.E. 1971: *The actor and the observer: Divergent perceptions of the causes of behavior*. Morristown, NJ: General Learning Press.

JOOS, M. 1967: *The five clocks*. New York: Harcourt, Brace & World.

JOURARD, S. 1971: *Self-disclosure: An experimental analysis of the transparent self*. New York: John Wiley.

JOURARD, S.M. and LASAKOW, P. 1958: Some factors in self-disclosure. *Journal of Abnormal and Social Psychology* **56**, 91–8.

KANOUSE, D.E. 1971: *Language, labeling and attribution*. Morristown, NJ: General Learning Press.

KANOUSE, D.E. and HANSON, L.R. 1971: *Negativity in evaluations*. Morristown, NJ: General Learning Press.

KASL, W.V. and MAHL, G.F. 1965: The relationship of disturbances and hesitations in spontaneous speech to anxiety. *Journal of Personality and Social Psychology* **1**, 425–33.

KAY, P. and McDANIEL, G. 1979: On the logic of variable rules. *Language in Society* **8**, 151–87.

KELLEY, H.H. 1967: Attribution theory in social psychology. In Levine, D., editor, *Nebraska symposium on motivation* (Lincoln, Nebraska: University of Nebraska Press).

—1971: *Attribution in social interaction*. Morristown, NJ: General Learning Press.

—1972: *Causal schemata and the attribution process*. Morristown, NJ: General Learning Press.

—1979: *Personal relationships: Their structures and processes*. Hillsdale, NJ: Lawrence Erlbaum Associates.

KELLY, G.A. 1955: *The psychology of personal constructs*, Vol. 1 and 2. New York: Academic Press.

KELVIN, P. 1977: Predictability, power and vulnerability in interpersonal attraction. In Duck, S., editor, *Theory and practice in interpersonal attraction* (London: Academic Press) 355–78.

KIESLER, C.A. 1969: Group pressure and conformity. In Mills, J., editor, *Advanced experimental social psychology* (New York: Macmillan).

KIESLER, C.A., KIESLER, S.B. and PALLAK, M.S. 1967: The effects of commitment to future interaction on reactions to norm violators. *Journal of Personality* **35**, 585–99.

KING, R.G. 1979: *Fundamentals of human communication*. New York: Macmillan.

KLECK, R., ONO, H. and HASTORF, A.H. 1966: The effects of physical deviance upon face-to-face interaction. *Human Relations* **19**, 425–36.

KLIMA, E.S. and BELLUGI, U. 1976: Poetry and song in a language without sound. *Cognition* **4**, 45–97.

KNAPP, M.L. 1978: *Social intercourse: From greeting to goodbye*. Boston, Mass.: Allyn & Bacon, Inc.

KNAPP, M.L., ELLIS, D.G. and WILLIAMS, B.A. 1980: Perceptions of communication behavior associated with relational terms. *Communication Monographs* **47**, 262–78.

KNAPP, M., HART, R. and DENNIS, H. 1974: An exploration of deception as a communication construct. *Human Communication Research* **1**, 15–29

KRUEGER, D. in press: Marital decision-making: A language-action analysis. *Quarterly Journal of Speech*.

LABOV, W. 1969a: Contraction, deletion, and the inherent variability of the English copula. *Language* **45**, 715–62.

—1969b: *The social stratification of English in New York City*. Washington, DC: Center for Applied Linguistics.

—1969c: The logic of nonstandard English. *Monograph Series on Language and Linguistics* (Washington, DC: Georgetown University) **22**, 1–31.

LAING, R.D. 1969: *The politics of the family*. New York: Random House.

LAING, R.D., PHILLIPSON, H. and LEE, A.R. 1966: *Interpersonal perception*: *A theory and a method of research*. London: Tavistock.

LAKOFF, R. 1975: *Language and woman's place*. New York: Harper & Row.

LAKOFF, G. and JOHNSON, M. 1980: *Metaphors we live by*. Chicago: The University of Chicago Press.

LANDERS, A. 1979: Ann Landers. *Hattiesburg American*, September 1.

—1981: Ann Landers. *Santa Barbara News Press*, June 28.

LANGER, E.J. 1978: Rethinking the role of thought in social interaction. In Harvey, J.H., Ickes, W.J. and Kidd, R.F., editors, *New directions in attribution research: Volume 2* (Hillsdale, NJ: Lawrence Erlbaum Associates) 35–58.

LANGER, E.J., BLANK, A. and CHANOWITZ, B. 1978: The mindlessness of ostensibly thoughtful action: The role of 'placebic' information in interpersonal interaction. *Journal of Personality and Social Psychology* **36**, 635–42.

LANGER, E.J. and WEINMAN, C. 1981: When thinking disrupts performance: Mindfulness on an overlearned task. *Personality and Social Psychology Bulletin* **7**, 240–3.

LARSEN, K.S., MARTIN, H.J. and GILES, H. 1977: Anticipated social cost and interpersonal accomodation. *Human Communication Research* **3**, 303–8.

LAVER, J. and TRUDGILL, P. 1979: Phonetic and linguistic markers in speech. In Scherer, K.R. and Giles, H., editors, *Social markers in speech* (Cambridge: Cambridge University Press) 1–32.

LENNEBERG, E. 1967: *The biological foundations of language.* New York: Wiley.

LESTER, D. 1977: The prediction of suicide and homicide rates cross-nationally by means of stepwise multiple regression. *Behavioral Science Research* **12**, 61–9.

LEVINGER, G. and RAUSCH, H. 1977: *Close relationships: Perspectives on the meaning of intimacy.* Amherst, Mass.: University of Massachusetts Press.

LIPPA, R. 1976: Expressive control and the leakage of dispositional introversion-extraversion during role-played teaching. *Journal of Personality* **44**, 541–59.

LUFT, J. 1969: *Of human interaction.* Palo Alto, California: National Press Books.

McARTHUR, L.A. 1972: The how and what of why: Some determinants and consequences of causal attribution. *Journal of Personality and Social Psychology* **22**, 171–93.

McARTHUR, L.Z. 1976: The lesser influence of consensus than distinctiveness information on causal attributions: A test of the person-thing hypothesis. *Journal of Personality and Social Psychology* **33**, 733–43.

Mc EWEN, W.J. and GREENBERG, B.S. 1970: Effects of message intensity on receiver evaluations of source, message, and topic. *Journal of Communication* **20**, 340–50.

McGEE, M.C. 1980: The 'ideograph': A link between rhetoric and ideology. *The Quarterly Journal of Speech* **66**, 1–16.

McGUIRE, W.J. 1980: The development of theory in social psychology. In Gilmour, R. and Duck, S., editors, *The development of social psychology* (London: Academic Press) 53–80.

McKIRNAN, D.J. and HAMAYAN, E.V. 1980: Language norms and perceptions of ethnolinguistic diversity. In Giles, H., Robinson, W.P. and Smith, P.M., editors, *Language: Social psychological perspectives* (Oxford: Pergamon Press) 161–9.

MAGNUSSON, D. and ENDLER, N.S. 1977: *Personality at the crossroads.* New York; John Wiley.

MAJOR, B. 1980: Information acquisition and attribution processes. *Journal of Personality and Social Psychology* **39**, 1010–23.

MARKEL, N.N., PHILLIS, J.A., VARGIS, R. and HOWARD, K. 1972: Personality traits associated with voice types. *Journal of Psycholinguistic Research* **1**, 249–55.

MARTIN, L.W., BRADAC, J.J. and ELLIOTT, N.D. 1977: On the empirical basis of linguistics: A multivariate analysis of sentence judgments. In Beach, W.A., Fox, S.E. and Philosoph, S. *Papers from the thirteenth regional meeting of the Chicago Linguistic Society* (Chicago: Chicago Linguistic Society) 357–71.

MEAD, G.H. 1934: *Mind, self, and society*. Chicago, Ill.: University of Chicago Press.

MEHRABIAN, A. 1980: *Basic dimensions for a general psychological theory*. Cambridge, Mass.: Oelgeschlager, Gunn and Hain, Publishers. Inc.

MEHRLEY, R.S. and McCROSKEY, J.C. 1970: Opinionated statements and attitude intensity as predictors of attitude change and source credibility. *Speech Monographs* **37**, 47–52.

MILLAR, F.E. and ROGERS, L.E. 1976: A relational approach to interpersonal communication. In Miller, G.R., editor, *Explorations in interpersonal communication* (Beverly Hills: Sage Publications) 87–104.

MILLER, G.R. and BASEHART, J. 1969: Source trustworthiness, opinionated statements, and responses to persuasive communication. *Speech Monographs* **36**, 1–7.

MILLER, G.R. and STEINBERG, M. 1975: *Between people: A new analysis of interpersonal communication*. Chicago, Ill.: Science Research Associates.

MILLER, N., MARUYAMA, G., BEABER, R.J. and VALONE, K. 1976: Speed of speech and persuasion. *Journal of Personality and Social Psychology* **34**, 615–24.

MISCHEL, W. 1973: Toward a cognitive social learning reconceptualization of personality. *Psychological Review* **80**, 252–83.

MONGE, P.R. 1973: Theory construction in the study of communication: The system paradigm. *Journal of Communication* **23**, 5–16.

MOTL, J.R. 1980: *Attitudes, attraction, and nonverbal indicators of uncertainty in initial interaction*. Unpublished doctoral dissertation, Department of Communication Studies, Northwestern University, Evanston, Illinois.

MOTLEY, M.T., CAMDEN, C.T. and BAARS, B.J. 1979: Personality and situational influences upon verbal slips: A laboratory test of Freudian and pre-articulatory editing hypotheses. *Human Communication Research* **5**, 195–202.

MULAC, A. and LUNDELL, T.L. 1980: Differences in perceptions created by syntactic-semantic productions of male and female speakers. *Communication Monographs* **47**, 111–18.

MURDOCK, J.I. 1978: *Conditional regulative rules: An empirical study of language within power relationships*. Unpublished doctoral dissertation, University of Iowa.

NEWCOMBE, N. and ARNKOFF, D.B. 1979: Effects of speech style and sex of speaker on person perception. *Journal of Personality and Social Psychology* **37**, 1293–303.

NEWMAN, S. and MATHER, V.G. 1938: Analysis of spoken language of patients with affective disorders. *American Journal of Psychology* **94**, 913–42.

NEWTSON, D. 1973: Attribution and the unit of perception of ongoing behavior. *Journal of Personality and Social Psychology* **28**, 28–38.

—1976: Foundations of attribution: The perception of ongoing behavior. In Harvey, J.H., Ickes, W.J. and Kidd, R.F., editors, *New directions in attribution research: Volume 2* (Hillsdale, NJ: Lawrence Erlbaum Associates) 223–47.

NISBETT, R.E. 1980: The trait construct in lay and professional psychology. In Festinger, L., editor, *Retrospections on social psychology* (New York: Oxford University Press) 109–30.

NISBETT, R.E. and ROSS, L. 1980: *Human inference: Strategies and shortcomings of social judgment*. Englewood Cliffs, NJ: Prentice-Hall.

NIXON, R.M. and THE STAFF OF *THE WASHINGTON POST* 1974: *The presidential transcripts*. New York: Delacorte Press.

NOFSINGER, R.E. 1974: The demand ticket: A conversational device for getting the floor. *Speech Monographs* **41**, 1–9.

NORTON, R.W. 1978: Foundation of a communicator style construct. *Human Communication Research* **4**, 99–112.

NORTON, R., FELDMAN, C. and TAFOYA, D. 1974: Risk parameters across types of secrets. *Journal of Counseling Psychology* **21**, 450–4.

O'KEEFE, D.J. 1977: Two concepts of argument. *Journal of the American Forensic Association* **13**, 121–8.

OLSON, D.R., editor 1980: *The social foundations of language and thought: Essays in honor of J.S. Bruner*. New York: W.W. Norton & Co.

ORVIS, B.R., CUNNINGHAM, J.D. and KELLEY, H.H. 1975: A closer examination of causal inference: The roles of consensus, distinctiveness, and consistency information. *Journal of Personality and Social Psychology* **32**, 605–16.

ORVIS, B.R., KELLEY, H.H. and BUTLER, D. 1976: Attributional conflict in young couples. In Harvey, J.H., Ickes, W. and Kidd, R.F., editors, *New directions in attribution research: Volume 1* (Hillsdale, NJ: Lawrence Erlbaum Associates) 353–86.

OSGOOD, C.E., SUCI, G.J. and TANNENBAUM, P.H. 1957: *The measurement of meaning*. Urbana, Ill.: The University of Illinois Press.

PARKS, M.R. 1979: Relational communication: Theory and research. *Human Communication Research* **3**, 372–81.

PEARCE, W.B. 1976: The coordinated management of meaning: A rules-based theory of interpersonal communication. In Miller, G.R., editor, *Explorations in interpersonal communication* (Beverly Hills: Sage Publications) 17–35.

PEARCE, W.B. and SHARP, S.M. 1973: Self-disclosing communication. *Journal of Communication* **23**, 409–25.

PIAGET, J. 1932: *The language and thought of the child*, 2nd edn. Preface by Claparede, E. Translated by Gabain, M. New York: Harcourt, Brace.

PLAYBOY 1976: 23, 86.

POPPER, K.R. 1963: *Conjectures and refutations: The growth of scientific knowledge*. London: Routledge & Kegan Paul.

PRONOVOST, W. and FAIRBANKS, G. 1939: An experimental study of the pitch characteristics of the voice during expression of emotion. *Speech Monographs* **6**, 87–104.

PRYOR, J.B., GIBBONS, F.X., WICKLUND, R.A., FAZIO, R.H. and HOOD, R. 1977:

Self-focused attention and self-report validity. *Journal of Personality* **45**, 513–27.

PYSZCZYNSKI, T.A. and GREENBERG, J. 1981: Role of disconfirmed expectancies in the instigation of attributional processing. *Journal of Personality and Social Psychology* **40**, 31–8.

RAPOPORT, A. 1960: *Fights, games and debates*. Ann Arbor: The University of Michigan Press.

ROBINSON, W.P. 1979: Speech markers and social class. In Scherer, K.R. and Giles, H., editors, *Social markers in speech* (Cambridge: Cambridge University Press).

ROBINSON, W.P. GILES, H. and SMITH, P.M. 1980: Epilogue. In Giles, H., Robinson, W.P. and Smith, P.M., editors, *Language: Social psychological perspectives* (Oxford: Pergamon Press) 425–30.

ROGERS, L.E., COURTRIGHT, J.A. and MILLAR, F.E. 1980: Message control intensity: Rationale and preliminary findings. *Communication Monographs* **47**, 201–19.

ROMMETVEIT, R. 1968: *Words, meanings and messages*. New York: Academic Press.

ROSCH, E. 1973: Natural categories. *Cognitive Psychology* **4**, 328–50.

ROSENTHAL, R. and JACOBSON, L. 1968: *Pygmalion in the classroom: Teacher expectation and pupils' intellectual development*. New York: Holt, Rinehart & Winston.

ROSS, J.R. 1967: *Constraints on variables in syntax*. Unpublished doctoral dissertation, MIT.

ROTTER, J.B. 1966: Generalized expectancies for internal versus external control. *Psychological Monographs* **80**, (609), 1–28.

RYAN, E.B. 1979: Why do low-prestige language varieties persist? In Giles, H. and St Clair, R.N., editors, *Language and social psychology* (Baltimore: University Park Press) 154–7.

RYAN, E.B. and CARRANZA, M.A. 1975: Evaluative reactions towards speakers of standard English. *Journal of Personality and Social Psychology* **31**, 855–63.

SAFIRE, W. 1975: *Before the fall*. New York: Belmont Tower Books.

SALZMAN, L. 1968: *The obsessive personality*. New York: Science House.

SANDERS, R.E. and MARTIN, L.W. 1975: Grammatical rules and explanations of behavior. *Inquiry* **18**, 65–82.

SANKOFF, D. and LESSARD, R. 1975: Vocabulary richness: A sociolinguistic analysis. *Science* **190**, 689–90.

SCHACHTER, S. 1951: Deviation, rejection and communication. *Journal of Abnormal and Social Psychology* **46**, 190–207.

—1964: The interaction of cognitive and physiological determinants of emotional state. In Berkowitz, L., editor, *Advances in experimental social psychology* (New York: Academic Press) 41–81.

SCHANK, R.C. and ABELSON, R.P. 1977: *Scripts, plans, goals and understanding*. Hillsdale, NJ: Lawrence Erlbaum Associates.

SCHEIER, M.F., BUSS, A.H. and BUSS, D.M. 1978: Self-consciousness, self-report of aggressiveness, and aggression. *Journal of Research in Personality* **12**, 133–40.

SCHEIER, M.F. and CARVER, C.S. 1977: Self-focused attention and experience of emotion: Attraction, repulsion, elation, and depression. *Journal of Personality and Social Psychology* **35**, 625–36.

SCHERER, K.R. 1979a: Personality markers in speech. In Scherer, K.R. and Giles, H., editors, *Social markers in speech* (Cambridge: Cambridge University Press) 147–209.

—1979b: Voice and speech correlates of perceived social influence in simulated juries. In Giles, H. and St Clair, R.N., editors, *Language and social psychology* (Baltimore: University Park Press) 88–120.

SCHERER, K.R., SCHERER, U., HALL, J.A. and ROSENTHAL, R. 1977: Differential attribution of personality based on multi-channel presentation of verbal and nonverbal cues. *Psychological Research* **39**, 221–47.

SCHNEIDER, M.J. 1979: *Cross-cultural communication and the acquisition of communicative competence.* Unpublished doctoral dissertation, University of Iowa.

SCHULMAN, L.S. 1976: *Compliments, reciprocity, and background information in initial interaction.* Unpublished doctoral dissertation, Department of Communication Studies, Northwestern University, Evanston, Illinois.

SCHUTZ, A. 1967: *The phenomenology of the social world.* Walsh, G. and Legnert, F., translators. Evanston: Northwestern University Press.

SCHWARZ, M.F. and RINE, H.E. 1968: Identification of speakers from whispered vowels. *Journal of the Acoustical Society of America* **44**, 1736–7.

SCOTTON, C.M. 1976: Strategies of neutrality: Language choice in uncertain situations. *Language* **52**, 919–41.

—1980: Explaining linguistic choices as identity negotiations. In Giles, H., Robinson, W.P. and Smith, P.M., editors, *Language: Social psychological perspectives* (Oxford: Pergamon Press) 359–66.

SEARLE, J.R. 1969: *Speech acts.* Cambridge: Cambridge University Press.

SEBASTIAN, R.J., RYAN, E.B., KEOGH, T.F. and SCHMIDT, A.C. 1980: The effects of negative affect arousal on reactions to speakers. In Giles, H., Robinson, W.P. and Smith, P.M., editors, *Language:* Social psychological perspectives (Oxford: Pergamon Press) 203–8.

SERMAT, V. and SMYTH, M. 1973: Content analysis of verbal communication in the development of a relationship: Conditions influencing self-disclosure. *Journal of Personality and Social Psychology* **26**, 332–46.

SHANNON, C. and WEAVER, W. 1949: *The mathematical theory of communication.* Urbana, Ill: University of Illinois Press.

SHAW, G.B. 1946: *Pygmalion, a romance in five acts.* Harmondsworth: Penguin Books.

SIEGMAN, A.W. and FELDSTEIN, S., editors, 1979: *Of speech and time: Temporal speech patterns in interpersonal contexts.* Hillsdale, NJ: Lawrence Erlbaum Associates.

SIEGMAN, A.W. and POPE, B. 1972: *Studies in dyadic communication.* New York: Pergamon Press.

SILLARS, A.L. 1980a: Attributions and communication in roommate conflicts. *Communication Monographs* **47**, 180–200.

—1980b: The stranger and the spouse as target persons for compliance-gaining strategies: A subjective expected utility model. *Human Communication Research* **6**, 265–79.

SIMARD, L., TAYLOR, D. and GILES, H. 1976: Attribution processes and interpersonal accommodation in a bilingual setting. *Language and Speech* **19**, 374–87.

SMITH, D.R. and WILLIAMSON, L.K. 1977: *Interpersonal communication: Roles, rules, strategies and games*. Dubuque, Iowa: William C. Brown Company.

SMITH, P.M. 1979: Sex markers in speech. In Scherer, K.R. and Giles, H., editors, *Social markers in speech* (Cambridge: Cambridge University Press) 109–46.

SNYDER, M. 1974: Self-monitoring of expressive behavior. *Journal of Personality and Social Psychology* **30**, 526–37.

—1979: Self-monitoring processes. In Berkowitz, L., editor, *Advances in experimental social psychology* (New York: Academic Press).

SNYDER, M. and CANTOR, N. 1980: Thinking about ourselves and others: Self-monitoring and social knowledge. *Journal of Personality and Social Psychology* **39**, 222–34.

SNYDER, M. and MONSON, T.C. 1975: Persons, situations and the control of social behavior. *Journal of Personality and Social Psychology* **32**, 637–44.

SORRENTINO, R.M. and BOUTILLIER, R.G. 1975: The effect of quantity and quality of verbal interaction on ratings of leadership ability. *Journal of Experimental Social Psychology* **11**, 403–11.

SPILICH, G.J., VESONDER, G.T., CHIESI, H.L. and VOSS, J.F. 1979: Text processing of domain-related information for individuals with high and low domain knowledge. *Journal of Verbal Learning and Verbal Behavior* **18**, 275–90.

STORMS, M.D. 1973: Videotape and the attribution process: Reversing actors' and observers' points of view. *Journal of Personality and Social Psychology* **27**, 165–75.

STREET, R.L. and GILES, H. in press: Speech accommodation theory: A social cognitive approach to language and speech behavior. In Roloff, M.E. and Berger, C.R., editors, *Social cognition and communication* (Beverly Hills: Sage Publications).

STREUFERT, S. and STREUFERT, S.C. 1969: The effects of conceptual structure, failure, and success on attribution of causality and interpersonal attitudes. *Journal of Personality and Social Psychology* **11**, 133–47.

TAJFEL, H. and TURNER, J.C. 1979: An integrative theory of intergroup conflict. In Austin, W.G. and Worchel, S., editors, *The social psychology of intergroup relations* (Monterey, Calif.: Brooks/Cole).

TANNEN, D. 1979: Ethnicity as conversational style. *Working Papers in Sociolinguistics* (Austin, Texas: Southwest Educational Development Laboratory) **55**.

THIBAUT, J. and KELLEY, H.H. 1959: *The social psychology of groups*. New York: John Wiley.

THOMPSON, T.L. 1981: The impact of a physical handicap on communicative characteristics of the marital dyad. *Western Journal of Speech Communication* **45**, 227–40.

THOMPSON, T.L. and SEIBOLD, D.R. 1978: Stigma management in 'normal'-stigmatized interactions: A test of the disclosure hypothesis and a model of stigma acceptance. *Human Communication Research* **4**, 231–42.

TIME, April 6, 1981: A sad baffling dependency. 45.

TRIANDIS, H.C., LOH, W.D. and LEVIN, L.A. 1966: Race, status, quality of spoken English and opinions about civil rights as determinants of interpersonal attitudes. *Journal of Personality and Social Psychology* 3, 468–72.

TURNER, R.G. 1978: Consistency, self-consciousness, and the predictive validity of typical and maximal personality measures. *Journal of Research in Personality* 12, 117–32.

VICK, C.F. and WOOD, R.V. 1969: Similarity of past experience and the communication of meaning. *Speech Monographs* 36, 159–62.

WALSH, R.H. and LEONARD, W.M. 1974: Usage of terms for sexual intercourse by men and women. *Archives of Sexual Behavior* 3, 373–6.

WATZLAWICK, P. 1977: *How real is real?* New York: Vintage Books.

WATZLAWICK, P., BEAVIN, J.H. and JACKSON, D.D. 1967: *Pragmatics of human communication: A study of interactional patterns, pathologies, and paradoxes.* New York: W.W. Norton.

WEGNER, D.M. and VALLACHER, R.R. 1977: *Implicit psychology: An introduction to social cognition.* New York: Oxford University Press.

WHEELESS, L.R. 1976: Self-disclosure and interpersonal solidarity. *Human Communication Research* 3, 47–61.

—1978: A follow-up study of the relationships among trust, disclosure, and interpersonal solidarity. *Human Communication Research* 4, 143–57.

WHEELESS, L.R. and GROTZ, J. 1977: The measurement of trust and its relationship to self-disclosure. *Human Communication Research* 3, 250–7.

WICKLUND, R.A. 1975: Objective self awareness. In Berkowitz, L., editor, *Advances in experimental social psychology* (New York: Academic Press) 233–77.

WIEMANN, J.M. 1977: Explication and test of a model of communicative competence. *Human Communication Research* 3, 195–213.

WIEMANN, J.M. and KELLY, C.W. 1981: Pragmatics of interpersonal competence. In Wilder-Mott, C. and Weaklund, J.H., editors, *Rigor and imagination: Essays from the legacy of Gregory Bateson* (New York: Praeger) 283–98.

WIEMANN, J.M. and KRUEGER, D.L. 1980: Dimensions of interpersonal relationships revisited. Paper presented at the meeting of the International Communication Association, Acapulco, Mexico.

WIENER, M. and MEHRABIAN, A. 1967: *Language within language: Immediacy, a channel in verbal communication.* New York: Appleton-Century-Crofts.

WOOD, R.V., YAMAUCHI, J.S. and BRADAC, J.J. 1971: The communication of meaning across generations. *Journal of Communication* 21, 160–9.

WORTHY, M., GARY, A. and KAHN, G.M. 1969: Self-disclosure as an exchange process. *Journal of Personality and Social Psychology* 13, 59–64.

ZAJONC, R.B. 1965: Social facilitation. *Science* 149, 269–74.

—1968: Attitudinal effects of mere exposure. *Journal of Personality and Social Psychology, Monograph Supplement* 9, 1–27.

ZIMMERMAN, D.H. and WEST, C. 1975: Sex roles, interruptions, and silences in conversation. In Thorne, B. and Henley, N., editors, *Language and sex: Difference and dominance* (Rowley, Mass.: Newbury House).

ZIPF, G.K. 1935: *The psycho-biology of language.* Boston: Houghton Mifflin Company.

Index